"*Turnip Greens & Tortillas* is a breath of fresh air. It's filled with colorful pages of mouthwatering recipes that celebrate the intersection of Mexican and Southern American cuisines in a unique and playful way. Chef Eddie's roots and his character shine brightly in this book, with great stories that grab your attention and make your stomach rumble for deep-flavored sauces, melty cheese, crispy tortillas, spicy chiles, and more. Whether you are an existing fan or a new one, you are bound to fall in love with this book." — STEVEN SATTERFIELD, JAMES BEARD AWARD–WINNING CHEF AND AUTHOR, *ROOT TO LEAF*

TURNIP GREENS & TORTILLAS

EDDIE
HERNANDEZ
AND SUSAN PUCKETT

TURNIP GREENS & TORTILLAS

A MEXICAN CHEF SPICES UP THE SOUTHERN KITCHEN

PHOTOGRAPHS BY ANGIE MOSIER

A RUX MARTIN BOOK
HOUGHTON MIFFLIN HARCOURT
BOSTON NEW YORK

For information about permission to reproduce selections
from this book, write to trade.permissions@hmhco.com or to
Permissions, Houghton Mifflin Harcourt Publishing Company,
3 Park Avenue, 19th Floor, New York, New York 10016.

hmhco.com

Library of Congress Cataloging-in-Publication Data
Names: Hernandez, Eddie, author. | Puckett, Susan, 1956- author. | Mosier,
Angie, photographer.
Title: Turnip greens & tortillas : a Mexican chef spices up the southern
kitchen / Eddie Hernandez and Susan Puckett ; photographs by Angie Mosier.
Description: Boston : Houghton Mifflin Harcourt, 2018. | Includes index. | "A
Rux Martin Book."
Identifiers: LCCN 2017052730 (print) | LCCN 2017051352 (ebook) | ISBN
9780544618848 (ebook) | ISBN 9780544618824 (hbk) |
ISBN 9780544618848 (ebk)
Subjects: LCSH: Cooking, Mexican. | LCGFT: Cookbooks.
Classification: LCC TX716.M4 (print) | LCC TX716.M4 H46 2018 (ebook) | DDC
641.5972--dc23
LC record available at https://lccn.loc.gov/2017052730

Book design by Anna Green, Siulen Design
Food styling by Eddie Hernandez, Thomas Driver, and Angie Mosier
Prop styling by Thomas Driver

Printed in China

SCP 10 9 8 7 6 5 4 3

4500713571

To my friend and mentor, Mike Klank, who took a chance on
putting a burned-out Mexican rock 'n' roll guy in charge of his
restaurant kitchen thirty years ago, made me a business partner,
and has stuck by me through thick and thin ever since.
—Eddie Hernandez

ACKNOWLEDGMENTS

FROM EDDIE HERNANDEZ

I would need many more pages to list all the people who have helped me get to where I am today. I am grateful to them all. Here are a few I would like to recognize by name.

First, my business partner, Mike Klank. Mike is the big guy with the heavy beard who can often be spotted on the restaurant floor or behind the bar mixing margaritas and chatting with customers at any of our Atlanta locations. He tends to keep a low profile, but make no mistake: If it weren't for him, there would be no Taqueria del Sol, no cookbook, or—for that matter—no Chef Eddie. No telling where I would be or what kind of trouble I'd be getting myself into if we hadn't met.

Thanks, Mike, for letting me show you what I could do behind a stove and believing we could put our heads—and our histories—together to build something great.

The best is yet to come.

My uncle José Chaires; my mother, Juana Chaires; and my grandmother Consuela Palomares, may they rest in peace, for instilling in me the values of hard work, a desire to learn, and being creative with what you have.

Susan Puckett, who offered to tell my story and has stuck with it for all these years. *Muchas gracias!*

Our longtime managers, Steve Shields and George Trusler, and the staffs at each of our Taqueria del Sol locations, who work hard every day at keeping our customers happy and coming back for more.

David Waller, Steve Murrell, Dan Krinsky, and the other talented chefs of all our restaurants present and past—Taqueria del Sol, Sundown Café, and Azteca Grill—who have contributed to my education as a chef and a born-again Southerner.

Jacques Pépin, Julia Child, and Rick Bayless—the chefs' chefs—who taught me things about cooking through their television shows and books that have made lasting impressions.

Christiane Lauterbach and Cliff Bostock, the first of many excellent food writers whose dining critiques, both positive and negative, helped me improve as a chef, especially early in my career.

John T. Edge and the members of the Southern Foodways Alliance, who do such great work bringing people of all backgrounds and cultures together to talk and share the foods of our heritage. We are proud to be part of this ongoing conversation.

Kate Medley, the documentarian who made my story part of a Southern Foodways oral history project about the diverse South, which inspired this book.

Kat Crawford and the rest of the Green Olive Media team, for getting our message out to an audience beyond our customers.

Most of all, I am thankful to God for my two beautiful children, Anna and Andrew, and for everything else He has done for me. I am a very blessed man.

FROM SUSAN PUCKETT

Mike Klank, words can't express my appreciation for your support, advice, and creative contributions to this project. Without your frequent reminders to stay on the "straight line," we might still be testing recipes!

Ralph Ellis, thanks for maintaining your good humor through all the grocery runs, recipe tests and retests, and pro bono proofreading. You've passed the "great husband test" with flying colors.

A shout-out to my mother, Nancy Puckett, for always being no more than a phone call away whenever I needed a listening ear.

I raise a margarita glass to my longtime journalist friends—Eileen Drennen, Michelle Hiskey, Jim Auchmutey, Deborah Geering, John Kessler, Jerry Sealy, Liz Rahe, and Anne Byrn—whose wise and encouraging words have carried me to the finish line on this project and others.

Eddie Hernandez, it has been an honor being your trusted scribe, and I can honestly say there has never been a dull moment! Thank you for the stories, the one-on-one cooking lessons, and your great friendship. I hope we will have many more delicious Saturday breakfasts together with Mike and Ralph at "the Taq"—to taste your latest kitchen experiments, catch up on life, and reminisce about the adventures of writing a book.

FROM EDDIE HERNANDEZ AND SUSAN PUCKETT

We both wish to express our deep gratitude to those who contributed to the making of this book:

Our agent, Amy Hughes, for helping us shape our rough nugget of a book idea and match us with the dream team that would produce it.

Our editor, Rux Martin, for believing in us and allowing us to stay true to our vision.

Angie Mosier and Thomas Driver, for illustrating the story beautifully in pictures and props, and Susan Rowe, for lending her creativity to the photo sessions.

Tamie Cook, Deborah Geering, Jeanne Besser, and Wendy Allen, for helping us test and fine-tune the recipes.

Julia Ellis, for her editorial assistance.

Shelley Berg, for her expert fact-checking and copyediting.

And the staff at HMH, for pulling the pieces together into a beautiful package: designers Anna Green and Rachel Newborn, production editor Jamie Selzer, typist Jacinta Monniere, and editorial assistant Sarah Kwak.

CONTENTS

BAPTISM BY POTLIKKER *1*

MY MEX-AMERICAN KITCHEN *8*

GOOD FOR BREAKFAST—OR ANY TIME *20*

CHIPS, DIPS, AND OTHER SNACKS *36*

TACOS *60*

WRAPPED, STUFFED, AND SAUCED *90*

SOUPS, STEWS, AND CHILIS *112*

EDDIE'S BLUE PLATE LUNCHES AND SPECIAL
   SUPPERS *134*

BREADS, BEANS, RICE, AND CORN *176*

SALSAS, SAUCES, RELISHES, AND CONDIMENTS *198*

SALADS, SLAWS, AND HOT VEGETABLE SIDES *218*

DRINKS TO COOL YOU DOWN AND WARM YOU UP *248*

SWEET TREATS FOR MY SOUTHERN FRIENDS *270*

BASIC RECIPES *288*

INDEX *301*

BAPTISM BY POTLIKKER

It all started with a bag full of turnip greens.

In 1989 I was cooking at a Tex-Mex restaurant on the outskirts of Atlanta called Azteca Grill when a regular customer came in with turnip greens from his garden. He said, "Eddie, if anybody can make these things good, it's you."

I thanked him, but they went bad because I didn't know how to cook them. Turnip greens don't grow in Mexico where I come from. The next Friday, the customer brought me more greens.

I went to my boss and said, "You need to tell me—how do you eat these things here in Georgia?" He said people in the South cook turnip greens with ham hocks and serve them with the juice they're cooked in—known as "potlikker"—on the side. But I wanted to do them the way Mexicans cook the wild greens that grow there like weeds.

I didn't have any ham hocks, so I used chicken stock instead. I sautéed onion with chopped fresh tomato, garlic, and chile de árbol—the chile I go with whenever I want to turn up the heat—and added that to the pot. We served the greens in little bowls and gave them away that day at the bar. People liked them so much that they came back and sat at the bar, waiting for the turnip greens.

We put the turnip greens (page 236) on the menu. A dining critic came to try them, and wrote a positive review. Another one came, and then another. The crowds got bigger.

My boss, Mike Klank, made me a business partner. And three decades later, our restaurants have been more successful than in our wildest dreams.

WHO I AM AND WHERE I'M FROM

I'm a born-again Southern boy.

I live in a city where I can listen to a bluegrass band on one night, and on another night I can go hear the blues. During football season I cheer for my two home teams—the UGA Bulldogs and the Georgia Tech Yellow Jackets—except when they play each other, and then I am a Tech fan all the way.

When I have a few days off, one of my favorite things to do is take a long, slow drive on the back roads of rural Georgia, along the bayous of Louisiana, or through the mountains of Tennessee. Wherever I go, I stop at every little café and roadside stand I can to try the fried chicken, the barbecue, the boudin sausage, or whatever it is the locals eat. As I taste, I start to get ideas about how I would re-create them—my way. In Nashville I try the famous hot fried chicken at a place called Hattie B's and think how it would taste cut into strips and wrapped in a tortilla together with lime and jalapeño mayonnaise and shredded lettuce to cool the spice.

So what if it doesn't work out? I will try it again until I get it right, or I will move on to the next thing. That is how I educate myself. I am not afraid to fail. Since I was a boy, I have always loved to figure out how to take things apart and put them back together—whether it was a truck engine or a tamale.

I have no family photographs to show because my family didn't own a camera. We didn't keep scrapbooks. I only have my cooking to trigger the memories. I was born in Monterrey, Mexico, one of the largest cities in the country. It lies in the foothills of the Sierra Madre Oriental about 115 miles from the Texas border. We lived in a working-class neighborhood of cement-block houses occupied by big families—up to thirty people. Every morning as

we kids walked to school—we walked pretty much everywhere—there would be five, ten, fifteen moms out sweeping the streets, criticizing our wardrobes. "Why are you wearing that shirt?" "I hope you changed your socks!"

My mother fed our family home-cooked food every day. We had lunch between twelve and one, and dinner between six and seven. Always. If you weren't there, you would either have to heat your meal up yourself, if there was anything left, or go hungry. The other kids and I did our share of arguing and fighting, but never at the table. That was our time to sit down together in peace.

Everything we ate was fresh. No one had gardens in my neighborhood, other than maybe some herbs or chiles in pots, because it was the big city and there wasn't space. Instead the mothers went to the market every day. They bought what looked good to them and was a good price.

Our markets were nothing like the mainstream supermarkets in the U.S. They were more like open-air farmers' markets with butcher shops, bakeries, and stalls filled with tomatoes, fresh corn, avocados, peppers, cabbages, zucchini, mangoes—you name it. Living in a climate that rarely dips below 70 degrees, even in winter, we were used to having access to a huge assortment of fresh produce year-round.

Most people didn't have refrigerators in their

homes, and in poor rural areas, that's often still the case. Electronics had to be imported and were very expensive. My family was fortunate enough to have those appliances. We even had a blender! But we still shopped daily. It was our way of life.

My dad was a mechanic. He worked on a steam engine in the railyard, and I watched him with fascination. He wore suits every day to work and came home covered in diesel oil, looking like he just crawled out of the earth. After he showered, he would put on a fresh suit and go out looking like a million bucks. I was nine when he died.

I lived with my mother and grandmother, neither of whom had a husband. Then my stepfather, Leonardo, came into the picture. And when he and my mother had kids—five of them—I couldn't help feeling neglected. I started to make my own course in life.

My mother's brother was like a father figure to me. Uncle José taught me mechanical skills like welding, bolting, and painting cars. He also taught me a lot about food. We ate things no one would eat but us—like goats' brains. He would buy whole pine nuts for us to crack and eat. He never bought them shelled because he thought it was more fun to crack them ourselves. When I got older, we liked to drink and listen to music together.

But it was my grandmother who gave me the desire to learn to cook. Her name was Consuela, but everybody called her Chelo. She was a strong-willed entrepreneur who owned seven different bars and convenience stores around Monterrey. One place was three doors down from where we lived. It didn't have a name. Everyone just knew it as Chelo's place. As a kid I hung out there.

Nobody messed with Chelo. She was a big woman, at least 5 foot 8, with blond hair and blue eyes. Her voice could make grown men run. We used to joke that she'd never die because neither God nor the devil would take her. She knew how to handle all kinds of situations. But whenever she raised her voice to me, I raised mine back. I think she liked that. We respected each other.

"If you want to eat it, then learn how to make it yourself, because I'm not going to be here one day and who is going to cook it for you?"

I'm not going to say Chelo was a chef, because back then there was no such thing as a chef. Everybody just cooked. Guys who would go to her pub for a beer liked the fact that they could get a good meal and free homemade snacks there. She was big on fresh food, and she never made the same things two days in a row.

I loved watching Chelo cook things that I had never seen anyone else make. Pickled pork skin was one of my favorites. In Mexico it's a good bar food and a side dish for tacos. I would ask her to make some just for me. But she would say, "If you want to eat it, then learn how to make it yourself, because I'm not going to be here one day and who is going to cook it for you?" And so I learned, and eventually became pretty good at it.

I taught myself to drive a truck when I was twelve, and Chelo would send me to the market to pick up groceries. I got my first job delivering newspapers when I was thirteen, and when I was fifteen, I bought a car and opened a torta stand on the street. I made a pot of *carnitas*—pork meat simmered in oil until tender— and served it on bread three different ways: with cold salsa made with tomatoes and chiles; with cooked salsa; and plain, with just some chopped avocado. It looked fancy but it was as simple as could be.

OVER THE BORDER—A *FASCINACIÓN* WITH FOOD

My dream was not to be a chef. Instead I wanted to travel the world as a musician. I discovered the drums and got all my frustrations out. It was the perfect instrument for me!

Some buddies and I formed a band called Fascinación. None of us knew any English, so we would just mimic-sing everything. We weren't very good, but we had ambition. When I was seventeen, we drove to Houston to get a recording deal. That never happened, but we stayed in Texas anyway. We got a house together, and I became the designated cook.

The Latino community in Texas at the time was predominantly Chicanos—Mexican descendants born in the U.S.—and they were not big on Mexican food. I craved what I used to eat at home: homemade tortillas; refried beans with my morning eggs; hearty soups simmered with whole cut-up chicken, chunks of pork, hominy, and chiles. Once I got acquainted with the stores, I started learning how to make them for myself.

I played music and held various day jobs for more than a decade, including working in factories and Tex-Mex restaurants. But the musician's life was killing me. I was eating bad food, getting too little sleep, and drinking too much, and I never knew when or where the next gig would be. Then in 1987 a friend who'd moved to Atlanta invited me to come visit while I figured out what to do next. I applied for a waiter's job at a Tex-Mex chain just south of Atlanta. The managing partner was Mike Klank.

Mike asked me if I was interested in being a line cook. I said no: I needed the tips that went with being a waiter. At that time, I looked like a standard-issue rock musician: hair down to my shoulders, pierced ear, and a lot of chunky gold jewelry—the exact opposite of my new boss! I liked Mike right away. But the food was totally wrong, and in my broken English, I told him that it lacked all the flavor of Mexican and good Tex-Mex. Instead of being insulted, Mike believed me. And he believed in me, eventually putting me in charge

of the whole kitchen. And because he trusted me, I worked really hard to do a good job. He'd lived in New Mexico and had an idea about what the food should taste like, but he didn't have anybody who could make it. He told me about the green chile pork stew he used to love in his ski bum days in the Southwest, and we added it to the menu.

Mike introduced me to the ways of the South and took me on a tour of all the good Southern restaurants in Atlanta. We ate breakfast at Waffle House, where I had grits for the first time—and I loved them! We had lunch at Mary Mac's Tea Room, known for having the best turnip greens in town. The greens were made as they used to do in the South, cooked for hours in a pork-flavored broth, with corn bread muffins for dipping.

On trips back home to Memphis, Mike returned with ribs and pulled pork from his favorite places and showed me how to put together a Memphis-style barbecue sandwich with slaw inside the bun. Soon we introduced a Memphis-style barbecue pork taco (page 67) that became one of our most popular menu items, especially when we added a side of greens— made my way, with the flavors of Mexico.

Southern food, I came to realize, is very similar to good Mexican cuisine. Southerners make corn bread, Mexicans make corn tortillas. They do pork cracklings, we do *chicharrones*. They smoke meats, we do *barbacoa*. Both cuisines are blessed with a huge variety of fresh ingredients and spices to work with.

Eventually Mike broke from the chain and turned it into an independent restaurant and made me a partner. People drove from all over the city to eat our food—especially after we started serving our famous turnip greens. A few years later, we opened Sundown

Café, another restaurant specializing in modern Southwest cuisine. I volunteered in the city's top restaurants to refine my techniques, and we hired classically trained chefs to work with us, who shared their knowledge with me.

We could see from the customers' responses that they wanted more dishes from the South, but done in a different way that was more exciting. I cooked buttermilk fried chicken, but instead of biscuits and gravy, I served it with tortillas and a creamy sauce spiked with green chiles and pickle relish (page 89). I flavored my mashed potatoes with cheese and pureed anchos and served them with spiced pork loin and jalapeño-infused gravy (page 142).

In the mid-1990s, I moved to Texas for a few years to attend to family matters. I returned to Atlanta every month to keep my hand in our restaurants, but I settled into the small-town life of Rosebud, Texas, a little town of about 1,400 people near Austin. I settled in so well that I opened a restaurant, joined the volunteer fire department, and even served as mayor for a little while. Having been a city guy all my life, I enjoyed being part of the community. I participated in barbecue championships and chili cook-offs and brought those experiences into my cooking. But I soon discovered that I like running a kitchen, not a town, and returned to Atlanta to stay.

What Mike and I craved most was good, cheap street food—the kind I grew up on in Mexico and Mike came to love in the Southwest. That's how our restaurant Taqueria del Sol came to be. We had started selling simple tacos and a few sides over the counter of our previous restaurant twice a week, as if it were a food truck. Long lines of customers quickly formed out the door and through the parking lot. Demand grew through word of mouth, and in 2000 we opened Taqueria del Sol, a counter-service restaurant in a repurposed repair shop with a limited menu of tacos, simple side dishes, several weekly specials, and a full bar with specialty margaritas. Today we have locations throughout Atlanta and in other cities, including Athens, Georgia; and Nashville.

A BORROWER AND A LENDER

I am always open to new ideas. I am not food correct. I put sugar in my grits—the quick-cooking kind—to balance the heat of jalapeños, even though some Southerners say this is a cardinal sin. I add sweet pickle relish to the gravy I serve over buttermilk fried chicken, and canned corn—creamed and niblets—to my shrimp chowder. I once won a barbecue contest with ribs I baked in the oven. If the food police don't like it, they can sue me! I don't play by any rules but Eddie's.

In Mexico we eat what we like and don't worry about what is authentic to this cuisine or that. We take shortcuts. We improvise. We adapt to whatever is around us. Our cuisine was built on borrowing ideas from other cultures, from the Spanish explorers who invaded us, to the French who briefly occupied us, to the native peoples who came thousands of years before us. The cuisine of the South is equally diverse. The cooks I have gotten to know here are generous in sharing their knowledge, and I am always honored to share what I can whenever I am asked.

My grandmother's sense of creativity—born of necessity—dominates my thinking in the kitchen. If I have a philosophy of cooking, it comes from the lessons instilled in me by her: Be creative. Don't be wasteful. Take pride in your work. And always pay attention so you learn to do things for yourself.

In Mexico we don't worry about what is authentic. We take shortcuts. We improvise. We adapt.

MY MEX-AMERICAN KITCHEN

We Mexicans tend to be thrifty by nature because we are a poor culture. That's what makes us such good cooks! For thousands of years, we have been making meals with beans, corn, squash, chiles, and not much else. Getting creative within the limitations of what is most affordable and available is the challenge, and the fun.

My shelves are not cluttered with fancy or exotic bottles and boxes of this and that. Other than a few dried chiles that may require a trip to an international market, most every ingredient in my recipes can be found at any grocery store. In fact, you probably already have them in your cabinets and refrigerators.

I use mostly fresh produce, but very basic: head lettuce, tomatoes, cabbages, onions, carrots, celery, and of course, a never-ending supply of peppers, avocados, herbs, and spices—and turnip greens! As for meat, I go for the most economical cuts—no filet mignon.

Keep in mind that whenever you are working with fresh ingredients, no matter how precise your measurements or instructions, the results will vary slightly. The tomatoes you buy may be sweeter and juicier one day than on another. You can never predict just how hot your chiles are going to be.

The biggest key to good cooking is to taste as you go. One thing I suggest: Follow my recipes the way I have written them the first time, so you will know how they are supposed to taste. Then you can decide if you want to change them the next time.

EQUIPMENT

For the most part, you will do just fine with what you have on hand. Here are a few fairly inexpensive specialized tools and appliances that may be useful.

BLENDER AND FOOD PROCESSOR

In most recipes they are not interchangeable. For a silky-smooth sauce or soup, a fresh fruit drink (*agua fresca*), or anything that calls for ice, you need the powerful motor of the blender. The depth of the container will hold more liquid and keep it from overflowing or leaking. For pureed soups, an immersion blender you can stick right in the pot is convenient but by no means essential. But many salsas and spreads are meant to be a little chunky, and for

them you will need the razor-sharp, whirling blade of a food processor—especially if they contain hard ingredients like nuts and seeds. You can control the texture better by pulsing.

CAST-IRON SKILLET

Like every good Southern cook, I love my cast-iron skillet. It is ideal for frying and searing because it holds heat so well and steadily. While a deep-fat fryer can be very handy, a cast-iron skillet will do the job just as well if you monitor the temperature with a thermometer. Use a deeper Dutch oven for large pieces that can splatter. Be sure to keep your skillet well seasoned to keep foods from sticking, and don't use strong detergents or abrasive scouring pads to clean it. Sprinkle in some salt to scrub stubborn bits. To reseason it, clean it well with a sponge, rub a little vegetable oil or melted vegetable shortening over the inside and outside, and set it upside down on the top rack of a 350-degree oven (with a pan underneath for catching drips) for about an hour. Turn off the oven and let the pan cool completely in the oven before using.

ELECTRIC GRIDDLE
Its even heat is ideal for heating tortillas, toasting spices, and dry-roasting chiles.

ELECTRIC SPICE OR COFFEE GRINDER OR MOLCAJETE/TEJOLETE
Centuries before there was electricity, Mexicans used a three-legged mortar (*molcajete*) and pestle (*tejolete*) made of volcanic rock, or basalt, to pulverize spices and other ingredients. Some purists still prefer to do it this way, but I rarely do. For small quantities, a spice grinder or a coffee grinder dedicated for this purpose will achieve the same results.

INDOOR SMOKER AND WOOD CHIPS
For the indoor smoking of pork barbecue and brisket and many other things, from tomatoes to salmon to butter, an indoor smoker is handy. If you don't want to make this investment, I show you how to rig your own device on page 64. Camerons makes a stainless-steel smoker for indoors or outdoors for under $60 that comes with small plastic containers of fine wood chips specially suited for stovetop smoking.

POTATO MASHER
You'll have more control over the texture of your mashed potatoes if you mash them by hand with a sturdy potato masher rather than a food processor or mixer. Overmixing potatoes can cause them to become gluey. A potato masher is also good for mashing up a small batch of refried beans.

SLOW COOKER
You can do so many things with it, from stews to beans, but I use mine mostly for an indoor version of barbacoa (meat traditionally cooked in an underground pit). It's also good for keeping cheese dip hot for a party.

STAND MIXER
Not a necessity for everyday cooking, but good to have for mixing the dough for *bolillos* (Mexican rolls).

TAMALE STEAMER
Any large pot can be used for steaming tamales, but the lidded aluminum pots found in Latin markets come with a steam rack that is ideal. They are also great for steaming seafood and cooking soups and chili. Bamboo steamers can be used, but the tamales will take longer to cook.

THERMOMETER
A reliable deep-fry thermometer is indispensable for regulating the temperature of hot oil, especially when frying food in batches. An instant-read meat thermometer is always a good idea, especially for leaner meats that are prone to overcooking.

TORTILLA PRESS AND ROLLING PIN
For corn tortillas, I use a press made of lightweight cast aluminum (less than $20 in Latin markets and many cookware stores). You set a ball of dough on the bottom plate and use the handle to press the top plate, lined with plastic wrap, down to flatten it. You can also press tortilla dough between dinner plates, with the bottom of a skillet, with a rolling pin, or even with your hands, but a tortilla press does a much better job of creating the uniform-size disks you want. I roll flour tortillas out with a small (8-inch) rolling pin, sold in Latin markets (or online) and designed for this purpose. A conventional rolling pin also works.

PRODUCE

AVOCADOS

The best-tasting avocados—and the only ones I use for guacamole—are Hass, which were first planted in California in the 1920s. They are the ones that are shaped like pears with very dark, pebbly skin that you see in any supermarket. Their flesh is creamy and buttery rich, perfect for guacamole. They are harvested while green, and ripen off the tree to a dark purplish-black. It's always a good idea to shop for them several days before you plan to use them, since there is a good chance you won't be able to find a single one in the bin that is ready to cut into that day. The best way to judge ripeness is to hold it in your palm and give it a gentle squeeze. Don't use your fingertips, since they can bruise it. If it yields slightly, it's ripe. If it feels mushy, it is over the hill. To speed the softening of a rock-hard avocado, put it in a paper bag with a banana or an apple. The bag will trap the ethylene gas released by those fruits, which will make the avocado ripen faster. Refrigerating slows the ripening.

Once you do cut an avocado open, the flesh will turn brown quickly. A few drops of lemon or lime juice or other acid will slow down that process. When I want to taste the avocado—not acid—I drizzle a little oil over the top. To save an avocado half, wrap it in plastic wrap, pressing the plastic against the flesh.

CHILES

Chiles are the lifeblood of Mexican cuisine and still the key to how I cook today. They are among the world's oldest crops and an important ingredient around the world. For about 6,000 years, poor Mexicans have relied on them to transform a bland diet of mostly dried beans and corn into something exciting and flavorful. That's a long time for us to get really good at using them!

I love to work with chiles because they can be manipulated in so many different ways to achieve different effects. People tend to associate them strictly with capsaicin, the natural chemical within them that makes them hot. But they also add color, texture, and layers of complex flavor to everything from salsas to main dishes, even to drinks and desserts. And they are really good for you, with lots of vitamins A and C and antioxidants.

To fully appreciate them, you have to understand what they can do in their different forms: raw, dried, pickled, boiled, fried, or roasted until black. Some chiles are mild enough to be stuffed with meat and grains like a main-dish vegetable; others are so hot that the only way to eat them is to infuse them in liquid and sprinkle them on food, drop by drop.

Because their heat levels can be so unpredictable, cooking with them can feel like a game of Russian roulette. The heat level can vary wildly even within the same variety. Each pepper releases its heat differently. Some peppers hit you in the back of the throat; with others, the heat immediately goes all over your tongue and lips.

The membranes and seeds are where most of the heat is concentrated, and for that reason, many recipes will play it safe and tell you to cut them out before proceeding. But I almost never do this. Besides getting rid of heat, you will also eliminate the flavor elements that round out a chile's character. I like to be able to taste the whole chile, and very often I will just toss the entire pepper, minus the stem, into the blender or food processor with the rest of a sauce's ingredients.

For these recipes, I give you the option of deciding how daring you want to be. Sometimes I provide a range, so you can start with the lesser amount, taste, and add more. Or you can chop up the membranes with the seeds separately and add them a little at a time.

HOW HOT IS THAT CHILE?

The heat of chiles is measured in Scoville heat units. More than a hundred years ago, a pharmacist in Detroit named Wilbur Scoville came up with a test to figure out the range of capsaicinoid compounds that determine a chile's heat. A bell pepper has 0 SHU (Scoville heat units), while a Trinidad Moruga Scorpion pepper or Carolina Reaper can have more than 2 million. Most chiles are somewhere in the middle and can have a wide range of heat within their own variety, depending on how old the chile is, the soil and weather conditions of where it was grown, and how it was grown.

GAUGING HEAT

- Cut the chile open and hold it close to your nose. If you feel a tingling sensation, you know there is heat. The stronger the sensation, the hotter it is.
- Smaller peppers are generally hotter than larger peppers.
- Peppers that have broad shoulders and rounded tips are milder than the ones with narrow shoulders and pointed tips.
- With some peppers, like jalapeños, thin, light brown stripes around the pepper can indicate heat. The more scarring, the older and the hotter it will likely be.
- The stem end tends to be the hottest part of the pepper because that is where most of the seeds are.
- Try this trick: Stick a toothpick into the seediest part of the chile, then touch the tip to your tongue. See if you feel a burn.

BUYING AND STORING CHILES

Choose peppers that are firm and free of wrinkles, bruises, or soft spots.

- Fresh peppers will keep for about 5 days in a plastic bag on the counter, or 10 or more in the refrigerator. Be sure to store them separately from other items, even other types of chiles. Their oils can rub off on other produce.
- Be very careful that you don't touch your eyes or other sensitive spots when working with chiles, especially with very hot ones. The capsaicin they contain is not water soluble and can linger on your skin even after you've washed your hands with soap and water. It's never a bad idea to wear rubber gloves, especially if you have a large quantity to chop.
- Buy loose dried chiles instead of pre-bagged whenever possible so you can choose the ones that look best. They should be richly colored and not dusty looking, free of blemishes, and slightly flexible. Place them in an airtight container and store in a cool, dry area for up to a year from when they were purchased.

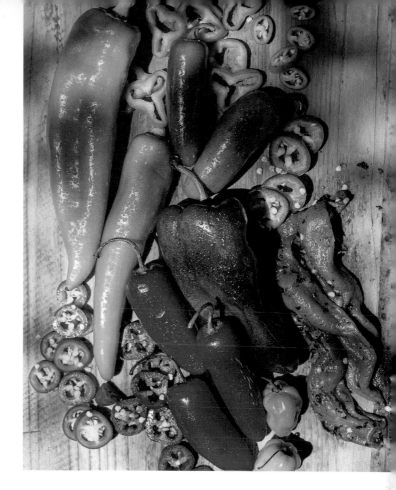

FRESH CHILES

Habanero (300,000–350,000 SHU)

These small, lantern-shaped chiles are about 2 inches tall and 1½ inches wide and extremely hot, with a hint of fruit flavor that works well raw, in salsas, and cooked in tomato sauces. They have smooth, thin, waxy skin and come in shades of pale green, yellow, orange, and red, with the red ones being the hottest. Habaneros came to Mexico and South America from the Amazons, where they were domesticated. They are often confused with their smaller cousin, the Scotch bonnet, which originated in Jamaica and is used extensively in Caribbean dishes. Scotch bonnets have a similar appearance and taste, but they are quite a bit hotter. Habaneros and Scotch bonnets can be used interchangeably, but be aware that they are not the same.

Jalapeño (3,500–11,000 SHU)

These meaty, smooth-skinned chiles are readily available in supermarkets around the world, and they're the variety we use the most by far at TDS. The name "jalapeño" comes from Jalapa, the capital of Veracruz, Mexico, where the pepper was first cultivated. Jalapeños are typically 2 to 4 inches long and are usually dark green, with some red ripe ones available during summer. The green ones have a grassy, juicy flavor similar to a green bell pepper, and some aren't much hotter than that. Others can set your mouth on fire. Red ones are more mature and a bit sweeter and hotter, and are the main ingredient in Sriracha sauce. (Red Fresnos are sometimes used in place of the red jalapeños.) I love working with jalapeños because they are so versatile. They are good raw, boiled, fried, or roasted, with or without the skin. A spoonful of minced jalapeño, including its seeds and membranes, can add a tingly undertone to a sauce or a dressing. Or you can chop up several whole ones and toss into a pan with other vegetables to spice up a quick sauté.

Smaller peppers tend to be hotter than larger ones. A jar of pickled jalapeños is great to have on hand for a taco or a cheese dip. I also like to pickle my own (page 214).

New Mexico, or Hatch (6,000–8,000 SHU)

New Mexico's Hatch green chiles (see photo above) come into season every August and September, when they are celebrated throughout the Southwest. These meaty long green chiles are grown around the village of Hatch, just west of the banks of the Rio Grande, and are considered by many people to be the best-tasting chiles in the world. They range in heat from very mild to hot and are often used interchangeably with Anaheim, poblano, or banana wax chiles, especially for *rellenos*. Every year, we bring in a large shipment and roast them in the restaurant parking lot to use in specials throughout the season.

Poblano (1,000–1,500 SHU)

Poblano peppers are dark green V-shaped peppers about 5 inches long and 3 inches wide, with a deep, earthy flavor that falls on a heat scale about halfway between a bell pepper and a jalapeño. They originated in Puebla, Mexico, where residents are called Poblanos, and they are one of Mexico's most popular chiles. Because of their size and thick skins, they are excellent for roasting and stuffing. They can also be diced and eaten raw, or

sautéed in dishes. Like bell peppers, their seeds are quite large and hard and should be removed along with the membranes before eating. Poblanos may also be labeled *pasillas* or *rellenos*. They are sometimes used in place of recipes calling for Hatch, Anaheim, or chilaca. The poblano reddens and becomes hotter as it ripens.

Serrano (10,000–23,000 SHU)

These slender green peppers are 2 to 3 inches long and are often used in place of jalapeños. But the flavor is different—usually hotter, greener, and more intense, with a quick burst of heat that goes away quickly. They are firmer and less juicy than jalapeños, and are rarely seeded or peeled before being used in salsas or cooked dishes.

ROASTING FRESH PEPPERS

Roasting peppers before adding them to dishes does two things: It allows you to easily peel away the skin, which on larger peppers can add an unpleasant texture to food if left intact, and it facilitates the caramelization of the peppers' naturally occurring sugars, mellowing, sweetening, and deepening the flavor of the peppers. In recipes like Salsa Asada (page 204), where the charred bits add a smoky-bitter flavor that I like, I don't remove the skins. The seeds and membranes can be removed, depending on how much heat you want.

Gas stove: This method is ideal if (1) you need to roast only a few peppers and (2) you have a gas stove.

Turn on the exhaust fan in your kitchen. Turn the gas flame on a stovetop burner to high. Place the peppers on the grate, spacing them evenly. Roast directly over the flame, turning occasionally, until the peppers' skins are blistered and blackened. Transfer the peppers to a paper bag and close to allow the peppers to steam. When they are cool enough to handle, peel away the blackened skins, and remove the stems and seeds, if desired.

Oven broiler: This method is especially good for larger quantities of peppers.

Move the oven rack to its highest position. Heat the broiler to high. Place the peppers on a baking sheet and lightly brush with vegetable oil. Roast under the broiler, turning occasionally, until the skins are blistered and blackened. Transfer the peppers to a paper bag and close to allow the peppers to steam. When they are cool enough to handle, peel away the blackened skins, and remove the stems and seeds, if desired.

Gas grill: Suitable for large or small quantities of peppers, and a good solution when you don't have a gas stovetop. The key is to blacken the skins as quickly as possible so the flesh remains firm.

Preheat the grill to high. Arrange the peppers on the grate. Brush lightly with vegetable oil. Grill, turning occasionally, until the skins are blistered and blackened. Transfer the peppers to a paper bag and close to allow the peppers to steam. When they are cool enough to handle, peel away the blackened skins, and remove the stems and seeds, if desired.

Skillet: Suitable for small quantities of peppers when you're in a hurry. Heat a skillet, preferably cast-iron, over high heat. Add the peppers. Cook, gently pressing the peppers against the skillet, until their skins are blistered and blackened. Transfer the peppers to a paper bag and close to allow the peppers to steam. When they are cool enough to handle, peel away the blackened skins, and remove the stems and seeds, if desired.

For jalapeños and other smaller peppers that don't need to be peeled, I often quick-fry them in a little oil, just long enough to caramelize them and soften the skins rather than char them. This mellows the flavor of the pepper in a way that works really well with some of my mayonnaise-based sauces.

DRIED CHILES

Ancho (1,000–2,500 SHU)

Dark brown, triangular-shaped ancho chiles are the dried version of a fully ripe, red poblano. They are about 3½ inches long, mildly spicy, with notes of dried fruit. I soak them first and puree them, then add the pulp to mashed potatoes, sautéed chicken, enchilada sauces, stews, and many other dishes.

Chile de árbol (15,000–25,000 SHU)

These skinny, bright red peppers are dried and sold whole, flaked, or ground. I use all three forms. I toast the whole peppers before pureeing them with roasted tomatillos for salsa, and I use flaked or ground chiles de árbol in recipes that typically call for cayenne pepper or red chile flakes. They are hotter than cayenne pepper and have a slightly different flavor profile, although many people can't tell the difference.

Chipotle (5,000–10,000 SHU)

These are the dried version of jalapeños that are smoked rather than air-dried, giving them a distinctive smoky, spicy flavor. In the U.S., they are most often reconstituted and packed into cans with adobo sauce, a hot and tangy puree of tomato, vinegar, and spices.

This product can be a convenient thing to have to liven up a sauce or soup in a hurry, but I have grown tired of the flavor. Now I use it only in a few dishes. I prefer the dried, unadulterated chile, which is a bit harder to come by but worth seeking out. It is a key flavor component of my homemade chorizo sausage (page 31).

Guajillo (3,000–6,000 SHU)

These dark red peppers are about 4½ inches long and 2 inches at their widest point, and have a fruity, earthy, mildly spicy flavor. They are a staple in my kitchen, and I often puree them as I do anchos. They are really good in chili and with pork.

CANNED AND BOTTLED CHILES

In most recipes that call for mild roasted chiles, canned are a fine substitute—and a practical choice, especially if the recipe calls for a large quantity. Canned chipotles in adobo, with their distinctive flavor, are an easy way to season a dish—maybe too easy. Jarred pickled jalapeños are great to have on hand for quickly dressing up a taco or flavoring a sauce. I also like to keep an assortment of bottled heat: Tabasco, Texas Pete, El Yucateco habanero sauce, and Sriracha.

CRANKING UP THE HEAT

It's fun and easy to grow chile peppers at home, and it's a good way to expand your knowledge. A few years ago, I asked a farmer friend of mine, Bill Yoder, to help me plant some varieties in my yard that I didn't know very well so I could understand them better. I am particularly interested in the really hot ones, designed for true chile-head people like myself. I planted some bhut jolokia, also known as the ghost pepper, after Guinness World Records named it "Hottest Chile" in the world. Chile-heads started posting videos of themselves eating the peppers whole on YouTube, and pretty soon you could buy ghost-pepper candy and Wendy's french fries covered in ghost-pepper sauce.

Ghost peppers are sneaky mothers. There is a fifteen- or twenty-second delay before the burn kicks in—that's why they are called ghosts. But I really like the flavor, both fresh and dried, and have introduced it in very small amounts to restaurant customers. Now every year, it seems, another grower sets a new world record. As of today, the hottest chile on record is the Carolina Reaper. I have grown it as well, and let me tell you, if you bite into one, you need to start praying before you start eating. They take your breath away. You will be on fire, sweating, with tears running down your face.

Unless your goal is to make yourself look like an idiot for all the world to see on a YouTube video, I would not advise attempting to eat one of these whole. You can appreciate their distinct flavors as well as their heat by turning them into a flavored vinegar (page 296).

Morita (2,500–10,000 SHU)

These dried, smoked, red-ripe chile peppers are similar to chipotles. They're hot when you put them in your mouth, but quickly mellow. Because they are not smoked as long as chipotles, they are softer and retain more rich, fruity flavor.

Mulato (3,000–5,000 SHU)

Mulatos are relatives of the ancho. They are brownish black and wrinkled when dried and yield a meaty pulp with chocolate and cherry undertones when rehydrated and pureed. They are often used in moles.

TOASTING AND GRINDING DRIED CHILES

Dried chiles release even more flavor when toasted. To do this, place them in a dry skillet and turn the heat on low to medium. Let them toast for 5 to 10 minutes, giving the pan an occasional shake, until the skins have darkened slightly. Be careful not to scorch them, as they can turn bitter.

Remove the stems and, for a milder spice, shake out the seeds. Grind the chiles in your spice or coffee grinder and store in a glass jar. They will be good to use for a year or more.

HERBS

The pungent leaves of the cilantro plant (whose seeds are called coriander) are an essential ingredient in many classic Mexican dishes, and I always keep plenty of bunches on hand. But we Mexicans are also accustomed to cooking with many other herbs, including basil, thyme, mint, and parsley.

To extend the freshness of these tender herbs, wash them well, dry with paper towels, and snip off the stem ends and wilted leaves. Then stick the stem ends into a jar with a few inches of water, like a bouquet of flowers. Cover the top with a piece of plastic wrap and seal it with a rubber band.

LEMONS AND LIMES

When I talk about limes, people often think I mean lemons because the Spanish word for "limes" is *limones,* and I often forget to translate. I use a lot of both, but in different ways. Limes are slightly more acidic than lemons, and lemons are higher in sugar. In a cocktail or a sauce for seafood, a shot of lime often provides just the refreshingly bitter edge I want. But I find that the high acid content can also quickly destroy a piece of fish in a marinade, or turn a salsa to mush. So for most of my everyday cooking, I will use lemons instead. I should point out that the limes I use today are the common dark green Persians you see everywhere, but the ones I was more accustomed to in Mexico were the small, yellow Key limes, whose juice is even more intense. Key limes are worth trying—if you can find them, which isn't easy—especially for a creamy custard dessert like the pie made famous in the Florida Keys.

LETTUCE

I am old-school when it comes to lettuce. Romaine and iceberg lettuce were the salad greens I knew growing up, and they are the only ones I still use regularly. Their mild, clean flavor and cool, crunchy texture work well with the chiles and other assertive ingredients in salads, tacos, and tostadas.

ONIONS

Mexican cooks use the whitest of white onions in their dishes more than any other onion, especially in relishes and salsas. White onions have a cleaner taste and a crisper texture than yellow ones, which are milder and sweeter. Yellow onions are good in slower-cooking dishes like soups and stews, where they are more of a background player. My general rule of thumb is to use yellow onions only in dishes where they become translucent and practically disappear from sight. I use red onions when I want to add crunch and vibrant color to raw dishes. Since coming to Georgia, I have also become a fan of the sweet Vidalia onion. I use them like a vegetable in dishes where I can showcase their naturally sweet flavor, such as Foil-Roasted Beets and Vidalia Onions with Butter, Lime, and Sea Salt (page 244).

TOMATILLOS

Tomatillos are sometimes called Mexican green tomatoes. Once you peel off their papery husks, they look like miniature versions of the green tomatoes that are sliced, rolled in cornmeal, and fried in restaurants all over the South. Both members of the nightshade family, tomatillos and green tomatoes have a similar tart flavor. But they are from two different plants and are good for different things. In addition to being fried, green tomatoes are often pickled and made into relishes and jams. Tomatillos are the basis for many green salsas and sauces. If fresh, they are usually simmered or roasted in the oven first. Canned tomatillos taste almost the same as fresh once they are pureed with fresh ingredients, and canned are what I use in green salsa dipping sauce. I use roasted fresh tomatillos when I'm dressing up the refried beans in my veggie tacos, or for a gravy that I serve over roast pork.

TOMATOES

In Mexico I was used to having easy access to ripe, flavorful tomatoes year-round. We never used canned tomatoes and I never developed a taste for them, even when I moved to the States, where good tomatoes are harder to come by in cooler months. While there's nothing that compares to the flavor of a perfectly ripe tomato picked fresh off the vine in the summer, the quality and availability of off-season tomatoes has greatly improved over the years. And fresh is still my preference, even in most sauces where canned are routinely used. Before using store-bought fresh tomatoes in a cooked dish, I let them ripen fully on the counter. Then I soften them by putting them in a pot, covering them with water, and turning the heat to high. When the water starts to boil and the skins begin to crack, I remove them to a blender or food processor.

Or instead of water, I may plunge them into hot oil for a few seconds. If I want to deepen and concentrate the tomatoes' flavor, I roast them in the oven first or toss them whole in a hot skillet until their skins are blistered. Some people core them and take the skins off, but if I am pureeing them, I see no reason to bother. To me it is wasteful, and I like to taste the whole tomato.

PANTRY INGREDIENTS

DRIED BEANS

Pinto means "spotted" in Spanish and refers to the speckles on the beans. Pinto beans are the most popular bean in northern Mexico and the ones we use most at Taqueria del Sol to make *charros* (stewed pinto beans) and refried beans, much like the ones my mother used to make. But if you visit any market in Mexico, you will see many more varieties in all colors, shapes, and sizes. I also grew up eating black beans regularly and sometimes other dried legumes that are popular in the South, like kidney beans and navy beans, and even black-eyed peas and butter beans.

For most bean dishes, I use dried beans, but canned work well when you are short on time. I soak the dried beans overnight before using them in the restaurant. It shortens the cooking time, and some people believe it makes them easier to digest. But I have also skipped this step and no one could tell the difference.

DRIED CORN PRODUCTS

Hominy, masa and masa harina, cornmeal, and grits (white and yellow) all start with dried *maize*, or field corn. But they are processed differently and cannot be used interchangeably.

Hominy: To make mature field-corn kernels edible, they must first be soaked in a mineral lime solution, lye, or wood ash. This ancient process, called nixtamalization, loosens the tough hulls surrounding the kernels, causing the kernels to swell up to double their size. This improves the corn's flavor and aroma and allows its nutrients, like niacin, to be absorbed by the body. Most Mexican cooks

have a few cans of whole hominy in the cabinet for soups and stews, or for eating as a side dish. You can also buy it dried and reconstitute it.

Masa and masa harina: *Masa* is Spanish for "dough," and it is made by grinding soaked hominy. This is used to make corn tortillas and tamales. The hominy dough is used fresh, or dried and ground into masa harina, a flour that is readily available in Mexican markets and many supermarkets. Maseca is the most popular brand in Mexico and the one I prefer (see photo, page 7).

Cornmeal: Do not attempt to make a tortilla using the cornmeal you use for making corn bread. It will not work because it is processed differently. There are two types of cornmeal: stone-ground and commercial. Stone-ground cornmeal is ground the old-fashioned way, between slow-moving stones, and still contains some of the hulls and germs, where most of the nutrients are. It's usually coarser and has a more distinctive corn flavor than commercial cornmeal, which is produced by passing corn kernels through metal rollers that remove most of the hulls and germs. Commercial cornmeal is less perishable and is typically enriched with the vitamins and minerals that are lost in the process. Cornmeal makes an excellent crunchy coating that is also gluten-free. It can be made with yellow, white, or blue corn and comes in different grinds: coarse, medium, and fine. Stone-ground and commercial cornmeal can be used interchangeably in recipes. If you buy stone-ground, you should refrigerate or freeze it to keep it from spoiling.

Self-rising cornmeal mix: You can find cornmeal mix, with flour, salt, leavening, and some sugar already added, in the cornmeal section of the grocery store. Food purists would not think of buying this because they say that corn bread has to be made with pure meal and no sugar. But I have no problem using it, especially if I am going to mix in other ingredients.

Precooked cornmeal: I travel to South America frequently and have become a big fan of Harina P.A.N. (Productos Alimenticios Nacionales), a brand of preboiled cornmeal made in Venezuela that is now sold widely in supermarkets in the U.S. It is mainly used for making *arepas*, the cornmeal flatbread native to Venezuela and Colombia that is griddled, fried or baked, and stuffed with a filling. Harina P.A.N. is highly versatile and also makes great empanadas, tortillas, and tamales, as well as many dishes from this side of the border: corn bread, muffins, waffles, pancakes, and hush puppies. (See Cornmeal Waffles, page 30.)

Grits: Grits are a coarser grind of cornmeal. Some, called hominy grits, are treated with lime first, but not all are. I still prefer the creamy texture of quick-cooking grits to the coarser stone-ground grits for most dishes. "Regular" grits are slightly coarser than quick, and take a little longer to cook, but the taste is similar. Don't confuse quick grits with instant grits, which are precooked and dehydrated to a near powder.

RICE

Rice is not native to Mexico, but we were quick to adopt it when the Spaniards brought it during their conquest in the 1500s, and it's been part of our daily diet ever since. The main reason is because it goes with just about anything. We eat it as a side dish, as a stand-alone course in *comida corrida*—our main meal of the day—and baked into sweet custard for dessert. We blend it into a cold drink called *horchata*. I can easily relate to the jambalayas and gumbos of Louisiana and the red rices and pilafs popular in the Carolinas. I mostly use broken rice, kernels that are broken in the milling process and sold very inexpensively (see photo above). I love its fluffy texture. It's not easy to find, though (check online or in Asian markets), so if you don't want to seek it out, any other white rice will produce good results. Jasmine rice has a floral aroma that I like.

DAIRY

CHEESE

The cheddar cheese that's grated into ground-beef tacos in Mexican chains everywhere is not something you see often in Mexico. Most tacos don't have any cheese, except for a few Americanized creations like the Sloppy José (page 72).

I do use several Mexican cheeses for other things.

Queso Cotija is a dry, strong, salty cow's milk cheese that is similar to Parmesan and sometimes sold in granular form. It can be sprinkled over most anything.

I like it on *chilaquiles*.

Queso fresco is a light, fresh cow's milk cheese with a salty tang that comes wrapped in round disks and is good for crumbling on top of enchiladas, beans, or *huevos rancheros*. It tastes a little like feta or goat cheese, which can be substituted.

Queso quesadilla is a part-skim natural cow's milk cheese that becomes stringy when melted, which is ideal for quesadillas, but not so good for dipping.

Other cheeses: Food snobs make a face when I tell them the key ingredient in my cheese dips and sauces is Land O'Lakes Extra Melt White American Cheese Loaf. But as most any honest Tex-Mex restaurant chef will tell you, it's hard to beat for achieving the velvety texture that's just the right consistency for dipping a chip into. Unfortunately it's hard to find (though it is available on Amazon), so I tell home cooks to use Kraft White American Singles or deli-style white American cheese (Boar's Head makes a good product). Velveeta makes a queso blanco cheese loaf that is similar to the familiar bright orange Velveeta but white. It melts well but has a more processed taste.

SOUR CREAM

Mexican crema is similar to American sour cream and crème fraîche, only runnier and not quite as tart. It's sold in plastic bottles in many U.S. supermarkets, or you can make a quick substitute by thinning regular sour cream with a little milk or buttermilk.

PORK, LARD, AND OTHER FATS

PORK

Old-time Southern cooks are famous for using every part of the pig, and Mexicans do the same thing. Most people don't know it, but one of the really good tacos in Mexico is made with chitlins (hog intestines). I know a taco maker back in my hometown, Monterrey, who sells only one kind of taco: It's filled with pork tripe and green salsa.

There is a key difference, though, in how many of our pork dishes taste: In Mexico we don't smoke our meats. You don't find a lot of cured meats, like bacon and ham. Our sausages are typically fresh. If we happen to have fresh ham hocks, we might throw them into a pork-based soup such as *posole* for the meat, but not into a pot of greens or beans, since they lack the flavor of a smoked hock.

PORK BUTT (SHOULDER)

At Taqueria del Sol, I probably use more pork butt than any other meat. It is what I use to make carnitas, and is also the meat of choice in the Memphis-style barbecue for my Memphis Tacos.

Pork butt, or Boston butt, is a confusing name because it is actually the upper part of a pig's shoulder, not its rear end. It may also be labeled pork shoulder. Because of all the connective tissue, the butt has enough fat marbling to keep it moist and tender when it is roasted slowly, or braised, or barbecued.

A whole pork butt weighs anywhere from 6 to

10 pounds and may be sold bone-in or boneless. You could ask the butcher to cut off the amount you need, but I highly recommend that you do that at home and freeze the rest. You will find many great ways to use it in this book.

LARD

When I see cooks cutting off the fat from a pork butt and throwing it in the garbage, it drives me crazy. I can't imagine being that wasteful. In Mexico, lard is a luxury that's more expensive than oil. Cooks keep cans on the stove to save the lard they have rendered themselves from a piece of meat, the way that cooks in the South save their bacon drippings. It is basically the same fat, except lard does not have a smoky taste.

At Taqueria del Sol, I take the fat from the pork butts I use for carnitas and Memphis Tacos with some of the meat underneath still attached, and render it in a big pot. I then immediately use some of that fresh lard in our beans, and pour the rest into a glass jar. Lard keeps forever in the refrigerator. Because of its high smoke point, it is ideal for frying the crispiest chicken you've ever tasted. And you can't beat homemade lard for country gravies or flaky pastries. Lard is so much better for you than most oils. (I am talking about pure lard, not the stuff on supermarket shelves that's full of chemicals.) Pure lard has no trans fats and more of the heart-healthy monounsaturated fats—and less of the artery-clogging saturated fats— than butter. (See page 299 for homemade.)

CHICHARRONES
The crispy browned pieces that cook in the pot as the lard is rendering turn into chicharrones, better known in the U.S. as cracklings. I may simmer them in green salsa for a staff breakfast to go with eggs and corn tortillas or save them to fold into a Southern-style corn bread. Or we'll just pop them in our mouths for a snack, like pork rinds. (See page 299 for homemade.)

COOKING OILS
For the majority of our dishes, I prefer a neutral vegetable oil or vegetable-olive oil blend that can add body and richness without competing flavors.

These oils also have the high smoke point needed for frying. I do not often cook with extra-virgin olive oil or flavored oils because they are expensive and have a bitter flavor when they're heated. I also find that olive oil clashes with chiles. I do keep bottles of olive oil and a few flavored oils on hand for drizzling over the tops of dishes as a finishing touch, when I want that extra flavor. If you sauté zucchini, for example, it's better to use plain vegetable oil first, and then drizzle a little olive oil or a flavored oil on top so the taste is really pronounced.

BUTTER AND MARGARINE
Many people look down on margarine as an inferior substitute for butter, and with all the bad press about trans fats, its reputation has only gotten worse. But for sautéing, it's often a better choice than butter because it is slower to burn yet still imparts some buttery flavor. This is especially true if the dish involves breading. Fine dining restaurants often sauté foods using clarified butter, in which the quick-to-burn milk solids have been removed. But this is a more expensive option, and those milk solids have a lot of flavor. For those who don't want to cook with margarine but also want to lessen the risk of burning their food, I suggest making a batch of Butter Blend (page 299) to have on hand. Or if you are in a hurry, just substitute vegetable oil for all or part of the butter. The higher the ratio of oil to butter, the less likely your food will burn.

SALT

Salt is a flavor enhancer, not a seasoning. For most of my cooking, I use regular table salt because it is more economical. But I do keep sea salt handy for when I want salt to be highlighted. For example, I will use regular salt in the dough for my Mexican rolls, and sprinkle a little coarse sea salt on the top where I want it to stand out. You can use sea salt for everything, if you prefer, but since it is coarser you may need to double the amount you use.

Other than salt, I use fresh and dried chiles to

season my food more than anything else. I never buy commercial chili powders or spice blends. I prefer to devise my own combinations of seasonings instead. You will see them throughout these pages, like the Memphis Spice Rub (page 145) for my ribs. The one I always have on hand is our Cajun Spice Mix (page 291). As you will soon discover, I love Cajun food. I find the flavors to be very compatible with the foods I like to cook. Other Creole seasoning blends on the market may be substituted, but I like mine best.

GOOD FOR BREAKFAST— OR ANY TIME

Chapter One

MY BREAKFAST MUFFINS *24*

SOPAPILLAS *26*

FRITOS CHILAQUILES *27*

CAJUN HASH *28*

CORNMEAL WAFFLES *30*

THREE-CHILE HOMEMADE CHORIZO *31*

  —CHORIZO WITH POTATOES *31*

  —CHORIZO WITH EGGS *31*

EDDIE'S BREAKFAST SAUSAGE *33*

HAM AND EGG TORTA *34*

To my way of thinking, breakfast has no rules.

Breakfast is my favorite meal of the day, because I get to make whatever sounds good to me and not worry about what anyone else thinks. To my way of thinking, and that of most every other Mexican I know, breakfast has no rules. You can eat a steak at ten o'clock in the morning or Frosted Flakes at ten at night. In my large household growing up, we sat down to eat as a family at set times for lunch and dinner. But for breakfast we fended for ourselves. We all knew how to cook. If we didn't feel like having the fried eggs and beans that everyone else was eating, we made scrambled eggs with potatoes and salsa instead. If we were in a hurry, we wrapped everything up in a tortilla to go.

I see a similar attitude here in the South at some of my favorite diners, especially the ones that are open twenty-four hours a day, where I can get a fried pork chop—or in some places, even a piece of catfish—with my eggs instead of bacon or sausage. I may not be able to eat my eggs with tortillas and salsas, but I can have toast or biscuits or waffles, with a choice of grits or hash browns, and jellies and syrups, or hearty gravies.

In my kitchen today, I have the best of both worlds. I always have eggs and grits and the double-thick white bread called Texas toast that is so good for sopping up runny egg yolks. But with Maseca corn flour, I can also make a quick batch of dough for fresh tortillas or *gorditas*. I keep packages of bacon and links of dried and cured Cajun- or Spanish-style sausages on hand, and sometimes I mix up a batch of fresh Mexican-style chorizo or a country-style breakfast sausage, more like what you see in Southern markets. Fry some eggs and ladle over some hot Salsa Frita or Tomato-Habanero Sauce, and you've got huevos rancheros, no recipe required!

Morning is my time to experiment. Sometimes I will try out an idea for a new dinner special on my business partner and some of the guys in the kitchen. I'll throw a fried egg on top, just as we do with almost anything in Mexico, and call it breakfast. I've come up with some of my best dishes this way.

This chapter will open your mind to the infinite possibilities of the first meal of the day and show you how easy and uncomplicated it can be. You don't need a strict list of ingredients or instructions, just some general guidelines to inspire you. Whatever rules you might have about breakfast, I say give yourself permission to break them. This is where creativity begins!

MY BREAKFAST MUFFINS

MAKES 12 MUFFINS

For a fast, convenient way to serve breakfast to a crowd that's far better than sugary pastries, fill some muffin tins with sprinkles of grated cheese and a couple of sausage slices. Then top with eggs that you've beaten with baking powder. Put them in the oven, and in a few minutes, they puff up like little soufflés! Serve them in a pool of leftover Mexican tomato sauce, or try them with Salsa Verde (page 205), Roasted Tomatillo Sauce (page 205), Tomato-Habanero Sauce (page 206), or Salsa Frita (page 204). You can substitute goat cheese or any other kind of cheese for the kinds below, or add crumbled bacon or leftover roasted vegetables in place of the sausage. Or bake a little salsa into the filling and wrap it up and take it to work. The muffins reheat well the next day in the oven or microwave.

---

12 large eggs

4½ teaspoons baking powder

½ teaspoon salt

4 ounces andouille or other smoked sausage, cut into 24 slices; or cooked, crumbled Eddie's Breakfast Sausage (page 33); or Three-Chile Homemade Chorizo (page 31)

¾ cup grated Monterey Jack or Colby cheese

2 cups Tomato-Habanero Sauce (page 206; see headnote)

Heat the oven to 425 degrees. Spray a 12-cup muffin tin with nonstick vegetable spray and set aside.

Whisk the eggs, baking powder, and salt in a large bowl until smooth. Place 2 slices of smoked sausage and 1 tablespoon of the cheese into the bottom of each muffin cup. Divide the egg mixture evenly among the muffin cups. Bake for 10 to 12 minutes, until puffed and lightly browned.

Meanwhile, heat the sauce. Ladle some of the sauce onto plates and top with the egg muffins.

SOPAPILLAS

MAKES 8 SERVINGS (32 SOPAPILLAS)

1 cup sugar

1½ teaspoons ground
   cinnamon

1 recipe bolillo dough
   (page 185, made without
   greasing the pans)

Vegetable oil for frying

Honey or jelly

I like to eat these hot cinnamon doughnuts for breakfast with hot chocolate or Mexican Cinnamon Tea (page 267), or as a snack any time of day.

———————

Mix the sugar and cinnamon together in a large wide bowl.

Set the bolillo dough in a bowl, cover with a cloth, and let rest for 10 minutes.

Roll out the dough to ¼-inch thickness. Cut into 2½-inch rounds with a sharp-edged biscuit cutter.

Line a baking sheet with several thicknesses of paper towels and place a cooling rack on top.

Heat 1½ inches of vegetable oil in a heavy pot or Dutch oven over medium-high heat to 350 degrees.

Gently add the rounds of dough, a few at a time, to the oil. Do not crowd the pot. Fry on both sides until crispy and golden, spooning hot oil over the tops as they cook, 2 to 3 minutes total. Transfer to the cooling rack using a slotted spoon. Drain for 1 to 2 minutes.

Roll the sopapillas in the cinnamon sugar. Repeat with the remaining dough, allowing the oil to return to 350 degrees between batches. Serve with honey or jelly on the side.

FRITOS CHILAQUILES

MAKES 4 TO 6 SERVINGS

This breakfast of eggs, tortillas, and salsa is famous for curing hangovers, but I eat it no matter what I did the night before. If there are some corn tortillas that have gone stale in a Mexican home, they will probably wind up in chilaquiles the next morning. I love to use Fritos because I like the texture—they're thicker and don't get as soggy.

---

6 large eggs

2 big handfuls (about 4 cups) Fritos

½ cup finely chopped onion

2 small jalapeños, stemmed and minced (remove some or all of the seeds and membranes for less heat)

¼ cup vegetable oil

1 to 1½ cups Salsa Frita (page 204)

1 cup grated Cotija or Parmesan cheese

1 cup sour cream or Mexican crema (optional)

Chopped avocado, red onion, fresh cilantro, and/or lime wedges for garnish (optional)

Whisk the eggs in a medium bowl. Add the Fritos, onion, and jalapeños and whisk to combine. Heat the oil in a medium skillet over medium heat until it shimmers. Add the egg mixture and cook, stirring occasionally, until the eggs are set, 1 to 2 minutes. Stir in 1 cup of the salsa and cook for 2 minutes, adding more if desired. Top with half of the cheese, cover the pan, and remove from the heat.

Set aside to rest for 3 minutes, then divide the chilaquiles among four to six plates, topping each serving with a sprinkling of the remaining cheese and a dollop of sour cream and the other garnishes, if desired.

CAJUN HASH

MAKES 6 TO 8 SERVINGS

To turn leftover potatoes into a hearty breakfast dish but with more of a Louisiana flavor, I add andouille, the spicy smoked pork sausage brought to Louisiana by French immigrants, along with some fresh jalapeño and my own Cajun Spice Mix seasoning. Carrots brighten up the color. Leftover diced cooked sweet potatoes or butternut squash would also be good. Serve with eggs on the side, or wrap it in a taco. This hash also makes a good side dish for a simple dinner entrée.

---

2 tablespoons butter

¼ cup diced onion

1 jalapeño, stemmed and
  minced (remove some or all
  of the seeds and membranes
  for less heat)

1 cup diced andouille sausage

2 cups diced cooked potatoes

1 cup diced cooked carrots

1½ teaspoons Cajun Spice Mix
  (page 291)

Melt the butter in a large skillet over medium heat. Add the onion and jalapeño and cook, stirring, until tender, about 1 minute. Add the sausage and cook, stirring, for 2 more minutes.

Add the potatoes and carrots, cook for another minute, then add the Cajun seasoning and cook for 1 minute more, until heated through. Serve.

CORNMEAL WAFFLES

MAKES 8 WAFFLES

Harina P.A.N., the Venezuelan-made preboiled cornmeal traditionally used to make the griddled corn cakes called arepas, adds a great corn flavor and aroma to these light, crunchy waffles (see photo, page 32). They're good not only for breakfast but also with a cup of tomato soup (page 122).

———————

2 cups Harina P.A.N. cornmeal

3 tablespoons sugar

4½ teaspoons baking powder

½ teaspoon salt

2½ cups whole milk

½ cup vegetable oil

4 large eggs

4 tablespoons (½ stick) butter, melted and slightly cooled

1 tablespoon vanilla extract

Spiced syrup (page 282; optional)

Heat the oven to 200 degrees.

Whisk the cornmeal, sugar, baking powder, and salt in a large bowl. Whisk the milk, oil, eggs, butter, and vanilla in another large bowl until well combined. Add the wet mixture to the cornmeal mixture and stir just to combine. Do not overmix; small lumps are okay.

Heat a waffle iron to high and spray with nonstick vegetable spray. When it is hot, add the batter ⅓ cup at a time and cook according to the manufacturer's directions. Keep the waffles warm in the oven until you've made them all. Serve with the spiced syrup, if desired.

THREE-CHILE HOMEMADE CHORIZO

MAKES 5 CUPS

Mexican chorizo is not like the red Spanish chorizo, which is cured and can be sliced and eaten as is. Ours is made of fresh ground pork, more like Southern-style breakfast sausage but flavored with vinegar, several kinds of dried chiles, and other spices. It does not have to be stuffed into casings, so it is easy to make a big batch and keep some in the freezer. Form it into patties or crumble and cook with potatoes and eggs for breakfast. I also add it to savory sauces and cheese dips.

4 dried guajillo chiles, stemmed and seeded

1 dried chipotle chile, stemmed and seeded

1 dried ancho chile, stemmed and seeded

1 cup apple cider vinegar

2 garlic cloves, peeled

2½ pounds ground pork

1 large egg

2 tablespoons ground cumin

1 tablespoon dried oregano

1 tablespoon salt

1 tablespoon ground black pepper

3 bay leaves

Soak the chiles in water overnight, or pour hot water over them and let soak for 30 minutes.

Drain the chiles and place in a blender. Add the vinegar and garlic and puree. Strain through a coarse strainer so you get a little of the pulp. Set aside.

Combine the pork, egg, cumin, oregano, salt, and pepper in a large bowl. Add the pepper puree and the bay leaves and mix well. Cover with plastic wrap and refrigerate for at least 2 hours and up to overnight. The sausage will keep in the freezer for up to 3 months.

Place the chorizo in a large skillet. Cover and cook over medium-high heat until cooked through, about 10 minutes for a full batch and 5 minutes for smaller batches. Remove the bay leaves. Serve or use as desired.

VARIATIONS

CHORIZO WITH POTATOES

Heat a little vegetable oil in a skillet over medium-high heat until hot, then add the chorizo. Cook and stir until browned. Remove the bay leaves. Transfer from the pan to a bowl. Add a little more oil to the skillet and cook sliced onions and diced, cooked potatoes until crusty, then stir in the chorizo. Season with salt and pepper.

CHORIZO WITH EGGS

Cook the chorizo in a skillet over medium heat until browned. Remove the bay leaves. Pour some beaten eggs over it and cook, stirring, until set.

Cornmeal Waffles (page 30) with
Eddie's Breakfast Sausage

EDDIE'S BREAKFAST SAUSAGE

MAKES 16 SERVINGS (ABOUT 16 PATTIES)

My sausage patties are similar to the Southern-style breakfast sausage available here, with lots of black pepper and sage. I give them extra heat with jalapeño, and mix in some of my homemade lard to keep the meat extra moist and juicy. You can use the sausage for a thousand different things other than breakfast, like Holy Trinity Rice and Sausage (page 195).

Divide it into portions, wrap tightly in plastic wrap, and freeze what you aren't using right away.

———

¼ cup chopped onion

1 garlic clove, crushed

1 large egg

2 pounds ground pork

1 jalapeño, stemmed and minced (remove some or all of the seeds and membranes for less heat)

1 tablespoon ground black pepper

2 teaspoons salt

1½ teaspoons ground sage

½ cup lard, preferably homemade (page 299)

In a food processor, grind the onion, garlic, and egg into a fine mash. Transfer to a large bowl. Add the pork, jalapeño, black pepper, salt, sage, and lard and mix well.

Form into 16 patties. The uncooked sausages will keep, wrapped in plastic wrap and refrigerated, for 2 days, or frozen for 3 months.

In a large skillet, in batches, fry the patties on both sides over medium-high heat until browned and cooked though, 8 to 10 minutes. Serve.

HAM AND EGG TORTA

MAKES 4 SERVINGS

The breakfast sandwich in Mexico came long before the Egg McMuffin. It starts with a really good roll. If you have some homemade bolillos, you are halfway there. A crusty French roll will work, too. I really like the combination of ham and eggs, even if it's just pressed, packaged lunch meat—one of the few smoked meats Mexicans could afford. But by all means use some high-quality mortadella or prosciutto if you have it. Smear both sides with mayonnaise, add a slice of really ripe and juicy tomato, some avocado and onion, and a runny fried egg. The only thing I recommend is that you never eat and drive with this torta, or you will have egg yolk all over the steering wheel and your pants, though it is well worth the mess!

---

4 tablespoons vegetable oil,
  butter, lard, or Butter Blend
  (page 299) for frying
4 large eggs
4 bolillos (page 185) or French
  bread rolls (wrapped in foil
  and warmed in the oven, or
  split and toasted, if desired)
Mayonnaise
Onion slices
Tomato slices
Avocado slices
4 slices smoked ham
Pickled jalapeño slices

Heat 1 tablespoon of the fat in a skillet over medium heat. When hot, crack the eggs one at a time into the skillet and cook until the whites are set. Flip, and cook to the desired doneness (I prefer mine runny).

Split open a warm bolillo and spread both sides with mayonnaise. Layer the bottom half with an onion slice, tomato slice, avocado slice, ham slice, and a few pickled jalapeño slices. Top with a fried egg. Add the top bun and assemble the remaining tortas.

CHIPS, DIPS, AND OTHER SNACKS

Chapter Two

CAJUN BOILED PEANUTS *41*

TAQUERIA DEL SOL JALAPEÑO-CHEESE DIP *42*

CHUNKY MEXICAN-STYLE GUACAMOLE *45*

DEVILED EGGS WITH PIMENTO CHEESE
   AND SPICY BREAD AND BUTTER PICKLES *46*
    —DEVILED EGGS WITH MEXICAN
     FLAVORS *48*

GUACAMOLE MINI TACOS *49*

CRISPY MINI TACO SHELLS *50*

SWEET AND TANGY CEVICHE TOSTADAS *51*

TOMATO AND PICKLED PORK SKIN TOSTADAS *52*

HOMEMADE TOSTADAS AND CHIPS *53*

FRIED GREEN TOMATILLOS WITH PEACH-
   HABANERO SAUCE *54*

MEXICAN "SUSHI" ROLL-UPS *56*
   —TAMARIND-GINGER SAUCE *57*

SMOKED SALMON–CHIPOTLE PIZZA ON
   FRY BREAD *58*
   —CHIPOTLE MAYONNAISE *59*

I choose not to complicate things.

Our appetizer list at Taqueria del Sol is short and basic: three kinds of salsa, guacamole, and queso (cheese) dip, served with baskets of chips warm from the deep fryer. We make them fresh daily.

I choose not to complicate things any more than that, and the reason is simple. I want to put everyone—no matter their age, color, or where they came from—in a comfortable mood for socializing, with flavors they recognize and enjoy. This is how conversations start and friendships are made. By treating these favorite appetizers with respect, I want to build your trust so you will want to try my less traditional specialties for the main meal.

Outside of the restaurant, I take a broader view. For parties, I often serve a variety of tostadas, more like the way my grandmother Chelo did at her bar in Mexico, with toppings such as ceviche, black-eyed pea salad, or refried beans topped with salsa. David Waller, who heads our catering operation, is from North Carolina and has showed me how Southern cocktail foods like pimento cheese and deviled eggs blend in well with Mexican flavors on a buffet table. Roasted peanuts are a standard bar food in Mexico, right along with the bowls of chicharrones and fried minnows. Then I discovered deliciously salty and soggy boiled peanuts on a road trip to Tennessee, and couldn't wait to simmer them with the spicy seasonings I like.

These recipes are built for ease. Break out the tequila, crack open some beers, and you're ready to join your guests!

CAJUN
BOILED PEANUTS

MAKES 2 POUNDS

When my kids were small, I used to take them in my little pickup truck on road trips to the Tennessee mountains in the fall. Along the way we would stop at small country stores and buy bags of boiled peanuts that had been simmering in slow cookers. I loved them! Years later, to kick off a barbecue fundraising event, I boiled peanuts in Cajun Spice Mix. The taste reminded me of Louisiana-style boiled crawfish. Instead of pinching the tails and sucking the heads of the crawfish, you crack the shells with your teeth, pop the peanuts into your mouth, and suck out the briny juices in the pod.

Unless you order them online, raw "green" peanuts are hard to find outside the growing area because they spoil quickly due to their high moisture content. Green peanuts are in season in summer and fall, depending on where they're grown. A good source for green Georgia peanuts is Hardy Farms (hardyfarmspeanuts.com).

---

1 gallon water, or more as
   needed
2 pounds raw green peanuts in
   shell (see headnote)
2 cups (4 recipes) Cajun Spice
   Mix (page 291)

Fill a pot with the water and heat over medium-high heat until the water is almost boiling. Add the peanuts, reduce the heat to medium, and maintain a low boil for 1 hour.

Add the seasoning and continue to cook for 1½ hours or longer, depending on how soft you like the peanuts, adding more water if needed to keep the peanuts submerged. Turn off the heat and let the peanuts cool for at least 30 minutes before draining and eating. The boiled peanuts will keep refrigerated, wrapped airtight, for 7 to 10 days, or frozen for up to 6 months.

TAQUERIA DEL SOL JALAPEÑO-CHEESE DIP

MAKES 2½ CUPS

People love our velvety cheese dip and are always asking us for the secret to how we make it. They can't believe how easy it is when we share the recipe. The key is in using the right cheese, and here is where it can get a little tricky. We use Land O'Lakes Extra Melt White American Cheese, the product most respectable Tex-Mex restaurants choose for achieving the smooth texture that's just the right consistency for dipping a chip into. Unfortunately it's hard to find retail, but other white pasteurized process American cheeses from the deli case, such as Boar's Head, can come very close. Velveeta is good for queso dips that are loaded with strong flavors like tomatoes and sausages, but because there are so few ingredients in this recipe, there's nothing to mask those artificial flavors that keep it shelf stable. And don't be tempted to use a more expensive, natural cheese—the sharper the cheese, the grainier it will be. Be sure to grate the cheese yourself just before using so it doesn't dry out—commercially pregrated cheese contains cornstarch or some other nonclumping ingredient that prevents it from melting smoothly.

Besides being a great dip, this also makes a delicious sauce for ground-beef tacos and enchiladas.

———————

1 cup whole milk

1 pound (about 4 cups) freshly grated white pasteurized process American cheese (such as Land O'Lakes or Boar's Head; see headnote)

2 to 4 tablespoons diced pickled jalapeños

Diced fresh jalapeños for garnish

Tortilla chips

Bring the milk to a boil in a medium saucepan. Remove from the heat. Stir in the grated cheese and pickled jalapeños. Whisk until smooth, about 5 minutes. Garnish with the fresh jalapeños. Transfer to a fondue pot or small slow cooker if you have one, or serve straight out of the pot if you don't. Serve with the chips. The dip will keep for up to 1 week, covered and refrigerated. Reheat for a minute or two in a microwave.

CHUNKY MEXICAN-STYLE GUACAMOLE

MAKES 3 CUPS

For our house guacamole, we use only Hass avocados—the almost-black, pebbly-skinned variety prized for its smooth, buttery flesh. Hass avocados are delicious on their own but even better when mixed with some finely chopped tomato, onion, cilantro, and chile, along with a dash of salt and citrus. (I prefer the less acidic taste of lemon rather than lime juice.) We fry the jalapeño first to mellow its flavor. In addition to being perfect for dipping chips into, this guacamole is also great paired with slices of grilled steak in a taco. (See page 10 for more about avocados.)

---

1 teaspoon vegetable oil

1 small jalapeño

4 ripe avocados

1 to 2 tablespoons fresh lemon juice (about ½ lemon)

½ cup chopped tomato

¼ cup chopped fresh cilantro

¼ cup chopped white onion

½ teaspoon salt

Heat the oil in a small skillet and cook the jalapeño over high heat until browned and blistered on all sides. Remove the stem and cut the jalapeño in half. (I like to leave in flecks of the toasted skin.) Remove some or all of the seeds and membranes for less heat, if desired. Mince the jalapeño.

Cut the avocados in half, remove the pits and peels, and dice into ½-inch pieces. Toss in a mixing bowl with the lemon juice. Stir in the jalapeño, tomato, cilantro, onion, and salt. Taste and adjust the seasonings as desired. Serve immediately if possible, or within a few hours of making. To keep it from browning, cover the top with an additional thin film of oil, and/or cover with plastic wrap, pressing down on the surface, before refrigerating.

DEVILED EGGS WITH PIMENTO CHEESE AND SPICY BREAD AND BUTTER PICKLES

MAKES 24 DEVILED EGG HALVES

No one eats boiled eggs this way in Mexico, but when David Waller, the chef of our catering operation, makes them, I can't get enough. He is a North Carolina native, and he sometimes adapts family recipes to fit our menus. This is a favorite from the Sol Catering menu and a great example of how the right chile can add a welcome and unexpected jolt to a classic Southern dish.

---

12 large eggs

1 recipe Pimento Cheese
   (page 48)

24 slices Spicy Bread and
   Butter Pickles (page 217)

Place the eggs in a large saucepan. Cover with water by 1 inch. Bring to a rolling boil over high heat. Boil for 1 minute. Turn off the heat and let the eggs rest in the water until you can immerse your hand in it, about 20 minutes. Drain off the hot water and cover the eggs with cold water and then drain. Crack and peel the eggs. Halve them lengthwise, remove the yolks, and reserve for another use. Or mash some or all of them into the Pimento Cheese with more mayonnaise to moisten, as needed.

Fill each egg half with 1 tablespoon of the pimento cheese mixture. Top with 1 slice Spicy Bread and Butter Pickle. Serve immediately, or cover and chill up to 1 day before serving.

*Deviled Eggs with
Mexican Flavors
(page 48)*

PIMENTO CHEESE

MAKES 1½ CUPS

10 ounces sharp cheddar cheese, grated
  (2½ cups)

2 tablespoons finely chopped pimentos
  or 2 tablespoons roasted (see page
  12), peeled, and finely chopped red bell
  pepper (about ½ medium)

2 tablespoons stemmed, dry-roasted (see
  page 12), finely chopped jalapeños
  (remove some or all of the seeds and
  membranes for less heat)

½ teaspoon ground black pepper

¼ teaspoon hot sauce (such as Texas
  Pete)

¼ teaspoon Worcestershire sauce

½ cup mayonnaise

Combine the cheese, pimentos, jalapeños, black pepper, hot sauce, and Worcestershire sauce in a medium bowl. Add the mayonnaise and gently stir to combine. Use immediately, or chill overnight to allow the flavors to develop.

VARIATION

DEVILED EGGS WITH MEXICAN FLAVORS

MAKES 24 DEVILED EGG HALVES

Mash the yolks from 12 halved hard-boiled eggs with about ¼ cup of one of the flavored mayonnaises in this book: Spicy Thousand Island Sauce/Dressing (page 209), Chipotle Mayonnaise (page 59), or Jalapeño-Lime Mayonnaise (page 211). Spoon into the whites. Garnish with a sprinkle of ground chile de árbol or cayenne pepper and some chopped cilantro.

GUACAMOLE MINI TACOS

MAKES 24 TACOS

For parties, I sometimes make hors d'oeuvres by filling mini taco shells in a variety of ways. This is a neat way to serve a crowd guacamole that can be passed on a tray.

_____

1½ cups Chunky Mexican-Style
    Guacamole (page 45)

24 Crispy Mini Taco Shells
    (page 50)

¾ cup Creamy Lemon–Black
    Pepper Dressing (page 212)

1 cup finely shredded lettuce

1 cup finely diced tomatoes

Spoon 1 tablespoon of the guacamole into each mini taco shell. Drizzle with ½ tablespoon of the Creamy Lemon–Black Pepper Dressing and top with the lettuce and tomatoes. Serve immediately.

_____

EDDIE'S WAY: *Any of the recipes on pages 65 to 77 calling for ground or shredded meat or beans can be scaled down to appetizer size. I especially like to tuck leftover Slow-Cooker Barbacoa (page 68) into a taco shell with chopped cilantro, chopped onion, and Salsa Verde (page 205).*

Sweet and Tangy Ceviche Tostadas (page 51), Guacamole Mini Tacos, and Tomato and Pickled Pork Skin Tostadas (page 52)

CRISPY MINI TACO SHELLS

MAKES 24 TACO SHELLS

These crunchy little containers are great for parties and can be purchased online at minitacoshells.com. They are also quite easy to make at home.

————————

12 store-bought or homemade (page 180) corn tortillas
2 tablespoons vegetable oil
Salt

Heat the oven to 350 degrees. Set a cooling rack (not the cross-hatch type) on top of a baking sheet.

Using a 2½-inch round biscuit cutter, cut 2 rounds from each of the tortillas.

Wrap the tortilla rounds in a damp towel and set in the oven for about 2 minutes to soften. Or wrap in damp paper towels and microwave for about 20 seconds.

Lightly brush both sides of the rounds with the oil and sprinkle with salt. Bend each round into a taco shape and set upright inside the grates.

Bake for 12 to 15 minutes, until crispy. Serve, or store in an airtight container at room temperature for up to several days until ready to use.

SWEET AND TANGY CEVICHE TOSTADAS

MAKES 12 TO 16 LARGE OR 24 TO 32 SMALL TOSTADAS OR MINI TACOS

After a trip to Panama, where ceviches are made with fruit, I devised this one using passion fruit juice and lemon juice, along with some sweet pickle relish. It's sweet, spicy, and vinegary, without being sour or bitter. I like to spoon this on top of homemade tostadas or on smaller tostadas or chips for a crowd.

1 pound very fresh snapper, catfish, tilapia, or other mild white fish, diced into ½-inch pieces

1 cup passion fruit juice or puree, or orange juice

½ cup lemon juice

½ cup diced red bell pepper

½ cup thinly sliced red onion

1 jalapeño, stemmed and finely diced (remove some or all of the seeds and membranes for less heat)

½ cup sweet pickle relish

¼ cup minced fresh cilantro

Juice of 1 lime

12 to 16 large (5½-inch) corn tostadas for serving, preferably homemade (page 53)

Combine the fish, passion fruit juice, and lemon juice in a medium bowl or container. Cover and refrigerate for at least 2 hours or overnight.

Add the bell pepper, onion, jalapeño, relish, cilantro, and lime juice and stir to combine. With a slotted spoon, top the tostadas with the ceviche and serve.

TOMATO AND PICKLED PORK SKIN TOSTADAS

MAKES 12 TO 14 TOSTADAS

1 cup diced cueritos (pickled pork skins, available in Latino markets; see headnote)

½ cup finely diced tomato

¼ cup finely diced red bell pepper

¼ cup finely diced yellow bell pepper

¼ cup finely diced white onion

¼ cup finely chopped fresh cilantro

1 jalapeño, stemmed and diced (remove some or all of the seeds and membranes for less heat)

¼ cup lemon juice

½ teaspoon salt

Garlic-Habanero Mayonnaise (optional)

½ cup mayonnaise

1 garlic clove, finely chopped

1 tablespoon green habanero sauce, such as El Yucateca

12 to 14 (5½-inch) tostadas, homemade (page 53) or store-bought

Shredded lettuce

This easy recipe is a good example of how I like to introduce traditional tastes from Mexico in a way that Americans can relate to. *Cueritos,* or pickled pork skins, have a soft, somewhat chewy texture, a little like calamari. I chop them up and mix them into a relish with tomatoes, peppers, onion, and lots of fresh cilantro; spoon the mixture on top of tostadas (see photo, page 38); and I often top them with a habanero-spiked aïoli that's the perfect creamy complement.

Cueritos are readily available in plastic jars at Mexican markets.

———————

Combine the pork skin, tomato, bell peppers, onion, cilantro, jalapeño, lemon juice, and salt in a medium bowl.

To make the mayonnaise, if using: Combine the mayonnaise, garlic, and habanero sauce in a small bowl.

Top each tostada with some of the tomato mixture and shredded lettuce. Garnish with a dollop of mayonnaise, or pipe it on with a squeeze bottle. Serve immediately.

HOMEMADE TOSTADAS AND CHIPS

Before there were tortilla chips, there were tostadas—a way to use up leftover or stale tortillas by toasting them on a comal, or frying them in hot oil until crispy.

Like salsa, tortilla chips have roots in Mexico, but the commercial products that made them a favorite snack in homes and restaurants were invented in the U.S. In the 1940s the family who owned the El Zarape Tortilla Factory in Los Angeles began using a machine to roll and cut their corn and flour tortillas. Rebecca Carranza, who ran the business with her husband Mario, didn't want the scraps to go to waste, so she took home the torn ones, cut them into triangles, fried them, and served them to guests at a party. People liked them so much she started selling them by the bag, and "Tort Chips" were the company's main source of business until it closed in the late 1960s.

There are many good commercial chips on the market now, but it's hard to beat ones hot out of the fryer.

Store-bought or homemade
corn (page 180) or flour
(page 186) tortillas,
preferably stale
Vegetable oil for frying
Table salt or sea salt (optional)

Line a cooling rack or baking sheet with paper towels.

For tostadas: Heat 1 inch of oil to 360 degrees in a large Dutch oven or heavy pot over high heat. Carefully add 1 tortilla. Fry for 10 to 15 seconds, flip, and continue to fry until golden and crispy. Transfer to the cooling rack. Allow the oil to return to 360 degrees before adding another tortilla. Season to taste with salt, if desired.

For tortilla chips: Cut the tortillas into quarters. Heat 1 inch of oil to 360 degrees in a large Dutch oven or heavy pot over high heat. Carefully add a small handful of tortilla quarters and fry for 20 to 25 seconds, until golden and crispy. Transfer to the cooling rack. Allow the oil to return to 360 degrees between batches. Season to taste with salt, if desired.

FRIED GREEN TOMATILLOS WITH PEACH-HABANERO SAUCE

MAKES ABOUT 24 SLICES

I've never understood why people in the South like fried green tomatoes so much. So many of the ones I have tasted are tough, greasy, and bland. I wanted to see what would happen if I used tomatillos instead. Tomatillos look like miniature tomatoes when you peel their husks, but they come from a different plant. They do have a tart flavor similar to that of green tomatoes, but they have a more delicate texture that takes well to a crispy fried coating—like a fried dill pickle but more refined. I garnish them with a creamy sauce flavored with fresh peach and habanero.

Make the peach sauce first.

---

8 tomatillos, husks removed, rinsed, and patted dry

1 cup whole milk

½ cup sour cream

1 large egg

1 cup self-rising cornmeal mix

1 cup Harina P.A.N. cornmeal (see page 17)

1 teaspoon salt

Vegetable oil for frying

Peach-Habanero Sauce (opposite)

Cut a thin slice off the blossom end and bottom of each tomatillo and cut each into ¼-inch-thick slices.

Whisk together the milk, sour cream, and egg in a shallow bowl.

Whisk together both cornmeals and salt in a second shallow bowl. Place a cooling rack in a sheet pan. Line a second sheet pan with paper towels.

Heat ½ inch of vegetable oil in a Dutch oven or a large, heavy pot or skillet over medium-high heat until it is 350 degrees.

One at a time, dredge the tomatillo slices in the cornmeal mixture, dip in the egg wash, dip again in the cornmeal mixture, and set on the rack. Gently place a few slices at a time into the hot oil; do not crowd. Fry on both sides until golden brown, 2 to 3 minutes per side. Remove to the paper towel–lined sheet pan. Repeat with the remaining slices, allowing the oil to return to 350 degrees between each batch.

Serve hot, with Peach-Habanero Sauce for dipping.

PEACH-HABANERO SAUCE

MAKES 2 CUPS

1 ripe peach, peeled and diced small,
about ½ cup (thawed frozen or canned
peaches may be used)
½ habanero, stemmed and minced
(remove some or all of the seeds
and membranes for less heat)
1 cup mayonnaise
½ cup sour cream
½ teaspoon salt

Combine all the ingredients in a small bowl and mix until blended. Taste and adjust the seasonings as desired. Refrigerate until ready to use.

MEXICAN "SUSHI" ROLL-UPS

MAKES 8 APPETIZER SERVINGS

I am fascinated with sushi and like to sit at the bar and watch the sushi chefs assemble the rolls. I have taught myself to make them just for fun and, with all the practice I've had building tacos and rolling tamales, I've gotten pretty good at it. For this appetizer, I use a large tortilla in place of nori to roll up rice, vegetables, and crabmeat, then slice it into rounds and serve it with a delicious creamy sauce that has both Asian and Latin flavors.

---

1 cup cooked white rice,
   at room temperature
   (½ cup uncooked)
1 (8- to 10-inch) flour tortilla,
   at room temperature
2 ounces cold cream cheese,
   diced
½ avocado, thinly sliced
½ cup lump crabmeat, picked
   over
½ small onion, thinly sliced
½ red bell pepper, thinly sliced
1 small jalapeño, stemmed,
   seeded, and cut into thin
   lengthwise strips
3 tablespoons Tamarind-Ginger
   Sauce (opposite), plus more
   for dipping

Spread the rice in the center of the tortilla, leaving a 1-inch border around the edges. Arrange the pieces of cream cheese in the middle of the rice and top with the avocado slices and crabmeat, followed by the onion, bell pepper, and jalapeño. Drizzle with the 3 tablespoons tamarind sauce.

Beginning on one side, roll up the tortilla as tightly as possible over the filling. With a sharp knife, trim off both ends. Then slice in 8 even pieces. Serve with extra Tamarind-Ginger Sauce for dipping.

TAMARIND-GINGER SAUCE

MAKES 1½ CUPS

½ cup frozen tamarind nectar concentrate (available in freezer sections of international markets and many supermarkets, or online)

½ cup sugar

¼ cup teriyaki sauce

2 tablespoons chopped fresh ginger

1½ teaspoons toasted sesame oil

½ to 1 dried ghost chile or minced fresh habanero (optional)

1 cup mayonnaise, or more or less, to taste

Make this sauce as creamy as you like. It's delicious over hot or cold vegetables or for glazing or dipping shrimp or seafood.

———

Combine the tamarind concentrate, sugar, teriyaki sauce, ginger, sesame oil, and chile pepper, if using, in a small saucepan over medium heat. Bring to a boil, reduce the heat to a simmer and cook, stirring, until reduced by half, about 10 minutes. Discard the ghost chile pepper, if using, transfer the sauce to a container, and refrigerate until completely chilled.

Put the mayonnaise in a small bowl and fold in the chilled sauce. Bring to room temperature for serving. The sauce will keep, covered and refrigerated, for up to 2 weeks.

SMOKED SALMON–CHIPOTLE PIZZA ON FRY BREAD

MAKES 2 PIZZAS, 16 WEDGES (ABOUT 8 SERVINGS)

Another great use for bolillo dough (page 185) is to roll it a little thicker than a tortilla and fry it in hot oil the way Native Americans do, but in hot-enough oil so it fries up crispy instead of soft and pliable. Rather than topping it with tomato sauce, use Chipotle Mayonnaise, which pairs really well with the smoked salmon that is sold presliced and packaged in supermarkets. The smoky, spicy flavors of the mayonnaise are also good with sliced grilled chicken or vegetables. With a salad, this is lunch. (If you prefer, divide the dough into 4 or 8 balls for mini pizzas.)

Vegetable oil for frying

¼ recipe bolillo dough (page 185)

¼ cup Chipotle Mayonnaise (opposite)

8 ounces thinly sliced smoked salmon

Microgreens or finely diced romaine lettuce for garnish

Line a platter with paper towels. Heat oil in a large, heavy skillet to 350 degrees.

Make the bolillo dough, cutting the dough into 2 (4- or 5-ounce) pieces. Set each piece of dough on a work surface. With the palm of your hand, roll vigorously into a smooth ball, then set in a warm place to rest, covered, for 10 minutes.

Roll each dough ball out into an 8-inch round about ¼ inch thick.

Lay one dough round in the oil and fry until golden brown, continually spooning hot oil over the top and turning once, 3 to 4 minutes. (If the dough isn't cooked through after it's browned, place a spatula under it and remove the pan from the burner; let it stand for about 5 minutes so the residual heat cooks it.)

Remove to the paper towel–lined platter and pat the top with another paper towel to absorb the grease. Repeat with the second piece, allowing the oil to return to 350 degrees before frying.

Set the fry bread on a plate. Spread the Chipotle Mayonnaise on each, top with the salmon, and garnish with the greens. Cut each pizza into 8 wedges.

CHIPOTLE MAYONNAISE

MAKES 2½ CUPS

1 tablespoon butter

½ cup finely chopped onion

1 garlic clove, crushed

2 to 3 canned chipotle chiles in adobo

½ cup dry red wine

2 cups mayonnaise

This is a great sandwich spread or vegetable dip.

———

Heat the butter in a small saucepan over medium heat. Add the onion and garlic and cook until the onion is translucent, 2 minutes. Add the chipotles and cook for 1 more minute. Add the wine and cook 2 more minutes, or until reduced by half. Remove from the heat and cool to room temperature. Puree in a food processor with the mayonnaise until smooth. This mayo will keep for up to 1 week, covered and refrigerated.

TACOS

Chapter Three

WACO TACOS *65*

MEMPHIS TACOS *67*

SLOW-COOKER BARBACOA TACOS PARTY
  PLATTER *68*

CUBANO TACOS *70*

SLOPPY JOSÉ TACOS *72*

BEEF BRISKET TACOS *74*

—CRISPY BEEF TACOS *74*

CHEESEBURGER TACOS *75*

PORK CARNITAS TACOS *76*

—CRISPY CARNITAS *76*

VEGGIE TACOS *77*

FRIED CHICKEN TACOS *78*

  —POTATO-CRUSTED CHICKEN TACOS
    WITH SPICY THOUSAND ISLAND SAUCE *80*

    —CRACKER CHICKEN TACOS
    WITH TABASCO-HONEY DRIZZLE *80*

CHICKEN VERDE TACOS *81*

NASHVILLE HOT CHICKEN TACOS *82*

—CHILE DE ÁRBOL SAUCE *83*

—HOT SHRIMP TACOS *83*

ANCHO CHICKEN TACOS WITH RED ONION
  AND JALAPEÑO ESCABECHE *84*

FAMOUS FISH TACOS *86*

—POBLANO TARTAR SAUCE *87*

NEW ORLEANS FRIED OYSTER TACOS *88*

—SWEET PICKLE REMOULADE *89*

Tacos are my way of making sense of where I am and how I got here.

Tacos are supposed to be simple. But make no mistake: A lot of thought goes into every component and how they go together. There is a reason for every decision I make. Is there something crispy to contrast with the soft tortilla? Is there enough acid in the salsa to cut the richness of that deliciously fatty meat?

Beyond flavor and texture, there's something else to consider: What is the story I want to tell? And how can I share it with my Southern customers in a way that they can understand?

In many ways, making tacos is like painting an abstract picture—which also happens to be something I like to do in my spare time. They are my way of making sense of where I am and how I got here. I think about the best and most interesting things I have eaten, from Monterrey to Atlanta and everywhere in between, and how they might taste wrapped up in one bite.

In this chapter you'll find recipes for different tacos—including a Memphis-style pork barbecue topped with creamy jalapeño-spiked coleslaw, hot fried chicken from Nashville, and New Orleans–inspired fried oysters with remoulade—all reimagined through a Mexican's taste buds.

My Fried Chicken Tacos, for example, were designed to remind our Southern customers of Sunday dinners at their grandmothers' houses, with a jolt of chile heat in the mayonnaise sauce. My spin-off is based on a fried chicken dinner I have eaten in diners all over the South, served with French fries and iceberg lettuce salad drenched in Thousand Island dressing. So I coated the chicken with mashed potato flakes from the supermarket and pulled everything together with my homemade version of Thousand Island dressing.

But I also want to walk you through my easy methods for re-creating an authentic taco just as you might experience it on a Mexican street corner before a soccer match: filled with brisket, carnitas, or barbacoa made with beef cheeks, and adorned with no more than a simple tomato salsa made from scratch.

I will show you how easy it is to adjust these basic formulas in many different ways to create something totally different-tasting yet equally delicious.

TO WRAP OR NOT TO WRAP?

Wrapping a taco in foil does more than keep it warm for traveling. It also steams it, changing the texture of both the tortilla and the filling inside. Fillings that are meant to be crispy go soft. But sometimes this can be a good thing, especially when I want people to get the saltiness and gooeyness of cheese as it melts into the meat or beans.

My veggie tacos with bean filling travel really well in foil. Golfers often pack a bag of them to carry with them on the golf course for this reason. The foil seals in juices and flavor and keeps the taco from being messy.

HOW TO SMOKE MEAT (OR ANYTHING ELSE) INDOORS

When I decided to create a pork barbecue taco, the biggest challenge was achieving the smoky barbecue flavor without a barbecue pit, since Taqueria del Sol didn't have one. So I worked out a two-step process, in which the pork is rubbed with spices and oven-roasted and then smoked briefly with hickory chips in a smoker I rigged for indoors. You can buy an indoor smoker (see page 9) or construct one yourself. I use it not only for pork but also for brisket, chicken, seafood, and tomatoes.

For indoor smoking, place two pieces of aluminum foil in the bottom of an old stockpot. (Cover the entire interior of the pot with foil to prevent blackening if you want.) Place a handful of wood chips on the bottom, and cover with another piece of foil. Set a steamer insert or metal colander over the foil and load with chopped meat. (Make sure the meat is an inch or more above the chips, or else the meat could have a scorched taste.) Cover the pot with a lid and wrap the edges of the lid tightly with aluminum foil to seal in the smoke. Place the pot over high heat for 5 minutes, or until the pot begins to smoke. Decrease the heat to the lowest setting and continue to smoke for 10 to 15 minutes, until the desired level of smokiness is achieved.

For smaller cuts and more delicate foods, you can turn the heat off once the pot starts smoking and leave the lid on for just a few minutes—just long enough for the smoky flavor to permeate. This can be done a day or two in advance and the food refrigerated until ready to serve.

WACO TACOS

MAKES 32 TACOS

Once you have roasted brisket, you can give it a Texas flavor by quick-smoking it as you would for pork, and then adding a tangy, peppery barbecue sauce, more like how I remember it in Texas. I give the same slaw we use for the Memphis taco a different twist by stirring in some yellow mustard, which perfectly complements the smoky beef and the tangy sauce. This combination is also good with smoked chicken or pork.

½ recipe (2 quarts) roast beef brisket (page 74), shredded

2 cups Jalapeño Coleslaw (page 233)

1 tablespoon yellow mustard

32 (6-inch) flour tortillas

2 cups Waco Barbecue Sauce (page 294)

Quick-smoke the shredded brisket (see opposite).

Meanwhile, mix the coleslaw with the mustard. The brisket will keep for up to 4 days, covered and refrigerated.

Set a dry skillet over medium-high heat. Add a tortilla and heat on both sides for a minute or two, until a few dark spots appear. Remove to a plate and place 3 to 4 tablespoons of the smoked brisket in the center of the tortilla. Top with 1 tablespoon barbecue sauce and 1 tablespoon slaw, and fold. Repeat with the remaining tortillas.

MEMPHIS TACOS

MAKES 24 TO 36 TACOS

I was introduced to barbecue in Texas, but being from Memphis, my business partner, Mike Klank, had other ideas about it. In Memphis pit masters go for pork shoulder more than brisket. They never brush it with barbecue sauce while it's cooking, but instead they barbecue it "dry"—with a rub. They then shred the pork and serve it on a bun with a thick, sweet barbecue sauce and a creamy slaw in the bun with the barbecue. We figured out that this combination would work just as well in a tortilla, and the Memphis taco is one of our biggest sellers. To smoke the meat at home, you can use the indoor smoking method on page 64, or if you prefer, your outdoor smoker or grill will work fine, too.

---

1 tablespoon granulated garlic

1 tablespoon granulated onion

1 tablespoon ground black pepper

3 tablespoons salt

1 (4- to 6-pound) bone-in Boston butt (pork shoulder) or 3- to 3½-pound boneless

1 to 2 cups hickory chips, for smoking

24 to 36 (6-inch) flour tortillas

Memphis-Style Barbecue Sauce (page 293)

Jalapeño Coleslaw (page 223)

Heat the oven to 350 degrees.

Combine the granulated garlic, granulated onion, black pepper, and salt in a small bowl. Rub the pork with the spice mixture, place in a roasting pan, cover with foil, and roast for 3 to 4 hours, until the meat is cooked through and falls apart easily. Remove from the pan and set aside to cool slightly. Finely chop the pork.

Quick-smoke the meat (see page 64). The meat can be smoked, covered, and refrigerated a day or two in advance.

Set a dry skillet over medium-high heat. Add a tortilla and heat on both sides for a minute or two, until a few dark spots appear. Remove to a plate. Place 3 to 4 tablespoons of the pork in the center of the tortilla, top with 1 tablespoon of the barbecue sauce and 1 tablespoon slaw, and fold. Repeat with the remaining tortillas.

SLOW-COOKER BARBACOA TACOS PARTY PLATTER

MAKES 16 TO 20 SERVINGS

¼ cup salt

1 tablespoon ground black
  pepper

8 bay leaves

5 pounds beef cheeks (see
  headnote), cut to fit in large
  slow cooker

5 pounds beef brisket, cut to fit
  in large slow cooker

Fresh Corn Tortillas (page 180);
  or store-bought, warmed

Salsa Fresca (page 202)
  or combination of salsas
  of choice

Finely chopped red onion
  for garnish

Chopped fresh cilantro for
  garnish

Lime wedges for garnish

In Mexico, instead of grilling meat, we put it inside a can with a lid, cover it up with leaves from the agave plant, and let it cook all day underground. Like me, my uncle José was not a patient guy. He wanted to find a way to cook in his house so he wouldn't have to dig a friggin' hole in his yard. And he found his answer: the slow cooker! You just plug the thing in, throw in the meat, and let it cook while you sleep. The next morning the meat tastes just as good as the stuff we had in the old days. I like a combination of half brisket and half beef cheeks, which are mostly fat and bone, but extremely flavorful. Although this sounds like a huge amount of meat, a lot of it is fat that will be removed. You can, of course, slow-cook just the brisket, but it will not be barbacoa, and you will miss out on the unique flavor only the cheeks provide. Trust me—they are well worth seeking out and special-ordering if you need to! I like to shred the meat and serve it on a platter for a crowd, with assorted garnishes and homemade corn tortillas that I make slightly thicker than the ones you buy, so everyone can assemble their own tacos. Barbacoa can be made ahead and frozen.

———————

In a large bowl, combine the salt, pepper, and bay leaves. Add the meat and toss to combine. Place in a large slow cooker. Cover and set on low. Cook for 12 hours or overnight, until the meat is falling apart.

Skim the grease and remove the fatty pieces and bone. Discard the bay leaves. Shred the meat and serve on a platter with the tortillas, salsa, and garnishes.

CUBANO TACOS

MAKES 24 TACOS

I won a cooking contest with this taco made from North Carolina sweet potatoes. The filling is similar to *picadillo*, a well-known dish in Mexico, Cuba, and other parts of Latin America that is composed of ground beef, chili spices, tomatoes, and dried fruit. I substituted cubed sweet potatoes for the more typical raisins to give bursts of color as well as sweetness. A drizzle of Roasted Tomatillo Sauce adds just the right spicy-tart balance.

---

3 cups peeled, ½-inch-diced sweet potatoes

2 tablespoons salt

4 tablespoons (½ stick) butter

2 pounds ground chuck

1 tablespoon ground chile de árbol or cayenne pepper

1 cup diced onions

1½ teaspoons ground black pepper

1½ teaspoons dried oregano

1 teaspoon dried basil

2 cups diced tomatoes

¼ cup chopped fresh cilantro

24 (6-inch) flour tortillas

1 cup grated white American cheese

1½ recipes (3 cups) Roasted Tomatillo Sauce (page 205)

Place the diced sweet potatoes in a medium saucepan, cover with 4 cups of water, and set over high heat. Add 1 tablespoon of the salt and bring to a boil. Reduce the heat to medium and simmer for about 5 minutes, or until the potatoes are crisp-tender but not mushy. Drain in a colander and rinse with cold water.

Melt the butter in a large skillet over medium-high heat. Add the beef and cook, stirring occasionally, until just cooked through, 5 to 7 minutes. Add the sweet potatoes and chile de árbol and cook for 2 minutes. Add the onions, black pepper, oregano, and basil and cook for 3 minutes. Add the tomatoes, cook for 2 minutes, then add the remaining tablespoon salt and the cilantro. Reduce the heat and simmer for 5 minutes to meld the flavors.

Set a dry skillet over medium-high heat. Add a tortilla and heat on both sides for a minute or two, until a few dark spots appear. Remove to a plate and place 3 to 4 tablespoons of beef mixture in the center of the tortilla. Add a sprinkle of cheese, 1 tablespoon tomatillo sauce, and fold. Repeat with the remaining tortillas.

SLOPPY JOSÉ TACOS

MAKES 24 TACOS

David Waller, one of our longtime chefs who heads the catering operation, created this frequent special inspired by a Tex-Mex Frito chili pie. The ground beef is simmered with onion, tomato, and chili spices, with mild roasted chiles folded in, and then garnished with grated cheddar and crushed corn chips, adding a subtle crunch and toasted corn flavor. This one is a real crowd-pleaser that's great for family entertaining.

---

1 tablespoon vegetable oil

½ cup finely chopped onion

1 tablespoon chopped garlic

2½ pounds ground chuck

¼ cup paprika

2 tablespoons sugar

1 tablespoon granulated onion

1 tablespoon granulated garlic

1½ teaspoons ground black pepper

2 teaspoons salt

1 teaspoon ground chile de árbol or cayenne pepper

1 cup tomato paste

1 cup water

1 cup roasted, peeled, seeded, and finely chopped green New Mexico chiles (see page 12)

24 (6-inch) flour tortillas

Garnishes: Crushed Fritos, grated sharp cheddar cheese, and sliced fresh jalapeños

Heat the oil in a large, heavy pot over medium heat until it shimmers. Add the onion and cook, stirring, until soft and translucent, 5 to 7 minutes. Add the garlic and cook for 1 minute more. Add the beef and increase the heat to medium-high. Cook, stirring frequently, until lightly browned and cooked through. Stir in the paprika, sugar, granulated onion, granulated garlic, black pepper, salt, and chile de árbol. Add the tomato paste, water, and roasted chiles and stir to combine. Reduce the heat to low and simmer for 20 minutes, stirring occasionally and adding more water if the mixture gets too thick. Taste and adjust the seasonings as desired.

Set a dry skillet over medium-high heat. Add a tortilla and heat on both sides for a minute or two, until a few dark spots appear. Remove to a plate and place 3 to 4 tablespoons of the beef mixture in the center of the tortilla; garnish with Fritos, cheese, and jalapeños; and fold. Repeat with the remaining tortillas.

BEEF BRISKET TACOS

MAKES 32 TACOS

This simple but delicious taco is about as authentically Mexican as you can get. The trick is getting a cut of brisket that has not been trimmed entirely of its fat, as this is where much of the moisture and flavor lies. Many instructions call for roasting at a very low temperature for many hours, but I find that the meat stays moist and juicy even when cooked more quickly at a higher heat if water is added to the pan before covering it with foil. You can also make this using a slow cooker.

1 tablespoon granulated garlic

1 tablespoon granulated onion

1 tablespoon salt

1 tablespoon ground black pepper

1 (4-pound) brisket, with ¼-inch layer of fat

Water for the pan

32 (6-inch) flour tortillas

Pico de Gallo (page 202)

Heat the oven to 375 degrees.

Combine the garlic, onion, salt, and pepper in a small bowl. Rub the mixture on both sides of the brisket. Place the brisket on a rack in a roasting pan, fat side up. Add an inch of water to the pan and cover tightly with foil.

Roast the brisket for 3½ to 4 hours, or until very tender and the meat pulls apart easily. Remove from the oven and cool. Reserve the cooking liquid. Shred the meat, removing any excess fat. If you're making it ahead, cover the meat with the reserved cooking liquid to keep it moist. The meat will keep, covered, in the refrigerator for up to 3 days.

Set a dry skillet over medium-high heat. Add a tortilla and heat on both sides for a minute or two, until a few dark spots appear. Remove to a plate and place 3 to 4 tablespoons of the brisket in the center of the tortilla. Top with a spoonful of Pico de Gallo and fold. Repeat with the remaining tortillas.

VARIATION

CRISPY BEEF TACOS

Heat a skillet over medium heat and brush it with a little oil. Add a corn tortilla and top one side of it with some brisket. Fold the other side over the filling and fry on both sides until crispy but still slightly pliable. Tuck in some shredded lettuce, chopped tomatoes, and Salsa Frita (page 204).

CHEESEBURGER TACOS

MAKES 16 TACOS

We once had a contest with customers to vote on our most popular taco, and the cheeseburger won hands down. You might expect that kids especially love it, but sophisticated adults are crazy about it, too. It has many layers of flavor.

---

2 pounds ground chuck

1 cup finely diced onions

1 jalapeño, stemmed and minced (remove some or all of the seeds and membranes for less heat)

1 large egg

2 tablespoons all-purpose flour

1 tablespoon ground black pepper

1½ teaspoons salt

2 tablespoons butter

16 (6-inch) flour tortillas

Taqueria del Sol Jalapeño-Cheese Dip, warmed (page 42)

1 cup Jalapeño-Lime Mayonnaise (page 211)

Shredded lettuce

Chopped tomatoes

Stir the beef, onions, jalapeño, egg, flour, pepper, and salt together in a large bowl.

Melt the butter in a large skillet set over medium heat. Add the meat mixture and cook, breaking up the mixture with a wooden spoon, until lightly browned and cooked through, 10 to 15 minutes. Keep warm.

Set a dry skillet over medium-high heat. Add a tortilla and heat on both sides for a minute or two, until a few dark spots appear. Remove to a plate and spread the tortilla with some of the warm cheese dip. Add 3 to 4 tablespoons of the meat mixture, top with 1 tablespoon of the mayonnaise, then a little lettuce and tomato, and fold. Repeat with the remaining tortillas.

PORK CARNITAS TACOS

MAKES 16 TACOS

The literal translation for *carnitas* is "piece of meat." I go with the cooking method that is closest to how I remember it. Taco vendors cooked the meat in a big pot of oil, sort of like a confit, and added some beer and fresh orange wedges, which flavored and helped break down the meat fibers. Then they finished it with a little sweetened condensed milk to give it caramelized notes.

———————

2 quarts vegetable oil

2 pounds Boston butt (pork shoulder), cut into 1-inch pieces

1 orange, quartered

1 tablespoon salt

2 cups Negra Modelo beer

¼ cup sweetened condensed milk

16 (6-inch) flour tortillas

Salsa Frita (page 204)

Mexican crema (see page 18) or sour cream thinned with a little milk or buttermilk

Lime wedges

Put the vegetable oil and meat in a large pot. Bring to a boil over high heat. Reduce the heat to a rapid simmer and simmer for about 20 minutes. Reduce the heat to maintain a slow simmer and cook for 30 minutes.

Add the orange pieces, salt, and beer. Simmer for 30 minutes more, or until the meat is tender.

Remove from the heat and set aside until bubbling stops, 2 to 3 minutes. Add the sweetened condensed milk and let stand for 5 minutes without stirring.

With a slotted spoon, transfer the meat to a cutting board and shred it using two forks, or your fingers once it's cool enough to handle, or mash with a potato masher.

Set a dry skillet over medium-high heat. Add a tortilla and heat on both sides for a minute or two, until a few dark spots appear. Remove to a plate, fill with 3 to 4 tablespoons of the carnitas, a spoonful of salsa, a drizzle of crema, and a squeeze of lime juice, and fold. Repeat with the remaining tortillas.

———————

VARIATION

CRISPY CARNITAS

Some people prefer their carnitas crispy and caramelized on the outside. To do this, place the cooked pork pieces in a dish and bake in a preheated 425-degree oven, turning occasionally, until nicely browned, about 10 minutes. Or quickly fry the pieces in a little oil in a hot skillet. Shred the meat as before, mixing the browned bits on the outside with the tender meat inside.

VEGGIE TACOS

MAKES 16 TACOS

This winning combination of mashed cumin-scented beans, tangy cheese, and spicy-tart green salsa is even better if you wrap the tacos in foil and let them stand for 5 minutes before eating, giving the flavors time to meld in the steamy packets. I often pack these when I am traveling.

———————

16 (6-inch) flour tortillas
1½ cups Veggie Refried Beans, warmed (page 77)
¾ cup crumbled queso fresco
1 recipe Roasted Tomatillo Sauce (page 205)

Set a dry skillet over medium-high heat. Add a tortilla and heat on both sides for a minute or two, until a few dark spots appear. Remove to a plate. Put about 1½ tablespoons refried beans, ½ tablespoon cheese, and 1 tablespoon sauce in the center of the tortilla and fold (or wrap in foil; see headnote). Repeat with the remaining tortillas.

FRIED CHICKEN TACOS

MAKES 16 TACOS

The main component of this taco is no fancier than any Southern grandma's fried chicken, but when you wrap the refried strips in a warm flour tortilla with Jalapeño-Lime Mayonnaise, the taste is unforgettable. I use this simple formula to create endless specials, such as the two popular variations on page 80.

1 large egg

2 cups whole milk

2 pounds chicken tenders

1 recipe Seasoned Flour
   Coating (page 290)

½ head iceberg lettuce,
   shredded

3 to 4 medium tomatoes,
   chopped

Vegetable oil for frying

16 (6-inch) flour tortillas

1 cup Jalapeño-Lime
   Mayonnaise (page 211)

Place three medium bowls on your work surface. In the first bowl, whisk together the egg with the milk. Add the chicken pieces and stir to coat. Cover and refrigerate until ready to use. You can do this the night before.

Place the seasoned flour in the second bowl. In the third bowl, toss the lettuce with the tomatoes.

Heat 1½ inches of oil in a Dutch oven or deep, heavy pot over high heat until it is 350 degrees.

Heat the oven to 200 degrees. Line a baking sheet with paper towels.

Remove a few pieces of chicken from the milk, dredge in the flour, and shake off the excess. Gently place in the hot oil. Cook until light brown, crispy, and cooked through, 6 to 8 minutes, turning as needed. Transfer to the paper towel–lined baking sheet to drain. Keep warm in the oven while you fry the remaining chicken. Allow the oil to return to 350 degrees between batches.

Set a dry skillet over medium-high heat. Add a tortilla and heat on both sides for a minute or two, until a few dark spots appear. Remove to a plate. Place 2 chicken tenders in the center of the tortilla, top with 1 tablespoon of the mayonnaise and some of the lettuce and tomato, and fold. Repeat with the remaining tortillas.

*Potato-Crusted Chicken Taco
(page 80) with Jalapeño-Lime
Mayonnaise (page 211) and Eddie's
Turnip Greens (page 236)*

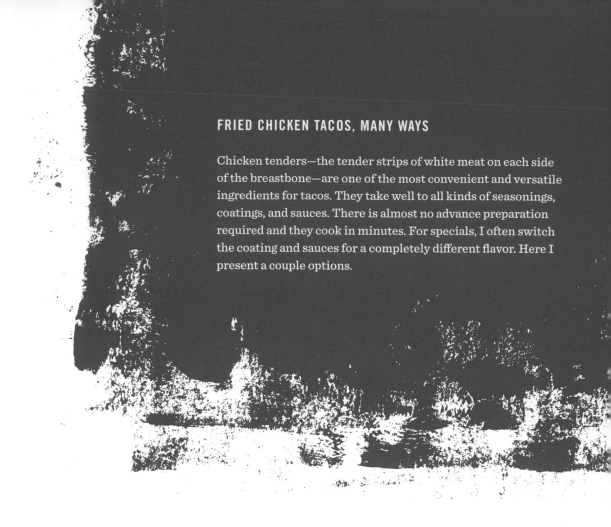

FRIED CHICKEN TACOS, MANY WAYS

Chicken tenders—the tender strips of white meat on each side of the breastbone—are one of the most convenient and versatile ingredients for tacos. They take well to all kinds of seasonings, coatings, and sauces. There is almost no advance preparation required and they cook in minutes. For specials, I often switch the coating and sauces for a completely different flavor. Here I present a couple options.

VARIATIONS

POTATO-CRUSTED CHICKEN TACOS WITH SPICY THOUSAND ISLAND SAUCE

Follow the instructions for the Fried Chicken Tacos, substituting 1 recipe Crunchy Potato Coating (page 290) for Seasoned Flour Coating, and Spicy Thousand Island Sauce/Dressing (page 209) for the Jalapeño-Lime Mayonnaise. (The photo is on page 79.)

CRACKER CHICKEN TACOS WITH TABASCO-HONEY DRIZZLE

Make the drizzle by mixing ½ cup honey, 2 tablespoons Tabasco, 1 teaspoon salt, and ½ cup mayonnaise in a small bowl. Follow the instructions for the Fried Chicken Tacos, substituting buttermilk for the whole milk in the egg wash, 2 cups Cracker Coating (page 290) for Seasoned Flour Coating, and the drizzle for Jalapeño-Lime Mayonnaise.

CHICKEN VERDE TACOS

MAKES 8 TACOS

Light and packed with the fresh flavors of cilantro and citrus, this taco comes together in no time. Don't let the chicken marinate for more than an hour, as the acid in the lime can make the meat too tart and break down its texture.

½ cup vegetable oil, plus more
  as needed for sautéing
½ cup lime juice
1 large garlic clove, chopped
1 tablespoon salt
1 tablespoon ground black
  pepper
1 pound chicken tenders
8 (6-inch) flour or (5½-inch)
  corn tortillas
Salsa Verde (page 205)
Chopped fresh cilantro
Chopped fresh white onion

Whisk ½ cup of the oil, the lime juice, garlic, salt, and pepper in a large bowl. Add the chicken, cover, and refrigerate for 1 hour.

Drain and discard the marinade from the chicken.

Heat 1 tablespoon vegetable oil in a large nonstick skillet over medium-high heat until it shimmers. Add the chicken in batches and cook, stirring, until cooked through, about 5 minutes per batch, adding more oil as needed. Remove to a plate and keep warm. Repeat until all the chicken is cooked.

Set a dry skillet over medium-high heat. Add a tortilla and heat on both sides for a minute or two, until a few dark spots appear. Transfer to a plate. Top the tortilla with a few pieces of chicken, Salsa Verde, cilantro, and onion and fold. Repeat with the remaining tortillas.

NASHVILLE HOT CHICKEN TACOS

MAKES 16 TACOS

Before we opened our first Taqueria del Sol in Nashville, I went there to get to know the food scene. That's when I first had hot chicken at Hattie B's. The chicken pieces are fried, tossed in a fiery sauce, and served on white bread with pickle chips. I instantly saw the possibilities for a taco. My interpretation includes three layers of heat: in the Spicy-Hot Coating for the tenders, in the chile de árbol–spiked sauce, and in the jalapeño mayonnaise.

---

1 recipe Chile de Árbol Sauce (opposite)

1 large egg

2 cups whole milk

2 pounds chicken tenders

1 recipe Spicy-Hot Coating (page 290)

½ head iceberg lettuce, shredded

3 to 4 medium tomatoes, chopped

Vegetable oil for frying

16 (6-inch) flour tortillas

1 cup Pickled Jalapeño Mayonnaise (page 211)

Keep the Chile de Árbol Sauce warm over low heat.

Place three medium bowls on your work surface. In the first bowl, whisk together the egg with the milk. Add the chicken pieces and stir to coat. Cover and refrigerate until ready to use. You can do this the night before.

Place the coating in the second bowl. In the third bowl, toss the lettuce with the tomatoes.

Heat 1½ inches of oil in a Dutch oven or deep, heavy pot over high heat until it is 350 degrees. Heat the oven to 200 degrees. Line a baking sheet with paper towels.

Remove a few pieces of chicken from the milk, dredge in the coating, and shake off the excess. Gently place in the hot oil. Cook until light brown, crispy, and cooked through, 6 to 8 minutes, turning as needed. Transfer to the paper towel–lined baking sheet to drain. Keep warm in the oven while you repeat with the remaining chicken. Allow the oil to return to 350 degrees between batches.

Drop the chicken into the Chile de Árbol Sauce and toss to coat.

Set a dry skillet over medium-high heat. Add a tortilla and heat on both sides for a minute or two, until a few dark spots appear. Remove to a plate. Place 2 chicken tenders in the center of the tortilla, top with 1 tablespoon of the mayonnaise and some lettuce and tomato, and fold. Repeat with the remaining tortillas.

CHILE DE ÁRBOL SAUCE

MAKES 1¼ CUPS

1 cup chicken stock, preferably
   homemade (page 99)

2 teaspoons ground chile de árbol or
   cayenne pepper

¼ cup lard, preferably homemade
   (page 299)

½ teaspoon minced garlic

½ teaspoon salt

Combine the stock, chile de árbol, lard, garlic, and salt in a large
saucepan. Bring to a boil over high heat, stirring occasionally.
Reduce the heat to low and cook for 2 to 3 minutes to meld the
flavors. Taste and adjust the seasonings as desired. The sauce will
keep, covered and refrigerated, for up to 3 days.

VARIATION

HOT SHRIMP TACOS

Substitute medium peeled and deveined shrimp for the chicken,
frying in batches just until the shrimp float to the surface. Replace
the lard in the Chile de Árbol Sauce with 4 tablespoons butter.
Garnish with Spicy Bread and Butter Pickles (page 217).

ANCHO CHICKEN TACOS WITH RED ONION AND JALAPEÑO ESCABECHE

MAKES 16 TACOS

A ruddy marinade of pureed dried chiles, vinegar, and garlic quickly transforms plain chicken tenders into something exciting, especially when folded into a taco with crisp and tangy pickled onions. It's also very healthy!

———

1 recipe Ancho (or Guajillo)
   Chile Puree (page 292)
½ cup apple cider vinegar
1 tablespoon crushed garlic
1½ teaspoons ground white
   pepper
1½ teaspoons salt
2 pounds chicken tenders
1 tablespoon vegetable oil,
   plus more as needed
16 (6-inch) flour tortillas
1 recipe Red Onion and
   Jalapeño Escabeche
   (opposite)
1 cup Salsa Verde (page 205)

Stir the ancho puree, vinegar, garlic, white pepper, and salt together in a large bowl. Add the chicken tenders and toss to coat. Cover and refrigerate for 30 minutes.

Heat the oil in a large nonstick skillet over medium-high heat until it shimmers. Add the chicken in batches and cook, stirring, until cooked through, about 5 minutes per batch, adding more oil to the skillet as needed. Remove the chicken to a plate and keep warm. Repeat until all the chicken is cooked.

Set a dry skillet over medium-high heat. Add a tortilla and heat on both sides for a minute or two, until a few dark spots appear. Transfer to a plate. Place 2 chicken pieces in the center of the tortilla. Top with 1 tablespoon escabeche and 1 tablespoon of the salsa. Fold and serve. Repeat with the remaining tortillas.

RED ONION AND JALAPEÑO ESCABECHE

MAKES 1 CUP

1 large red onion, halved and thinly sliced

1 thinly sliced jalapeño, stemmed and
   thinly sliced (remove some or all of the
   seeds and membranes for less heat)

2 bay leaves

1½ teaspoons crushed garlic

½ cup apple cider vinegar

1 teaspoon salt

The acidity of the vinegar and the crunch and pungency of the onion go well with chicken.

————

Combine the onion, jalapeño, bay leaves, garlic, vinegar, and salt in a small bowl. Set aside for at least 5 minutes, or cover and refrigerate for up to several days. (The onion will wilt the longer it stands.)

FAMOUS FISH TACOS

MAKES 8 TACOS

Baja California—a Mexican state close to San Diego that includes Tijuana—gets the credit for popularizing the fish taco, which is now on restaurant menus in every form imaginable coast to coast. But my business partner and I were serving them in the late 1980s, long before they became trendy. The Taqueria del Sol version is much less complicated than most and geared to the Southern palate. It's nothing more than strips of lightly breaded and fried fish wrapped in a tortilla with poblano-laced tartar sauce and pickled jalapeño slices. The fish has just enough crunch and corn flavor, and customers can't seem to get enough.

1 recipe Extra-Crispy Coating (page 290)

1 cup whole milk

1 large egg

1 teaspoon salt

1 pound tilapia or other mild fish, cut into 16 (1½-inch-wide) strips

Vegetable oil for frying

8 (6-inch) flour tortillas

½ cup Poblano Tartar Sauce (opposite)

Sliced pickled jalapeños for garnish

Heat oven to 200 degrees. Line a baking sheet with paper towels.

Place the coating in a shallow dish.

Whisk together the milk, egg, and salt in another shallow dish. Add the fish and stir to coat.

Heat 1½ inches of oil in a Dutch oven or deep, heavy pot over high heat until it is 350 degrees.

Remove the fish from the milk one piece at a time, dredge in the coating, shake off the excess, and set aside. Repeat until all the fish is coated. Gently place a few pieces at a time into the oil and cook until light brown, crispy, and cooked through, 2 to 3 minutes, turning as needed. Transfer to the paper towel–lined baking sheet and place in the oven to keep warm. Repeat until all the fish is cooked. Allow the oil to return to 350 degrees between each batch.

Set a dry skillet over medium-high heat. Add a tortilla and heat on both sides for a minute or two, until a few dark spots appear. Top the tortilla with 2 pieces of fish and 1 tablespoon tartar sauce. Garnish with the jalapeños and fold. Repeat with the remaining tortillas.

POBLANO TARTAR SAUCE

MAKES 1¼ CUPS

¼ cup diced poblano pepper (about ½ medium), cored, and seeds and ribs removed

½ small jalapeño, stemmed (remove some or all of the seeds and membranes for less heat)

2 tablespoons diced onion

1 cup mayonnaise

2 tablespoons lemon juice

Pinch of salt

Pulse the poblano, jalapeño, and onion in a food processor until finely chopped but not pureed. Transfer to a small bowl. Add the mayonnaise, lemon juice, and salt and stir to combine. Taste and adjust the seasonings as desired. This sauce keeps refrigerated, covered, for up to 1 week.

NEW ORLEANS FRIED OYSTER TACOS

MAKES 8 TACOS

In my tribute to the famous New Orleans po' boy, I pair oysters fried in a light cornmeal jacket with a sauce based on the traditional remoulade, with confetti-like bits of sweet pickle, sweet and hot peppers, celery, and onion, and wrap it all in a flour tortilla.

———————

Coating

1 cup yellow cornmeal

½ cup all-purpose flour

¼ cup cornstarch

1½ teaspoons salt

¼ teaspoon baking powder

Tacos

Vegetable oil for frying

2 dozen shucked large oysters

8 (6-inch) flour tortillas

Sweet Pickle Remoulade
    (opposite)

¼ head iceberg lettuce,
    chopped (2 cups)

2 medium tomatoes, chopped

To make the coating: Whisk the coating ingredients in a shallow bowl.

To make the tacos: Heat 1½ inches of oil in a Dutch oven or deep, heavy pot over high heat until it is 350 degrees. Line a baking sheet with paper towels and set aside.

Heat the oven to 200 degrees.

Working in batches, dredge the oysters in the coating and drop into the hot oil, stirring occasionally with a slotted spoon, until golden brown, about 2 minutes. Transfer to the paper towel–lined baking sheet to drain. Keep warm in the oven. Allow the oil to return to 350 degrees between each batch.

Set a dry skillet over medium-high heat. Add a tortilla and heat on both sides for a minute or two, until a few dark spots appear. Remove to a plate. Spread 1½ tablespoons of the remoulade across the middle of the tortilla and top with 3 oysters, lettuce, and some tomato. Fold the tortilla in half and serve hot. Repeat with the remaining tortillas.

SWEET PICKLE REMOULADE

MAKES ABOUT 2¼ CUPS

⅔ cup sweet pickle relish

1 cup mayonnaise

6 tablespoons finely chopped
   red bell pepper

¼ cup finely chopped celery

¼ cup finely chopped onion

1 jalapeño, stemmed and minced
   (remove some or all of the seeds
   and membranes for less heat)

1½ teaspoons Tabasco or other hot
   pepper sauce

½ teaspoon ground black pepper

Pinch of salt

Place the relish in a fine-mesh strainer set over a small bowl. Let drain for 10 minutes. Transfer the relish to a medium bowl. Stir in the mayonnaise and remaining ingredients. Taste and adjust the seasonings. The sauce keeps, covered and refrigerated, for up to 3 days.

WRAPPED, STUFFED, AND SAUCED

Chapter Four

ENCHILADAS MEXICANAS 94
CHEESE ENCHILADAS WITH MORITA
    PEPPER SAUCE 96
CHICKEN ENCHILADA CASSEROLE
    WITH LEMON-CREAM SAUCE 98
    —BASIC CHICKEN FILLING AND STOCK 99
BLACK BEAN ENCHILADAS WITH CILANTRO-AVOCADO
    DRIZZLE 100
CORN, POBLANO, AND CHEESE TAMALES 102
PORK HOT TAMALES 104
CREOLE RED BEANS AND RICE BURRITOS 107
NEW MEXICAN CHILES RELLENOS 109

I wore a suit and played by the company rules. Now I get to play by my own.

"Give me a chicken Laredo!"

"I need an enchilada dinner combo and two orders of guacamole!"

As the waitress called out the orders, I stayed quiet and kept washing dishes. That was the job I was hired to do. But I was listening to everything going on around me. El Chico's menu was about six pages long and had a zillion things on it, but I was determined to memorize it. I watched the line cooks and kept a log in my brain of how they made each item.

This is how I learned Tex-Mex cooking. It's also how I learned English.

Language wasn't a problem when I first went to Houston, Texas. I lived in Mexican communities and played music in clubs where everyone spoke Spanish. Then I met a girl named Cindy who I wanted to ask out, but all I knew how to say was "Cindy, Cindy, Cindy." Finally I learned how to say "Cindy, can you go to the movies with me?" She went with me on the date, but that was as far as our "conversation" went.

The language barrier also limited my career options. I knew I wanted to do more with my life than live from gig to gig as a drummer in a band that was never going to make the big time. I had many jobs—in landscaping, manufacturing, construction, you name it. Working for a large Tex-Mex chain catering to gringos helped me realize that I wanted to be part of a bigger society, and I would need to be open to everything.

Building tacos, tamales, tortas, and enchiladas came naturally to me. But the ones they made in El Chico's were Texas inventions, mostly by Chicanos. Their versions of tacos and enchiladas were not what we made in Mexico—not right or wrong, just different.

So I watched and listened and learned from the sidelines—just as I did in Uncle José's garage while he worked on engines, and in my mother's and grandmother's kitchens as they rolled tamales for the holidays. I could see how, once you mastered the basic techniques, you could make those same recipes 14,000 ways. And when I proved that to my supervisor, he made me a line man. Later I became the traveling cook for the chain—the guy without the title who did everything. They asked me to go help in Waco in the front of the house. I had to wear a suit. I continued to work on my English and played by the company rules. And now I get to play by my own.

ENCHILADAS MEXICANAS

MAKES 6 SERVINGS (12 ENCHILADAS)

The baked enchilada with chili and melted cheese on top is a Texas invention. To us Mexicans, an enchilada is something much simpler: just a warm corn tortilla rolled around crumbly queso fresco cheese, topped with whatever salsa we have on hand, or just a little more cheese. It was created, like so many Mexican dishes, as a tasty way to dispose of leftovers. There were never any fixed ingredients, except for the corn tortillas we used to roll them. Typically they were made to be eaten immediately, with or without a salsa on the side. Over time they evolved to become center of the plate. Enchiladas Mexicanas are enchiladas in their most traditional form. To give the tortillas a nice color and deep, earthy flavor, I mix together equal parts vegetable oil and water with several big spoonfuls of paprika. Right before serving, I heat a little of this mixture in a saucepan with a tortilla, warming the tortilla and coating it on both sides while making it soft and pliable for rolling. In minutes you have a meal!

Serve these hot, with Mexican Rice (page 194) and Veggie Refried Beans (page 187) if you like. They are also a great breakfast dish, with a fried egg on top.

———————

Heat the oven to 200 degrees.

To make the filling: Mix together the crumbled cheese and the onion in a medium bowl.

To make the coating: Mix together the paprika, oil, and water in another bowl.

To make the enchiladas: Heat a small skillet over medium heat until hot. Add 1 tablespoon of the coating mix, rotating the pan to coat. Before the water evaporates, quickly add a tortilla and coat by swirling the pan. Carefully flip the tortilla to coat on the other side,

Filling

1 pound queso fresco,
   crumbled

½ cup finely diced red onion

Coating

¼ cup paprika

½ cup vegetable oil

½ cup water

Enchiladas

12 (5½-inch) fresh Corn
   Tortillas (page 180) or
   store-bought

Salsa Verde (page 205) for
   serving

Salsa Frita (page 205) for
   serving

less than 30 seconds total. Remove to a plate. Repeat with another tortilla and remove to the plate. Spoon about ½ cup of the cheese mixture down the middle of each, then roll. Sprinkle the top with a little more cheese mixture. Keep warm in the oven while you assemble the remaining enchiladas. Repeat with the remaining tortillas, serving 2 enchiladas to a plate.

Serve hot, with Salsa Verde and Salsa Frita on the side.

VARIATIONS

Store-bought tortillas are fine for these, but because the recipe is so simple, it is a great way to showcase the natural corn flavor and texture of a homemade tortilla. See the instructions on page 180. Instead of warming the tortilla in the coating mixture, you can knead the paprika or other seasoning—like Cuban Bijol seasoning or minced serranos—right into the tortilla dough. Brush both sides of the tortilla with a little oil before placing on a griddle or nonstick pan set over high heat, flip, heat, and remove to a plate. Proceed with filling as above.

These enchiladas are also good served atop Morita Pepper Sauce (page 96).

For a Tex-Mex-style enchilada, substitute grated Colby cheese for the queso fresco, then top the enchiladas with a ladleful of Waco Chili (page 127), more grated cheese, and sour cream if you like.

CHEESE ENCHILADAS WITH MORITA PEPPER SAUCE

MAKES 6 SERVINGS (12 ENCHILADAS)

Morita peppers are smoked red-ripe jalapeño peppers with a rich, earthy flavor similar to chipotles, only milder and slightly fruitier. When boiled and pureed, they produce a sauce as dark and complex-flavored as the mole poblano sauces the regions of Oaxaca and Puebla are famous for. The big difference is this sauce has only a few ingredients instead of a thousand.

Moritas are quite hot for most people's tastes. You can tame this sauce but still get the complexity of flavors by substituting the milder mulato pepper for about half of the moritas.

Sauce

20 dried morita peppers (see headnote), stemmed

3 cups chicken stock, preferably homemade (page 99)

4 garlic cloves, peeled

1 tablespoon dried basil

½ teaspoon salt

Enchiladas

About ½ cup vegetable oil for softening the tortillas

12 (5½-inch) corn tortillas

1 pound queso fresco, crumbled

Pico de Gallo (page 202)

Sour cream for garnish (optional)

Heat the oven to 200 degrees.

To make the sauce: Put all the ingredients in a large saucepan over high heat. Bring to a boil, reduce the heat to a simmer, and cook until the peppers are soft, about 15 minutes.

Transfer the mixture to a blender and puree until smooth. Return to the saucepan and keep warm over low heat while you assemble the enchiladas.

To make the enchiladas: Line a baking sheet with paper towels. Heat enough vegetable oil to cover the bottom of a small skillet over medium-high heat. Place 1 tortilla in the oil. Cook until the tortilla begins to bubble, about 30 seconds. Use tongs to gently turn the tortilla. Heat for another 30 seconds, then remove to the paper towel–lined baking sheet to drain. Repeat with the remaining tortillas, adding oil as necessary to the skillet and layering the tortillas on the paper towels to drain.

Place about ½ cup cheese in the center of each tortilla, roll it up tightly, and place on a plate. Keep warm in the oven while you assemble the remaining enchiladas. Spread about ½ cup of the sauce on the plate and top with the enchiladas (or drizzle the sauce on top of the enchiladas). Serve 2 enchiladas to a plate with Pico de Gallo, and garnished with sour cream, if desired.

*Enchiladas Mexicanas
(page 94) with Morita
Pepper Sauce (opposite)*

CHICKEN ENCHILADA CASSEROLE WITH LEMON-CREAM SAUCE

MAKES 6 OR 7 SERVINGS (12 TO 14 ENCHILADAS)

Lemon-Cream Sauce

3 cups chicken stock
   (opposite)

Juice of 1 large lemon
   (3 tablespoons)

⅓ to ½ cup Blond Roux
   (page 298)

1½ cups sour cream

½ teaspoon salt

Enchiladas

2 tablespoons butter

1 medium onion, chopped

2 garlic cloves, smashed

1 bay leaf

2 cups chopped tomatoes

3 cups cooked, shredded
   chicken (opposite)

About ½ cup vegetable oil for
   softening the tortillas

12 to 14 (5½-inch) corn
   tortillas

8 ounces Monterey Jack
   cheese, grated

1 to 2 teaspoons ground
   paprika for garnish

¼ cup sliced pickled jalapeños
   for garnish

These enchiladas are not spicy-hot, just full of flavor. At Taqueria del Sol, we roll them to order, topping each enchilada with about ¼ cup of sauce, sprinkling with cheese, and running them under the broiler just until the cheese is bubbly. If you're making these for just a few people and don't want to wait for the enchiladas to bake, you can do this as well. The sauce can easily be cut in half. Here I have turned it into a casserole that makes a great dish to carry to a potluck, or to have on hand in the refrigerator for several days. It can be cut into pieces like a lasagna and served to a crowd.

If you are short on time, you can buy a rotisserie chicken and shred it. But the chicken will be more tender and flavorful if you cook it as I suggest here, and you will also have the bonus of a wonderful stock.

———

To make the Lemon-Cream Sauce: Put the chicken stock and lemon juice in a medium saucepan over high heat and bring to a boil. Stir in the roux, a spoonful at a time, until the stock is very thick. You may not need all of it. Remove from the heat and stir in the sour cream and salt. Taste and adjust the seasonings as desired. The sauce will keep, covered and refrigerated, for up to 1 day.

To make the enchiladas: Heat the butter in a large skillet set over medium heat. Add the onion, garlic, and bay leaf and cook until the onion is soft and translucent, 5 to 7 minutes. Add the tomatoes and cook until softened, about 2 minutes. Stir in the chicken. Taste and adjust the seasonings as desired.

Heat the oven to 375 degrees. Line a baking sheet with paper towels.

Heat enough vegetable oil to cover the bottom of a small skillet set over medium-high heat. Place 1 tortilla in the oil. Cook until the tortilla begins to bubble, about 30 seconds. Use tongs to gently turn the tortilla. Heat for another 30 seconds, then remove to the paper towel–lined baking sheet to drain. Repeat with the remaining tortillas, adding vegetable oil as necessary to the skillet and layering the tortillas on paper towels to drain.

Place about ⅓ cup of the chicken filling in the center of a tortilla. Roll it up tightly and place it, seam side down, in a 9-by-13-inch baking dish. Repeat with the remaining tortillas and filling, arranging tightly in the dish so they all fit. Cover with the sauce and sprinkle the top evenly with the cheese. Bake until bubbly and beginning to brown, about 30 minutes.

To serve, place 2 enchiladas on each plate. Garnish with a sprinkling of paprika and the pickled jalapeños. Serve hot.

BASIC CHICKEN FILLING AND STOCK

MAKES ABOUT 6 CUPS SHREDDED CHICKEN AND 4 CUPS STOCK

1 (3½-pound) whole chicken, cut into pieces

2 stalks celery, coarsely chopped

1 small carrot, coarsely chopped

2 tablespoons salt

2 quarts cold water

Place the chicken, celery, carrot, and salt in a large pot and cover with the water. Bring to a boil over high heat. Reduce the heat to maintain a simmer and cook until the chicken is just done, about 25 minutes. Remove the chicken from the liquid and, when it is cool enough to handle, remove the skin and bones and set aside. Use two forks or your fingers to shred the chicken. Set aside. Return the skin and bones to the pot with the cooking water. Return to a boil and cook for an additional 20 minutes. Strain and reserve the stock. The stock and chicken will keep, refrigerated separately and covered, for up to 3 days.

BLACK BEAN ENCHILADAS WITH CILANTRO-AVOCADO DRIZZLE

MAKES 8 SERVINGS (16 ENCHILADAS)

Spiced with dried chile, cumin, and garlic, refried black beans make a delicious dip or side dish on their own. Here they are wrapped in corn tortillas, topped with cheese dip, and drizzled with an emerald avocado and herb sauce for a vegetarian enchilada that everyone loves.

¼ cup vegetable oil, plus more
    for heating tortillas

1 cup finely chopped onions

1 tablespoon crushed garlic

1 tablespoon chile de árbol
    flakes or dried red chile
    flakes

1 teaspoon salt

3 cups cooked or canned black
    beans, drained

1 tablespoon ground cumin

1 tablespoon white vinegar

16 (5½-inch) corn tortillas

1 cup Taqueria del Sol
    Jalapeño-Cheese Dip
    (page 42)

Cilantro-Avocado Drizzle
    (opposite)

Heat the ¼ cup oil in a large saucepan over medium heat until it shimmers. Add the onions, garlic, chile de árbol, and salt. Cook for 5 to 7 minutes, until the onions are soft and translucent. Add the beans and cook for 2 more minutes. Add the cumin and vinegar, cook for 2 more minutes, then mash with a potato masher or fork until they reach the consistency you prefer. Taste and adjust the seasonings as desired. Keep warm.

Heat a small skillet over high heat. When it is hot, brush with oil, add a tortilla, and heat on both sides. Remove the tortilla to a plate and spoon the bean mixture into the center and roll up. Place 2 enchiladas on a plate. Top with the cheese dip, then the drizzle. Repeat with the remaining tortillas. Serve.

CILANTRO-AVOCADO DRIZZLE

MAKES 2 CUPS

1 cup vegetable oil

2 ripe medium avocados, pitted and peeled

½ cup chopped fresh cilantro

1 jalapeño, stemmed (remove all or some of the seeds and membranes for less heat)

1 garlic clove, peeled

Salt to taste

Avocados, cilantro, and jalapeño blended with oil create a vibrantly colored and flavored emerald-green sauce. If you prefer more of the solid and less oil, strain it after you have blended it and use the oil to drizzle on fish, salads, vegetables—even toss in pasta.

———

Combine the oil, avocados, cilantro, jalapeño, and garlic in a blender and puree until smooth. Taste and adjust the seasonings as desired.

CORN, POBLANO, AND CHEESE TAMALES

MAKES 6 TO 7 SERVINGS (12 TO 14 TAMALES)

About ¾ of a 1-pound package of fresh or thawed frozen banana leaves (available at many Hispanic and Asian markets; see headnote)

Filling

4 to 6 poblano peppers, roasted, peeled, cored, and seeded (see page 12)

1 tablespoon butter

2 cups fresh corn kernels

12 ounces mild white cheese, such as queso Chihuahua or Monterey Jack, cut into 3-inch-by-¾-inch-by-½-inch sticks

Dough

3 cups Maseca masa harina

1 tablespoon salt

¾ cup melted lard, preferably homemade (page 299)

3 cups warm water or pork stock (page 129) or chicken stock, preferably homemade (page 99), plus more as needed

Once you get the hang of rolling tamales, tamale making does not have to be that difficult or time consuming, especially if you have someone helping you roll. This very simple filling comes together in no time and the combination is delicious. While you can use the more familiar corn husks, banana leaves are also traditional, and I find them easier to work with.

———————

To prepare the banana leaves: Rinse the leaves and pat dry with a towel. Cut away the stems and thick edges of leaves, then cut into twelve to fourteen 8-by-10-inch rectangles. It's good to have extra, since some will tear.

To make the filling: Cut the poblanos into 2-inch-long strips.

Melt the butter in a medium skillet over medium heat. Add the corn and cook until tender, 3 to 5 minutes.

To make the dough: Combine the masa harina and salt in a large bowl. Add the melted lard and 3 cups of the warm water. Knead with your hands to make a smooth dough, adding more liquid as needed, until the mixture is the consistency of mashed potatoes.

To assemble and steam: Using tongs, hold a banana leaf directly over a hot burner for a few seconds to soften, just until it turns bright green. Don't let it heat any longer or it will turn brittle.

Set the leaf on a work surface so that the lighter, smoother side is facing up. Place ⅓ to ½ cup of dough in the center of the leaf and flatten with your hand or a spatula. Place a piece or two of cheese in the center of the dough. Add a few strips of poblano and a heaping spoonful of corn.

Fold the long sides over the dough, overlapping them, then fold the short sides under, forming a snug but not too tight rectangular package. If desired, you can secure them by tying with string or thin strips of banana leaf like a package, although this is not essential.

Topping

Mexican crema (see page
  18), crème fraîche, or sour
  cream thinned with a little
  milk or buttermilk

Repeat with the other banana leaves, dough, and filling until all the dough is used.

Fill the bottom of a steamer or large pot with just enough water to come up to the bottom of the steamer basket. Set the steamer basket on top. Line the bottom with extra banana leaves. Arrange the tamales in the steamer basket in layers on top of the leaves, then top with more leaves to help hold in steam. Cover with a lid and bring the water to a gentle simmer. Cook for 50 to 60 minutes, until the dough begins to pull away from the sides of the leaves.

Remove from the heat and let the tamales rest for 5 minutes. Set on plates, unfold, and drizzle with crema. The cooked tamales will keep, wrapped airtight, in the freezer for 2 months. Thaw in the refrigerator overnight before serving and reheat in a steamer basket over simmering water, covered, for 15 to 20 minutes. The tamales may also be reheated in the microwave for about 2 minutes.

*From left: Corn, Poblano,
and Cheese Tamales, and
Pork Hot Tamales (page 104)*

PORK HOT TAMALES

MAKES 12 TO 15 SERVINGS (24 TO 30 TAMALES)

40 to 50 dried corn husk
  wrappers (from an 8-ounce
  package)

Filling

1½ pounds Boston butt (pork
  shoulder)

2½ quarts water plus 4 cups

10 dried guajillo chiles,
  stemmed and seeded

5 dried chiles de árbol,
  stemmed and seeded

2 tablespoons vegetable oil

½ cup diced onion

1 tablespoon minced garlic

1 cup chicharrones (page 299)
  or pork cracklings (see
  page 19; optional)

2 tablespoons ground cumin

1 tablespoon salt

1 tablespoon ground white
  pepper

Dough

6 cups Maseca masa harina

¼ cup ground cumin

2 tablespoons salt

1 tablespoon ground white
  pepper

1½ cups melted lard,
  preferably homemade (page
  299), cooled slightly

I didn't know the Mississippi Delta was famous for hot tamales until I was invited to compete in the celebrity chef competition of the 2013 Delta Hot Tamale Festival. The little city of Greenville, where the festival is held, even calls itself the Hot Tamale Capital of the World. Legend says Mexican migrant workers came over from Texas to work in the cotton fields and brought tamales in their lunch buckets to eat. African American sharecroppers got a taste and figured out how to make them with cornmeal and whatever ingredients they had. A hundred years later, they're still being made—often by descendants of the original tamale makers—and sold from roadside stands and even in fine restaurants. They are different from what I grew up with: smaller and grittier in texture; some with pork, but most with ground beef; simmered in spicy juices instead of steamed; and served with saltine crackers and sometimes little cups of chili filling on the side.

In both the Delta and Mexico, tamale making is a group activity. Everyone in my family made tamales—my grandmother, mother, uncle, aunts—mostly for holidays like Christmas. Sometimes I would come into the kitchen to watch, and then they would draft me into rolling them for the rest of the afternoon. This is not how a thirteen-year-old boy wants to spend his day! But after I moved to the U.S., I was glad I had the skill. Good homemade tamales are hard to come by because they are so labor-intensive. After I won the tamale festival's chef competition, we ran my winning tamales—the Pork Hot Tamales and Corn Poblano Cheese Tamales—on the menu as a special and they were a big hit. This recipe is involved, but if you recruit some friends to pitch in, they can be fun to make, and you will be rewarded with dozens of delicious packets that will be the hit of the party. Plus they freeze well, and reheat beautifully in the microwave in the shucks they are wrapped in. The photo is on page 103.

Soak the corn husks in cold water until soft, several hours and up to overnight.

To make the filling: Place the pork in a large pot and cover with 2½ quarts of the water. Bring to a boil over high heat. Reduce the heat to maintain a simmer and cook until the meat is tender and falling apart, about 2 hours. Transfer the meat to a work surface to cool slightly. Be sure to reserve the liquid for the dough. Shred the meat with your fingers. You should have about 4 cups. Reserve all of it in case you need it.

Place both kinds of chiles in a medium saucepan, cover with the remaining 4 cups water, and bring to a boil over high heat. Reduce the heat to a simmer and cook until the chiles are soft, about 15 minutes. Transfer the chiles, with ½ cup of the cooking liquid, to a blender and puree. Add more of the cooking liquid if necessary to create a smooth puree. Press the chile puree through a fine-mesh strainer into a bowl.

Heat the oil in a large saucepan over medium heat until it shimmers. Add the onion and garlic and cook for 3 to 5 minutes, or until the onion is soft and translucent. Add the chicharrones or cracklings, if using, and cook for 1 minute more. Add the chile puree, cumin, salt, and white pepper and cook for 2 minutes. Add the pork, reduce the heat to low, and cook for 5 minutes more. Set aside to cool slightly.

To make the dough: Combine the masa harina, cumin, salt, and white pepper in a large bowl. Add the melted lard and 4 cups of the warm pork stock. Knead with your hands to make a smooth dough, adding more stock or water as needed.

To assemble the tamales: Remove a softened husk from the water and pat dry. Hold in one hand, smooth side up and pointed end facing outward. (If one rips, place two together, overlapping slightly.) Place about ⅓ cup of dough on the widest end, and spread out with your hand or a spatula into a ¼-inch-thick rectangle to cover about two-thirds of the husk.

Place 3 to 4 tablespoons of the meat filling down the center of the dough. Fold one long side of the husk over the dough, then the other, then fold the pointed end of the husk so it slightly overlaps the dough, forming a snug but not too tight package. Place a spoonful of dough in the open end of the tamale to seal.

Repeat until all the dough and filling is used.

Fill the bottom of a steamer or large pot slightly taller than the tamales with a few inches of water and set a perforated rack on top. Stand the tamales, open end up, around the edge. Continue adding rows until the pot is filled, being careful not to pack too tightly. Fill any gaps with leftover husks and lay some of the husks over the top. (This will help hold in steam.) If necessary, place a ball of foil in the center to hold the tamales upright. Bring the water to a gentle simmer, cover tightly, and steam for about 40 minutes, until the dough pulls away from the sides of the husks.

Remove from the heat and let the tamales rest for 5 minutes.

To serve, place one tamale on a plate. Unfold and top with some of the remaining meat filling if desired. Cooked tamales will keep, wrapped airtight, in the freezer for 2 months. Thaw in the refrigerator overnight before serving and reheat in a steamer basket over simmering water, covered, for 15 to 20 minutes, or in the microwave for about 5 minutes.

CREOLE RED BEANS AND RICE BURRITOS

MAKES 12 BURRITOS (8 BURRITOS IF PLATED)

¼ cup vegetable oil

1 cup chopped onions

1 cup chopped celery

1 cup chopped green bell
   pepper

1 red or green jalapeño,
   stemmed and minced
   (remove some or all of the
   seeds and membranes for
   less heat)

1 teaspoon finely chopped
   garlic

2 tablespoons Cajun Spice Mix
   (page 291), plus more if
   desired

1 (15-ounce) can tomato sauce

2 (16-ounce) cans red kidney
   beans, with liquid

1 tablespoon finely
   chopped fresh parsley

8 to 12 (8-inch) flour tortillas

4 to 6 cups cooked white or
   brown rice

Red beans and rice is a signature dish of New Orleans. It started out as something mothers would leave on the stove to simmer with bits of leftover ham from Sunday's dinner while they washed clothes on Monday. Now it is eaten any day of the week at home and in restaurants, especially during Mardi Gras. Mexicans, of course, have loved beans and rice forever.

These burritos are fast and easy to make, since you start with canned beans. Plus, they're vegetarian. If you are a meat eater and happen to have some leftover ham or andouille sausage, by all means chop it up and throw it in. The final, very important step is to wrap the cooked burritos in tinfoil and heat in the oven for fifteen to twenty minutes. That helps the burrito hold together in a nice cylinder and makes all the stuffing ingredients blend together into one flavorful package. These make great handheld meals, but if you want a nicer, plated presentation, make only eight burritos and then ladle some of the extra bean filling onto plates to serve as a sauce, slice the burritos in half diagonally, and set the halves on top of the sauce.

———————

Heat the oil in a large skillet over medium heat until it shimmers. Add the onions, celery, bell pepper, jalapeño, and garlic and cook, stirring, for 5 to 7 minutes, until the vegetables are softened, but still a little crunchy. Stir in 2 tablespoons of the spice mix and the tomato sauce and cook, stirring, for 2 minutes to blend the flavors.

Stir in the red beans with their liquid, reduce the heat to medium-low, and simmer for 15 to 20 minutes, until the mixture is thickened to a gravylike consistency. Taste and add more spice mix if desired. Stir in the parsley.

Recipe continued

To assemble the burritos: Heat the oven to 400 degrees.

Set a dry skillet over medium heat. Add 1 tortilla and heat on both sides for a few seconds, just long enough to warm through and soften.

Transfer to a work area. Spread ½ cup of the rice across the center of the tortilla, leaving a 2- to 3-inch border on each side. Spread ½ to ¾ cup of the bean mixture on top of the rice. Fold in the opposite sides of the tortilla toward the center. Beginning at the bottom, roll up the tortilla tightly toward the top edge to enclose the filling, making a well-sealed package. Wrap the burrito tightly in foil and place on a baking sheet. Repeat with the remaining tortillas and filling. Heat in the oven for 15 to 20 minutes, until hot.

Remove from the oven, unwrap the foil, and cut each burrito diagonally in half. If desired, ladle some of the extra red-bean mixture on a plate and set the burrito halves on top.

NEW MEXICAN CHILES RELLENOS

MAKES 8 SERVINGS (8 CHILES RELLENOS)

New Mexico's Hatch green chiles come into season every August and September. These meaty, medium-hot, long green chiles are grown around the village of Hatch, just west of the banks of the Rio Grande, and are considered by many people to be the best-tasting chiles in the world. Hatch celebrates this fact each year by hosting a chile festival that draws thousands of people from around the world.

I roast and stuff the chiles with cheese, coat the outside with a crispy batter, and serve them over fresh tomato sauce with jalapeños. We host our own Hatch chile festival as a charity fundraiser, where we serve the rellenos along with other dishes that include the chiles, from cheeseburgers to ice cream. Each year we order around 5,000 pounds that our guys roast in a special roaster in the parking lot and peel by hand. We freeze what we don't use right away to incorporate into specials throughout the year.

If you can't get your hands on Hatch chiles, you can also get very good results using Anaheims or poblanos, though the taste won't be quite the same.

---

8 green New Mexico chiles
   (see headnote) or 8 large
   Anaheim or poblano chiles
1 pound Monterey Jack cheese,
   grated
1 cup all-purpose flour
½ teaspoon salt
About 1 cup water
2 cups panko
Vegetable oil for frying
2 to 3 cups Salsa Frita
   (page 204)

Place the chiles over a medium-high flame on a gas stove or on a very hot grill, turning frequently until the skins are evenly blistered or blackened. Remove from the heat and wrap in a dishtowel or paper bag to steam for 15 minutes. When they are cool enough to handle, rub the peppers with a paper towel to remove the skins. Leaving the stem intact, cut a slit down the side of each chile to remove the membranes and seeds. Stuff each pepper with ½ cup of cheese. Place in the refrigerator to firm up, about 20 minutes.

Combine the flour and salt in a small bowl. Stir in enough water to create a mixture as thick as pancake batter. Place the panko on a small plate. Working with one chile at a time, dip and roll the chile in the batter, hold over the bowl for a few seconds to let the excess drip off, then roll the chile in the panko. Return the breaded chiles to the refrigerator for 20 minutes to set.

Line a baking sheet with paper towels. Heat 1 inch of oil in a Dutch oven or heavy skillet over high heat to 350 degrees. Gently add the chiles to the pot and fry in batches, turning, until browned, 5 to 6 minutes. Allow the oil to return to 350 degrees between batches. Transfer to the paper towel–lined baking sheet and drain. Serve hot over the salsa.

SOUPS, STEWS, AND CHILIS

Chapter Five

CALDO DE POLLO (CHICKEN SOUP) *116*
ZUCCHINI AND CORN SOUP WITH BRIE *118*
   —TORTILLA CROUTONS *119*
POBLANO CORN CHOWDER WITH SHRIMP *121*
SPICY TOMATO SOUP *122*
RED POSOLE *124*
   —GREEN POSOLE *125*
PORK BROTH WITH VIDALIA ONIONS
   AND SMOKED GOUDA CHEESE *126*
WACO CHILI *127*
PORK, PEANUT BUTTER, AND BLACK BEAN
   CHILI *128*
GREEN CHILE STEW *129*
REAL MEXICAN CHILI CON CARNE *130*
THE DISHWASHER'S SOUP (MEXICAN-COCKTAIL
   SEAFOOD SOUP) *132*

At the house I shared with the other members of the rock band, I would make big pots of soup for all of us.

———

The first thing that I missed about Mexico when I came to the U.S. was soup. In Texas everybody makes chili. I could not find a good, nicely made soup to save my life. I was seventeen or eighteen and didn't know anything about fine dining in the U.S. But I definitely was not satisfied with chicken and noodles out of a can. Back home I ate homemade soup in some form every day—usually chicken or vegetable, always with homemade corn tortillas on the side. And no matter how simple, it was always good.

Soups are a staple in Mexico. There are places that sell only chicken soup, and others that sell only posole, a thick soup of pork, hominy, and chiles. At home or in restaurants, soups are not typically a special-occasion dish but everyday fare, and a way to use what we have left over from the day before. They vary, from the high plains to the low plains, from sunny beaches to volcanic regions where it snows year-round. In the north where I'm from, we like meatier soups—usually with chicken or pork. As far as vegetables go, it's lots of tomatoes, zucchini, and corn. And we all eat menudo, a very labor-intensive soup made with tripe (beef stomach) and other tough cuts of beef that take many hours to tenderize. That was the one traditional Mexican soup that I could get in Houston, at a café in the Latino community where I lived.

I realized the only way I could eat what I liked on a regular basis was to cook it myself. I started experimenting. I made a lot of mistakes, but I didn't care. At the house I shared with the other members of the rock band I played with, I would make big pots of soup for all of us to eat. They were great to have in the refrigerator because we came and went as we pleased and we could just heat them up whenever we felt like it.

Later in the kitchens of fine-dining restaurants in the South, I learned how to make seafood chowders and bisques and use beef bones for stocks that had to simmer forever. For years I worked beside chefs from Louisiana who taught me all about gumbos.

In this chapter I present a collection of my favorite meals in a bowl that need only some tortillas or bread, and maybe a salad, to make a meal. None of them calls for tripe.

CALDO DE POLLO (CHICKEN SOUP)

MAKES 8 TO 12 SERVINGS

Comida corrida, the Mexican version of the Southern meat and three (main dish and three sides), always starts with a soup, and 85 percent of the time it's chicken. This is the soup we had most often at home as well. I like a chicken soup with a clean broth—shiny and golden looking, fortified with fresh vegetables, and intensified with extra bouillon cubes. Once the chicken is cooked, we may take the meat off the bones and use it for something else—tacos, enchiladas, tostadas—and stretch out the broth with rice, noodles, or vegetables. Or we will cut up the whole chicken first and serve it, bones and all, in the soup, using corn tortillas to pick up big pieces of meat. If you have some leftover tortillas, you can shred them and fry in hot oil for a garnish.

---

1 (4-pound) whole chicken

3 quarts cold water

2 cups finely chopped celery

1½ cups thinly sliced onions

2 jalapeños, stemmed and cut in half (remove some or all of the seeds and membranes for less heat)

3 chicken bouillon cubes

2 vegetable bouillon cubes

1 teaspoon salt

3 cups diced tomatoes

Pico de Gallo (page 202)

Lime wedges

Mexican Rice (optional; page 194)

Cut the chicken into pieces small enough to fit into soup bowls, including the bones and skin. Place the chicken in a large pot, cover with the water, and bring to a boil over high heat. Boil for 3 minutes.

Add the celery, onions, jalapeños, bouillon cubes, and salt. Bring back to a boil and boil for 5 minutes longer. Add the tomatoes, bring back to a boil, then lower the heat to maintain a rapid simmer for 25 minutes or until the chicken is cooked through. Remove and discard the jalapeños and the large bones. Taste and adjust the seasonings as desired.

To serve, place 1 or 2 pieces of chicken in a soup bowl. Ladle the broth and vegetables over the chicken. Garnish with the Pico de Gallo, a lime wedge, and Mexican Rice, if desired.

ZUCCHINI AND CORN SOUP WITH BRIE

MAKES 6 TO 8 SERVINGS

I love all kinds of cheeses—especially Brie. The Brie adds creaminess and body to this simple vegetable soup and gives it another layer of flavor. I recommend topping the soup with Tortilla Croutons, or serving with toast, grilled cheese sandwiches, or chips. The photo is on page 114.

2 large tomatoes

1 medium red or green jalapeño

2 vegetable bouillon cubes

4 tablespoons (½ stick) butter

1 tablespoon vegetable oil

½ cup chopped onion

1 garlic clove, crushed

1 teaspoon salt

3 cups diced zucchini

3 cups fresh corn kernels

1½ cups water

1½ teaspoons ground cumin

8 ounces Brie, cut into thin slices

Tortilla Croutons (opposite; optional)

Place the tomatoes and jalapeño in a large saucepan, cover with water, and bring to a boil over high heat. Just as the tomato skins begin to crack, remove the tomatoes with a slotted spoon and transfer to a blender or a food processor. Remove the stem from the jalapeño and some or all of the seeds and membranes for less heat, if desired. Add to the tomatoes, along with the bouillon cubes. Process until smooth.

Dump out the water from the saucepan and set over medium heat. Heat the butter and vegetable oil until they shimmer. Add the onion, garlic, and salt and cook for 5 to 7 minutes, until the onion is translucent. Add the zucchini and corn and cook, stirring, for 3 more minutes, until the vegetables begin to soften. Add the tomato mixture, water, and cumin and cook for 3 more minutes, or until the vegetables are tender. Taste and adjust the seasonings as desired.

Ladle into soup bowls. Top each serving with several slices of cheese and with the Tortilla Croutons, if desired.

TORTILLA CROUTONS

MAKES 1 CUP

4 (6-inch) flour tortillas
1 large egg, beaten
Vegetable oil for frying
Cotija cheese (optional)

Line a baking sheet with paper towels and set aside.

Brush 1 tortilla with some of the beaten egg. Press a second tortilla on top of the first and brush with more egg. Repeat with the remaining tortillas. Cut into crouton-size squares.

Heat 1 inch of vegetable oil in a Dutch oven or a large, heavy pot or skillet over high heat to 350 degrees. Carefully add a small handful of tortillas to the oil and fry until golden, 30 to 45 seconds. Remove with a slotted spoon to the paper towel–lined baking sheet and sprinkle with Cotija cheese, if desired. Repeat with the remaining tortillas, allowing the oil to return to 350 degrees between each batch.

POBLANO CORN CHOWDER WITH SHRIMP

MAKES 8 TO 10 SERVINGS

3 celery stalks, coarsely
chopped

¼ large onion, coarsely
chopped (½ cup chopped)

2 tablespoons butter

1 poblano pepper, cored,
seeded, and diced

1 teaspoon salt, plus additional
as desired

4 cups heavy cream

4 cups half-and-half

8 ounces shrimp, peeled,
deveined, and diced

⅓ cup sugar, plus additional as
desired

1 teaspoon lobster base
(optional; see headnote)

1 teaspoon ground black
pepper

Pinch of ground chile de árbol
or cayenne pepper, plus
additional as desired

½ to ¾ cup Blond Roux (page
298)

1 (15-ounce) can whole corn,
drained

1 (15-ounce) can creamed
corn

Before Mike Klank and I opened our previous restaurant together, he wanted to make me a better chef. So he called a friend of his at City Grill, one of the top-rated dining rooms in Atlanta, and suggested that I do an exchange with the chef for a week so I could learn classic techniques. We made stocks where you roast the bones first and then reduce them for twenty-four hours. It takes forever, and I thought I would go out of my mind! But nevertheless I did it. One of the dishes I did enjoy making was lobster corn chowder. Later I modified it by adding a bit more heat and using more affordable ingredients, like shrimp instead of lobster, with a spoonful of lobster base. (This concentrated flavor paste is sold in jars at many supermarkets and can be ordered online, but the chowder will still be good without it.) And while I hardly ever recommend canned vegetables for anything, the creamed and whole-kernel niblets serve the purpose well here and contribute to the creaminess. (You can use fresh kernels in place of the niblets if you prefer.) This chowder is now one of our regular and most popular offerings at Taqueria del Sol.

———————

Put the celery and onion in a food processor and process just until pureed. Drain off any liquid with a slotted spoon and reserve the solids.

Melt the butter in a large pot over medium heat. Add the celery-onion puree, the poblano pepper, and salt and cook until the pepper is softened, 5 to 7 minutes. Add the cream, half-and-half, shrimp, sugar, lobster base (if using), black pepper, and chile de árbol and stir to combine. Bring to a simmer, add ½ cup of the roux, and cook, stirring frequently, for 3 minutes, or until thickened and the shrimp is cooked through. Add the whole corn and creamed corn and heat through, stirring to combine. If you prefer it thicker, slowly stir in more roux, a spoonful at a time, and cook for a minute or two longer until the chowder reaches the desired thickness. Ladle into bowls and serve.

SPICY TOMATO SOUP

MAKES 8 SERVINGS

The flavor of this quick soup is as bright as its red color. Fresh tomatoes and red jalapeños are boiled, pureed, and cooked with sautéed sweet Vidalia onions and reduced white wine. To thicken the soup, I add some ketchup, which gives a nice smooth texture and intensifies the tomato flavor. A garnish of sour cream and crumbled bacon makes the soup even better. It goes great with a grilled cheese sandwich or a simple quesadilla.

6 medium ripe tomatoes

2 to 3 medium red jalapeños

8 tablespoons (1 stick) butter

2 cups diced Vidalia onions

1 teaspoon salt

2 cups dry white wine

2½ cups ketchup

Garnishes

Sour cream

Crumbled, cooked bacon
  (optional)

Pico de Gallo (optional; page
  202)

Chopped parsley or cilantro
  (optional)

Place the tomatoes and jalapeños in a large saucepan, cover with water, and bring to a boil over high heat. Just as the tomato skins begin to crack, remove them with a slotted spoon and transfer to a blender or a food processor. Remove the stems from the jalapeños and some or all of the seeds and membranes for less heat, if desired. Add the jalapeños to the blender. Process until smooth.

Dump out the water from the saucepan. Add the butter and melt over medium heat. Add the onions and salt and cook until the onions are soft and translucent, 5 to 7 minutes. Turn the heat up to high. Add the wine and reduce by half, about 5 minutes.

Add the tomato mixture and ketchup, reduce the heat to a simmer, and cook for 3 minutes. Taste and adjust the seasonings as desired.

Ladle into bowls and garnish with the sour cream and bacon, and Pico de Gallo and parsley, if using.

RED (OR GREEN) POSOLE

MAKES 10 TO 12 SERVINGS

Hominy is traditional in the South, though many of my Southern friends think of it only as poor people's food their grandparents ate during the Depression. Our attitude is much different in Mexico, where hominy's earthy corn flavor and chewy texture are prized in some of our favorite dishes, especially posole. This hearty soup made with pork and hominy is eaten throughout Mexico for holidays and special occasions, such as Christmas Eve. At our house we had it anytime. Even though it's economical, it can be very festive. You serve it at the table with bowls filled with all kinds of things—lemon or lime wedges, diced onions, diced radishes, shredded cabbage, cilantro—and let everyone garnish their soup as they like. The broth may be enriched with a puree of dried red chiles or roasted green chiles. Many recipes for posole are very labor-intensive, but mine is quite simple. You can easily make a double batch—one red and one green—to serve around Christmastime. I like to eat this soup with French bread, but corn tortillas or your favorite corn bread are fine, too.

---

2 pounds Boston butt (pork shoulder), cut into 3-inch chunks

1 pound pork backbones or other pork bones

1 onion, peeled, trimmed, and cut in half

2 garlic cloves, peeled

3 chicken bouillon cubes

2 tablespoons salt

4 quarts water

20 dried guajillo chiles (remove some or all of the seeds for less heat)

10 dried chiles de árbol (remove some or all of the seeds for less heat)

4 cups canned hominy (juice included)

Garnishes

Lemon wedges

Diced onions

Diced radishes

Place the pork meat, bones, onion, garlic, bouillon cubes, and salt in a large pot. Add 3 quarts of the water, or just enough to cover the meat, and bring to a boil over high heat. Reduce the heat to maintain a simmer and cook for 1 hour, or until the meat is cooked through and tender.

Meanwhile, in a medium pot, bring the remaining 1 quart of water to a boil over high heat. Add all the chiles and boil until softened, about 15 minutes. Remove from the heat. When they are cool enough to handle, remove the stems. Transfer to a blender and puree. Set aside.

Remove the meat from the broth, and when it is cool enough to handle, chop into ½-inch cubes. Discard the bones. Return the meat to the broth. Add the hominy and chile puree and heat through. Ladle into bowls and garnish with the lemon wedges, onions, and radishes.

GREEN POSOLE

Blend together 4 cups diced roasted (see page 12) fresh green chiles or canned diced roasted mild green chiles with 2 stemmed jalapeños in a blender or food processor until pureed. Add to the broth in place of the red puree.

PORK BROTH WITH VIDALIA ONIONS AND SMOKED GOUDA CHEESE

MAKES 8 SERVINGS

Whenever I'm feeling under the weather, I have a soup remedy that I like even better than chicken soup: chunks of pork simmered with lots of Georgia's famous sweet Vidalia onions and just enough spice to wake up the taste buds. A handful of smoked Gouda stirred in at the end adds a creamy, slightly nutty flavor that complements the pork and the onions. For crunch, I like to top it with croutons that I make out of tortillas.

---

1 pound Boston butt (pork shoulder), cut into 1-inch cubes

2 chicken bouillon cubes

2 quarts water

4 cups thinly sliced Vidalia onions (3 or 4 large)

1 habanero, stemmed and thinly sliced (remove all or some of the seeds and membranes for less heat)

1½ teaspoons ground cumin

1 large tomato, chopped

1 teaspoon salt

8 ounces smoked Gouda cheese, grated

Tortilla Croutons (page 119)

Place the pork, bouillon cubes, and water in a large pot over medium-high heat and bring to a boil. Reduce the heat to maintain a rapid simmer and cook for 30 minutes. Add the onions, habanero, cumin, tomato, and salt and continue to cook until the pork is tender, about 15 minutes more. Taste and adjust the seasonings as desired. Ladle the soup into bowls, top each bowl with cheese, and garnish with the croutons.

WACO CHILI

MAKES 8 SERVINGS

3 large tomatoes

2 medium jalapeños

Vegetable oil for brushing

1 teaspoon lard, preferably
   homemade (optional;
   page 299)

½ pound ground beef

½ pound ground pork

1 small onion, finely chopped

1 green bell pepper, cored,
   seeded, and finely chopped

2 teaspoons salt

2 garlic cloves, minced

½ cup paprika

1 teaspoon ground cumin

1 teaspoon ground black
   pepper

4 cups chicken stock,
   preferably homemade
   (page 99), or pork stock
   (page 129)

2 to 3 tablespoons Ancho Chile
   Puree (page 292)

⅓ cup Blond Roux (page 298)

Sour cream and salsa for
   garnish

When I was working in restaurants in Texas, I noticed how people judged a restaurant by their chili. I studied chili. I took part in some chili cook-offs. My chili uses both ground beef and pork and has a soupy base that is thickened with a roux, giving it a shiny look and a texture that is more smooth than chunky. Instead of chili powder, I flavor it with roasted tomatoes and jalapeños, pureed dried chiles, and other seasonings. It is very versatile. You can eat it right out of the bowl, or you can ladle it over enchiladas as a sauce (page 94). It is also great on a hot dog with slaw, in a bun or a flour tortilla. Make a big batch and freeze what you aren't using right away.

——————

Heat the oven to 425 degrees.

Place the tomatoes and jalapeños on a baking sheet, brush each with vegetable oil, and roast for 15 to 20 minutes, until the skins begin to soften and burst. Remove the stems from the jalapeños and some or all of the seeds and membranes for less heat, if desired. Transfer to a blender or food processor and process until smooth.

If using lard, melt it in a Dutch oven or large, heavy pot over medium-high heat. Add the beef and pork and cook, stirring, until browned. Add the onion, bell pepper, and salt and continue to cook until the onion is soft and translucent, 5 to 7 minutes. Reduce the heat to medium. Add the tomato and jalapeño mixture and cook, stirring occasionally, for 3 minutes. Add the garlic, paprika, cumin, black pepper, stock, and ancho puree. Increase the heat to high and boil for 5 minutes.

Reduce the heat to medium, stir in the roux, and simmer, stirring frequently, for 5 minutes or until thickened. Taste and adjust the seasonings as desired. Ladle into bowls, garnish with sour cream and salsa, and serve.

PORK, PEANUT BUTTER, AND BLACK BEAN CHILI

MAKES 8 TO 10 SERVINGS

2 pounds Boston butt (pork shoulder), cut into ½-inch cubes

3 chicken bouillon cubes

1 tablespoon salt

3 quarts water

4 tablespoons (½ stick) butter

1 cup diced onions

1 cup diced red bell pepper

1 cup diced yellow bell pepper

1 cup diced zucchini

1 tablespoon minced garlic

3 cups cooked or canned black beans, drained and rinsed

1 cup diced tomatoes

1 cup diced roasted (see page 12) mild fresh green chiles, or canned diced roasted mild green chiles

1 tablespoon ground cumin

1 cup smooth peanut butter

⅓ to ½ cup Blond Roux, at room temperature (page 298)

Putting peanut butter in chili may not sound like a good idea. But I hope you will trust me and give it a try anyway. I got this idea while living in Texas, where people put all kinds of crazy stuff in chili, and was curious to see how it would taste. People loved it! And if you do a little research, you will discover that this combination of broth, spices, ground peanuts, and sometimes meat and vegetables is nothing new. Groundnut stew has been a popular dish in West Africa for centuries, and cream of peanut soup is a specialty in Virginia, where peanuts are a major crop. My chili has a smooth, savory base that has elements of those dishes. It's equally good with crusty bread or warm corn tortillas on the side.

———

Place the pork, bouillon cubes, salt, and water in a large pot and bring to a boil over high heat. Reduce the heat to maintain a simmer and cook until the meat is tender, about 30 minutes.

Drain the liquid through a fine-mesh strainer into a large container, reserving the stock and meat separately.

Melt the butter in the now-empty pot over medium heat. Add the reserved meat and cook, stirring frequently, until browned, about 3 minutes.

Add the onions, bell peppers, zucchini, and garlic and cook, stirring frequently, for about 2 minutes, or until the vegetables are soft. Add the black beans, tomatoes, and chiles and cook for 2 minutes. Add 2 quarts of the reserved stock, along with the cumin and peanut butter, and cook for 5 minutes. Stir in ⅓ cup of the roux and simmer, stirring frequently, for 5 minutes, until the chili is slightly thickened. Stir in a little more roux if needed until the chili reaches the desired thickness. Taste and adjust the seasonings as desired. Ladle into bowls and serve.

GREEN CHILE STEW

MAKES 8 TO 10 SERVINGS

Pork Stock

2 pounds Boston butt (pork
   shoulder), cut into ½-inch
   cubes, or ground pork

3 quarts water

3 chicken bouillon cubes

¼ cup vegetable oil

2 cups chopped green bell
   peppers

1½ cups chopped onions

3 large garlic cloves, minced

1 teaspoon salt

2 cups chopped tomatoes

2 jalapeños, stemmed and
   minced (remove some or all
   of the seeds and membranes
   for less heat)

2 tablespoons ground cumin

¼ to ½ cup **Blond Roux**
   (optional; page 298)

3 cups diced roasted (see page
   12), peeled mild fresh green
   chiles, such as Hatch (see
   page 12), or canned diced
   roasted mild green chiles

2 jalapeños, roasted and
   chopped (see page 12),
   stemmed, (remove some
   or all of the seeds and
   membranes for less heat)

This stew is similar to what you'll find on menus throughout
the Southwest, and nothing like the chili con carnes of Texas or
Mexico. It is a brothy chili, made of chopped pork with lots of
roasted mild and hot chiles, that's heavy on the cumin. I saw how
people in the South like their gravies, so I thickened it with roux,
but this is a personal preference. This chili is good with chopped
or ground pork.

To make the pork stock: Combine the pork, water, and bouillon
cubes in a large pot and bring to a boil over high heat. Reduce the
heat to a rapid simmer and simmer for 45 minutes. You should have
about 4 cups broth left—add a little more water if needed while
cooking. Pour through a fine-mesh strainer, reserving the stock and
the meat separately.

Heat the oil in a large, deep saucepan over medium-high heat
until it shimmers. Add the pork and cook, stirring frequently, until
browned, about 5 minutes. Add the bell peppers, onions, garlic, and
salt and cook for 5 to 7 minutes, until the onions are translucent.

Add the tomatoes and jalapeños and cook for 5 minutes. Add the
reserved stock and the cumin. Increase the heat to high and boil for
3 minutes. Stir in ¼ cup of the roux, if using.

Reduce the heat to medium and simmer, stirring frequently, for
5 minutes. Stir in a little more roux if needed until the stew reaches
the desired thickness. Add the mild green chiles and jalapeños and
simmer for 5 minutes longer. Ladle into bowls and serve.

REAL MEXICAN CHILI CON CARNE

MAKES 8 SERVINGS

Chili con carne in Mexico looks and tastes nothing like the pots of slow-simmered meats and spices Texans are famous for. The meat, the peppers, and the tomatoes are all fresh and quickly sautéed before some stock is added and it simmers for ten minutes or so. That's it! The chili will be very brothy, so it is up to you if you want to eat it more like soup, or dish it out with a slotted spoon so it is more like a stew and save the broth for a later meal. It's great over beans or rice, but I like it best served in a wide bowl along with a ladleful of the Mexican spaghetti that we call Sopa de Fideo (page 197). The juices of each are even more delicious when they blend together, and the noodles give it a nice texture contrast.

_____

2 tablespoons vegetable oil

2 pounds flank steak, cubed (or sirloin, cube, or skirt steak)

1½ cups finely chopped onions

1 jalapeño, stemmed and minced (remove some or all of the seeds and membranes for less heat)

1 finely chopped green bell pepper

1 tablespoon crushed minced garlic

2 cups chopped tomatoes

½ teaspoon ground cumin, or to taste

1 teaspoon salt, or to taste

1 chicken bouillon cube

1 cup water, or more as needed

In a large saucepan, heat the oil over medium-high heat until it shimmers. Add the meat. Cook, stirring, until browned on all sides, about 5 minutes. Add the onions, peppers, and garlic. Cook for 5 to 7 minutes, until the vegetables are soft, then add the tomatoes and cook for 5 minutes longer. Add the cumin, salt, bouillon cube, and water and cook for 10 minutes. Ladle into bowls and serve.

THE DISHWASHER'S SOUP (MEXICAN-COCKTAIL SEAFOOD SOUP)

MAKES 12 TO 14 SERVINGS

Seafood

1 gallon water

4 bay leaves

1 onion, peeled and halved

3 tablespoons salt

1 pound octopus (see headnote)

1 pound shrimp, peeled and deveined

8 ounces snapper or other white fish, cut into 1-inch pieces

Soup Base

5 cups ketchup

2 cups water

2 cups chopped tomatoes

1 cup finely chopped onions

1 cup finely chopped fresh cilantro

2 jalapeños, stemmed and minced (remove some or all of the seeds and membranes for less heat)

½ cup lime juice

1 tablespoon Worcestershire sauce

1 tablespoon Tabasco sauce

We call this Dishwasher's Soup because I learned to make it from Serafín Rojas, who came to wash dishes at our previous restaurant, the Sundown Café, in 1991, and is still with the company today. Serafín was born in Oaxaca and lived near Acapulco before he emigrated to the U.S. He used to sell tamales out of his car, and to this day, they are some of the best I have ever tasted. He sometimes made a cold seafood soup with leftover shrimp or fish from the kitchen as a staff lunch that was so good we occasionally ran it as a special. The tomato base is like a cross between a Southern shrimp cocktail and Spanish gazpacho. Once you start eating it, it is hard to stop.

Serafín has never had a desire to move up in the company. But he always shows up, and his tremendous work ethic runs in his family. Two of his sons and one of his grandsons have worked for Taqueria del Sol, and his nephew, who started working for us when he was seventeen, became a kitchen manager. I'm the godfather to one of Serafín's children. So I am honored to be able to include one of his recipes in this book.

You can simplify this soup by using any combination of seafood, including just shrimp. Crabmeat is delicious in it. You can substitute baby octopus for regular octopus: Cook as directed, but reduce the total time to 7 minutes, or just until tender.

To make the seafood: Put the water, bay leaves, onion, and salt in a large pot, place over high heat, and bring to a boil. Add the octopus and cook for 1 minute. Remove with a slotted spoon and return the water to a boil. Add the octopus again and cook for 1 minute. Remove with a slotted spoon and bring back to a boil. Add the octopus and cook for 20 minutes. Remove, coarsely chop, and chill.

Bring the water back to a boil, add the shrimp, and cook for 2 minutes. Remove using a slotted spoon. Coarsely chop and chill.

Garnish
2 cups diced avocados
Crackers, such as saltines
Tabasco sauce

Bring the water back to a boil, add the fish, and cook for 1 minute. Remove with a slotted spoon. Coarsely chop and chill. Reserve 2 cups of the stock.

To make the soup base: Combine all the ingredients in a large bowl, including the stock, and refrigerate.

Ladle 1 cup of soup base into each bowl and add some octopus, shrimp, fish, and diced avocados. Serve with the crackers and Tabasco sauce.

EDDIE'S BLUE PLATE LUNCHES AND SPECIAL SUPPERS

Chapter Six

SPICED PORK TENDERLOIN
   WITH SWEET POTATOES, CHILE
   GLAZE, AND SHIITAKES *138*
   —FLUFFY SWEET POTATOES *140*
EDDIE'S PORK WITH ROASTED JALAPEÑO
   GRAVY *142*
PAN-FRIED PORK CHOPS WITH RANCHERO
   BROWN GRAVY *143*
OVEN-BAKED MEMPHIS-STYLE RIBS *145*
MEATLOAF WITH TOMATO-HABANERO GRAVY *146*
STEAK CHURRASCO WITH CHIMICHURRI
   SAUCE *148*
TEXAS CHICKEN-FRIED STEAK
   WITH TABASCO CREAM GRAVY *151*
BLUE CORNMEAL—CRUSTED CHICKEN
   WITH MINT-JALAPEÑO DRIZZLE *154*
BUTTERMILK FRIED CHICKEN WITH GREEN
   CHILE—HORSERADISH SAUCE *156*
CHICKEN—GREEN CHILE POTPIE IN PUFFY
   TORTILLA SHELLS *159*
REMOULADE-TOPPED FISH FILLETS OVER
   MEXICAN MAQUE CHOUX *161*
BLACK PEPPER—CRUSTED TILAPIA WITH
   ARTICHOKE AND JALAPEÑO RELISH *163*
MAC AND CHEESE WITH FETA AND JALAPEÑO *164*
SAUTÉED SNAPPER WITH CILANTRO—ROASTED
   PECAN PESTO *165*
MEXICAN-STYLE BARBECUED SHRIMP *168*
SHRIMP FRIED RICE TOPPED WITH BRONZED
   SCALLOPS AND TABASCO OIL *171*
SHRIMP AND GRITS, MY WAY *173*
CREAMY GRITS *175*
   —LIGHTER CREAMY GRITS *175*
   —CREAMY BLUE CHEESE GRITS *175*

I don't care about expensive cuts.

When I first moved to Texas from Mexico, I used to go to Kentucky Fried Chicken all the time. I knew barely any English, and I would go there and look at the menu and say, "*Grande* chicken and *grande* Coke?" and they would give me a whole bucket of chicken and a two-liter Coke. Every week for the first month, I craved chicken, so I would go back. The girls who worked there got to know me and they'd laugh and go, "*Grande* chicken?" I was paying $16.20 just so that I could have the chicken, but I liked it so much that I kept ordering it.

Southern-style fried chicken is still one of my favorite things to this day, whether it comes in a bucket at a drive-through window or at a small-town café that may have only one old lady in the kitchen doing the cooking. People around here call those cafés meat and twos or meat and threes, meaning you get an inexpensive home-cooked lunch that consists of one meat and two or three vegetable side dishes, and maybe rolls or corn bread.

These places remind me of the family-run *cocinas* where Mexicans go for comida corrida—a cheap, hot midday meal served in courses, beginning with a soup and warm tortillas on the side. The customers are working people of all classes who can't go home for lunch. You don't have a menu with choices; you just eat whatever the cook is preparing for her family that day, depending on what looks good at the market.

When Mike Klank and I opened our taqueria, we decided to incorporate a blue plate special into our lunch menu—similar to what's served in a traditional Southern diner but with some dishes you might also find in a cocina. These dishes change weekly, giving me an opportunity to try out new dishes on customers and experiment with the flavors of the season.

People ask us how we can serve these full-course meals that are like those in fine-dining restaurants but for half the price. In this chapter you will find out. It is no big secret. I cook from the bottom up. First I think about the sauce, then the starch and the vegetable, and last, the meat, chicken, or fish. I don't care about expensive cuts. These recipes feature lower-cost meats, which you may have to cook longer, cut a certain way, or marinate to get the texture and flavor you want. Add a good gravy or salsa and a vegetable that perfectly complements them, and you won't miss that expensive ingredient!

SPICED PORK TENDERLOIN WITH SWEET POTATOES, CHILE GLAZE, AND SHIITAKES

MAKES 8 SERVINGS

Sometimes the littlest detail can make the biggest difference in a dish. In this case, it's the shiitake mushrooms. Pork and sweet potatoes go well with one another, and a chile-infused syrup ties the two together. To add a little crunch and take the edge off the sweetness, I thinly slice and quickly sauté a handful of the mushrooms and sprinkle them on top as a garnish. Cook the sweet potatoes while the pork is roasting and whip them after the pork comes out of the oven.

———————

Pork

½ cup chopped fresh parsley

¼ cup chopped fresh basil

2 tablespoons fresh thyme
  leaves

1 tablespoon crushed
  coriander seeds or
  1½ teaspoons ground

1½ teaspoons minced garlic

1 tablespoon salt

1 tablespoon ground black
  pepper

½ cup vegetable oil

2 (1-pound) pork tenderloins,
  trimmed

Chile Glaze

1 cup light corn syrup or maple
  syrup

¼ cup Chile de Árbol Vinegar
  (page 296)

1 tablespoon ketchup

Pinch of salt

To make the pork: Combine the herbs, salt, pepper, and oil in a container large enough to hold the tenderloin. Add the tenderloin and turn to coat on all sides. Refrigerate for 2 hours or overnight.

Heat the oven to 425 degrees.

Heat a large ovenproof skillet over medium-high heat. Unwrap the tenderloin and add to the pan. Sear on all sides until browned, 5 to 6 minutes total. Transfer to the oven and cook for 15 to 20 minutes, until the center of the loin reaches 145 degrees.

Remove from the oven, cover, and let rest for 10 minutes.

Meanwhile, make the glaze: Place the corn syrup, vinegar, ketchup, and salt in a small bowl and set aside at room temperature.

Mushrooms

2 tablespoons butter

8 ounces shiitake mushrooms, stemmed and thinly sliced

Salt

Fluffy Sweet Potatoes (page 140)

To make the mushrooms: Melt the butter in a medium skillet set over medium-high heat. Add the mushrooms and cook, stirring frequently, until lightly browned, 2 to 3 minutes. Season to taste with salt. Set aside.

Slice the pork into ½-inch-thick slices. Place a mound of sweet potatoes on each plate, top with some pork slices, drizzle with some of the glaze, and garnish with the sautéed mushrooms.

FLUFFY SWEET POTATOES

MAKES 8 SERVINGS

6 medium sweet potatoes, peeled and cut
    into 2-inch chunks
½ cup heavy cream, at room temperature
8 tablespoons (1 stick) butter, melted
Salt

Put the sweet potatoes in a large pot and cover with water. Bring to a boil over high heat. Reduce the heat to maintain a simmer and cook until the potatoes are tender, 10 to 15 minutes. Drain. While they are still warm, place the potatoes in a food processor with the cream and butter and puree just until smooth. (Or you can use an electric mixer.) Add salt to taste. Keep warm.

EDDIE'S PORK WITH ROASTED JALAPEÑO GRAVY

MAKES 8 SERVINGS

1 tablespoon salt

1 tablespoon ground black pepper

1 tablespoon granulated garlic

1 tablespoon granulated onion

2½ to 3 pounds boneless pork loin (with some fat on it)

Roasted Jalapeño Gravy

2 jalapeños

1 teaspoon vegetable oil

1 cup half-and-half

2 cups pork stock (page 129) or chicken stock, preferably homemade (page 99)

1 teaspoon salt, plus additional as desired

4 to 5 tablespoons Blond Roux (page 298)

This interpretation of a traditional Sunday supper in the South is one of our most requested specials. I roast the pork quickly at a high heat to give it an extra-crusty exterior and keep it moist inside, and smother it in a creamy gravy flecked with savory bits of roasted jalapeño.

———

Heat the oven to 475 degrees.

Mix together the seasonings. Place the pork on a rack set in a roasting pan and sprinkle all over with the spice rub. Roast for 30 to 40 minutes, until the pork reaches an internal temperature of 145 degrees. (Tent the pork loosely with foil if it begins to brown too much.) Cover and let rest for 10 minutes to allow the juices to redistribute.

To make the gravy: Reduce the oven heat to 450 degrees. Place the jalapeños in a small pan, brush with the oil, and roast for 6 minutes, or until soft. Remove the stems and remove some or all of the seeds and membranes for less heat, if desired. Dice the jalapeños. Place the half-and-half, stock, salt, and jalapeños in a medium saucepan. Bring to a boil over high heat (watch carefully so the mixture doesn't boil over); reduce the heat to medium, and cook, stirring, for about 5 minutes, until reduced slightly.

Stir in 4 tablespoons of the roux and simmer for 2 to 3 minutes, whisking continually, until the sauce is thickened and bubbly. Stir in a little more roux if needed to reach the desired thickness.

Serve the pork with the gravy.

———

EDDIE'S WAY: *Serve with Ancho Mashed Potatoes (page 247).*

PAN-FRIED PORK CHOPS WITH RANCHERO BROWN GRAVY

MAKES 8 SERVINGS (WITH ABOUT 5½ CUPS GRAVY)

Ranchero Brown Gravy

¼ cup lard, preferably
   homemade (page 299)

1 cup thinly sliced onions

2 poblano peppers, cored,
   seeded, quartered, and
   thinly sliced

2 medium jalapeños, stemmed
   and minced (remove some
   or all of the seeds and
   membranes for less heat)

1 cup diced tomatoes

4 cups chicken stock,
   preferably homemade
   (page 99)

1½ teaspoons ground cumin

1 teaspoon ground black
   pepper

1 teaspoon salt

½ cup all-purpose flour

1 cup cold water

Pork Chops

1 cup all-purpose flour

1 teaspoon salt

1 tablespoon ground black
   pepper

8 (5-ounce) boneless pork
   chops or pork loin steaks

¼ cup vegetable oil, plus more
   if needed

Here is a Mexican's answer to how to make a fried pork chop a lot more exciting. I serve the chops in an old-time flour-thickened country gravy that gets its richness and silky texture from homemade lard that I use to sauté the onions, poblanos, and tomatoes that go in it. Cumin and black pepper add to its robust flavor.

———

To make the gravy: Melt the lard in a large saucepan over medium heat. Add the onions, poblanos, and jalapeños and cook, stirring, until the onions are translucent and peppers are soft, 5 to 7 minutes. Add the tomatoes and cook for 2 minutes. Add the chicken stock, cumin, black pepper, and salt and bring to a boil.

Meanwhile, whisk the flour and cold water in a small bowl until smooth. Slowly add to the boiling gravy, stirring constantly, until the gravy is thickened and smooth. Taste and adjust the seasonings as desired.

To make the pork chops: Combine the flour, salt, and pepper in a shallow dish. Dredge the pork chops in the flour on both sides. Heat the oil in a large cast iron skillet over medium-high heat until it shimmers. Add the pork chops in batches and cook, turning and adding more oil as needed, until lightly browned and no longer pink inside, 4 to 6 minutes on each side. Remove to a plate and keep warm.

Add the porkchops to the gravy and simmer for 5 minutes to heat through. Serve the pork chops covered in gravy.

———

EDDIE'S WAY: *Serve with black-eyed peas, and collards or turnip greens. Or serve with Fluffy White Rice (page 192) and Collards and Black-Eyed Peas with Lemon-Habanero Dressing (page 238).*

OVEN-BAKED MEMPHIS-STYLE RIBS

MAKES 6 TO 8 SERVINGS

While living in Texas, I got good at barbecue and was part of a team with my fellow volunteer firemen that won several trophies in competitions. Here in Atlanta, I wanted to make ribs Memphis style, the way my business partner, Mike Klank, likes them, with a spicy rub. My ribs are flavorful enough that you don't need to cook them on the grill, and they don't even need sauce. Unlike most oven-baked ribs that cook for hours on low heat until the meat falls off the bone, mine roast at a high temperature and come out firm but still juicy, succulent, and nicely caramelized in less than an hour. Smoking them is optional, but the taste will be different.

Memphis Spice Rub

¼ cup sugar

1 tablespoon salt

1 tablespoon granulated onion

1½ teaspoons ground white
    pepper

1½ teaspoons granulated
    garlic

1½ teaspoons cayenne pepper

1½ teaspoons paprika

1½ teaspoons dried tarragon

4 to 5 pounds spare ribs

Memphis-Style Barbecue Sauce
    (optional; page 293)

To make the rub: Place all the seasonings in a glass jar and shake to combine. Rub the ribs with the spice mix, place on a rack in a roasting pan, meaty side up, and set aside at room temperature for 30 minutes.

Heat the oven to 425 degrees. Bake the ribs without turning for 45 to 55 minutes, until a knife easily pierces the meatiest portion.

Meanwhile, if you'd like a smoky flavor, prepare an indoor smoker (see page 64).

Remove the ribs from the oven and smoke them in the indoor smoker for 15 minutes.

EDDIE'S WAY: *Serve with Roasted Potato Salad with Mustard-Orange Dressing (page 233) and Jalapeño Coleslaw (page 223).*

MEATLOAF WITH TOMATO-HABANERO GRAVY

MAKES 8 SERVINGS

Every culture has its own take on meatloaf. This is one of my favorites. The meat is flavored with fresh herbs and jalapeño and served over a simple habanero-spiked tomato gravy. It's baked in a casserole dish instead of a loaf pan, making it easy to cut it into squares and serve to a crowd. Another thing that makes it unique is that it does not contain either eggs or bread crumbs. Cornstarch holds it together, making it a good option for customers sensitive to gluten or eggs.

———

Heat the oven to 425 degrees. Rub the bottom and sides of an 8½-by-11-inch baking dish with the butter and set aside.

Mix all the ingredients except the gravy in a large bowl thoroughly to combine. Pat the meat mixture evenly into the prepared dish.

Bake until the meat reaches an internal temperature of 160 degrees in the center, 35 to 40 minutes. Garnish with fresh parsley if desired. Serve the meatloaf with the gravy.

———

EDDIE'S WAY: *Serve with whipped potatoes and buttered green beans. You'll have a meal that tastes like what your grandmother might have made, but better!*

1 tablespoon butter, at room
   temperature

1½ pounds ground pork

1½ pounds ground chuck

1 cup finely chopped onions

1 cup finely chopped celery

1 jalapeño, stemmed and
   minced (remove some or all
   of the seeds and membranes
   for less heat)

1 garlic clove, minced

½ cup minced fresh parsley,
   plus more for garnish

1 teaspoon fresh thyme leaves

1½ teaspoons salt

½ cup cornstarch

Tomato-Habanero Gravy
   (page 206)

STEAK CHURRASCO WITH CHIMICHURRI SAUCE

MAKES 8 SERVINGS

In Mexico our version of a neighborhood cookout was *carne asada*, which also is the name for a piece of beef—usually flank, skirt, or seven-bone steak—that we grilled along with sliced onions and other vegetables. South Americans do something similar with a dish called *churrasco*. The meat is typically cooked on a grill or a spit over hot coals and served with a tangy herbed sauce called *chimichurri*. If you don't want to light your grill, do what I do and sear the steak in a hot cast-iron skillet instead. This technique creates a nice caramelized exterior.

½ medium onion, thinly sliced

1 garlic clove, mashed

Juice of 1 large lemon (about ¼ cup)

2 tablespoons soy sauce

3 pounds skirt or flank steak, cut into 8 (6-ounce) portions

2 tablespoons olive oil

1 recipe Chimichurri Sauce (page 150)

8 sprigs fresh cilantro for garnish (optional)

Place the onion, garlic, lemon juice, and soy sauce in a shallow dish. Add the steaks, turn once to coat, cover, and refrigerate, turning occasionally, for 2 to 4 hours. Remove from the refrigerator for 30 minutes before cooking to allow the steaks to come to room temperature.

Heat a large cast-iron skillet over high heat. Remove the steaks from the marinade and pat dry with a paper towel. Brush lightly with the olive oil and place the steaks in the pan, a few at a time if necessary so as not to overcrowd. Cook for 2 to 3 minutes on each side to sear, then remove the pan from the heat and allow the steaks to finish cooking in the residual heat for 3 to 5 minutes, until medium-rare. Remove the steaks from the pan, cover with foil, and let rest for 5 minutes. Serve each steak topped with 2 tablespoons Chimichurri Sauce and garnished with a sprig of cilantro, if desired.

CHIMICHURRI SAUCE

MAKES 1 CUP

2 garlic cloves, peeled

1 jalapeño, roasted, peeled, and
  stemmed (see page 12; remove some
  or all of the seeds and membranes
  for less heat)

1 cup lightly packed fresh parsley

1 cup lightly packed fresh cilantro

½ cup olive oil

2 tablespoons white vinegar

½ teaspoon salt, plus additional as
  desired

This simple, flavorful sauce makes a great marinade or steak sauce. Use leftovers on hamburgers or baked potatoes.

———————

Place the garlic, jalapeño, parsley, and cilantro in a food processor and pulse a few times until coarsely chopped. Add the oil and vinegar and pulse a few more times until combined and finely chopped. Transfer to a bowl and add the salt. Store covered in the refrigerator for up to 2 days.

———————

EDDIE'S WAY: *I like to pair this with Green Pea Salad with Roasted Chiles and Red Onion (page 225).*

TEXAS CHICKEN-FRIED STEAK WITH TABASCO CREAM GRAVY

MAKES 4 SERVINGS

I rarely crave a T-bone, but I will never turn down a chicken-fried steak. I ate them all the time when I lived in Waco, where they were on every diner menu. Chicken-fried steak is made from a cheap cut of beef that's been tenderized, dipped in an egg wash, dusted with seasoned flour, then dropped into hot oil until it's nice and crunchy. Then it's covered in a simple pan gravy made of drippings and flour and milk. This flourless cream gravy spiked with Tabasco is more refined. It's best if you can buy cube steak because the meat has already been tenderized. You can substitute boneless pork chops.

---

4 (4-ounce) cube steaks

1 large egg, lightly beaten

1 cup whole milk

Pinch of salt

1 recipe Seasoned Flour
   Coating (page 290)

Vegetable oil for frying

Tabasco Cream Gravy
   (page 153)

Line a baking sheet with paper towels. Place each steak between 2 pieces of plastic wrap and pound to about 1/4-inch thickness.

Combine the egg, milk, and pinch of salt in a shallow dish.

Place the seasoned flour in a second shallow dish.

Heat 1 inch of oil in a wide, deep skillet or Dutch oven over high heat to 350 degrees.

Dredge one steak on both sides in the flour and shake off the excess. Dip in the egg wash on both sides and dredge again in the flour mixture on both sides.

Recipe continued

Carefully lay the steak in the oil and cook until the edges begin to brown, about 2 minutes, spooning hot oil over the top. Flip and cook on the other side for about 2 minutes longer, or until golden brown. Remove to the paper towel–lined baking sheet. Repeat with the remaining steaks. Allow the oil to return to 350 degrees between batches.

To serve, ladle some of the gravy onto a plate and top with the steak.

TABASCO CREAM GRAVY

MAKES ABOUT 1½ CUPS

2 cups heavy cream

1 tablespoon Tabasco sauce

8 tablespoons (1 stick) cold unsalted butter, cut into small pieces

Salt

Bring the cream to a boil in a medium saucepan over medium-high heat, watching carefully to make sure it doesn't boil over. Reduce the heat to maintain a simmer and reduce the liquid by half, then stir in the Tabasco.

Whisking continually, add the butter a few pieces at a time, until incorporated. Taste and add salt if needed.

EDDIE'S WAY: *Serve with Ancho Mashed Potatoes (page 247) or Cajun Hash (page 28).*

BLUE CORNMEAL–CRUSTED CHICKEN WITH MINT-JALAPEÑO DRIZZLE

MAKES 6 SERVINGS

Here is a way to get juicy, crispy-crusted chicken in a fraction of the time of traditional fried chicken, and it happens to be very healthy as well.

Mint-Jalapeño Drizzle

¼ cup fresh mint leaves

1 jalapeño, stemmed (remove some or all of the seeds and membranes for less heat)

½ cup vegetable oil

Pinch of salt

Chicken

1 cup all-purpose flour

1 cup blue cornmeal, or white or yellow

1½ teaspoons salt

1 tablespoon ground black pepper

2 large eggs

2 cups whole milk

Vegetable oil for frying

6 (6-ounce) boneless, skinless chicken breasts

To make the drizzle: Combine the mint, jalapeño, and oil in a blender and puree until smooth. Season with salt.

To make the chicken: Heat the oven to 350 degrees. Place a rack in a roasting pan or a large baking pan. Line another baking sheet with paper towels.

Combine the flour, cornmeal, salt, and pepper in a shallow dish. Place the eggs and milk in a second shallow dish and whisk to combine.

Heat ½ inch of oil in a large cast-iron skillet over medium heat to 350 degrees. Dip 2 chicken breasts first in the egg wash, then in the blue cornmeal mix, coating on all sides. Carefully place in the oil, top side down, and cook for 3 minutes, or until crispy and lightly browned, being careful not to burn. Flip and cook on the other side, until crispy and lightly browned, about 3 minutes. Transfer to the paper towel–lined baking sheet to drain, then set on the rack in the other pan. Repeat with the remaining chicken. Allow the oil to return to 350 degrees between each batch.

Cut into the thickest part of a piece of chicken to see if the juices run clear. If not, place in the oven for 5 to 10 minutes, until cooked through. Serve with some of the drizzle spooned over and around the chicken.

EDDIE'S WAY: *The perfect way to serve this chicken is on top of a mound of tender and sweet Melted Cabbage with Carrots (page 243). Garnish with some Creamy Lemon–Black Pepper Dressing (page 212) and sprinkle the minty emerald-green drizzle around the edge. The entire dish, including both sauces, can be made, start to finish, in less than an hour.*

BUTTERMILK FRIED CHICKEN WITH GREEN CHILE–HORSERADISH SAUCE

MAKES 8 SERVINGS

These cutlets have the same flavor profile as traditional Southern fried chicken. The difference is that they cook in less than ten minutes. I added horseradish to the cream sauce, and of course I had to throw some chiles in there for another layer of mild heat. Pickle relish adds tartness and sweetness. When Martha Stewart visited while she was in town, this was the special that day and she ordered it. She called over one of our servers and asked what was in the sauce that made it so good. I imagine she was surprised when he told her.

———————

2½ pounds chicken breast
   cutlets, ¼ inch thick or less
2 cups buttermilk
1 cup Seasoned Flour Coating
   (page 290)
Vegetable oil for frying
Green Chile–Horseradish
   Sauce (opposite)
Sriracha sauce (optional)

Line a baking sheet with paper towels.

Put the chicken and buttermilk in a large bowl, cover, and refrigerate for 2 hours. Put the seasoned flour in a shallow dish.

Heat 1 inch of oil in a large, heavy skillet or Dutch oven over high heat to 350 degrees.

Remove the chicken from the buttermilk and dredge in the flour on both sides. Gently place in the oil and cook in batches, turning, until golden brown and crispy on the outside and cooked through, 5 to 10 minutes. Remove with a slotted spoon to the paper towel–lined baking sheet. Allow the oil to return to 350 degrees between each batch.

Serve each cutlet with ¼ cup of the sauce and Sriracha, if desired.

GREEN CHILE– HORSERADISH SAUCE

MAKES 2 CUPS

8 tablespoons (1 stick) plus 1 tablespoon
   unsalted butter
1 (4-ounce) can mild green chiles
2 teaspoons prepared horseradish
½ cup sweet pickle relish
2 cups heavy cream
Pinch of salt

Melt 1 tablespoon of the butter in a small saucepan over medium heat. Add the chiles, horseradish, and pickle relish. Cook for 3 minutes and add the heavy cream. Increase the heat to medium-high and let boil for 3 minutes, watching closely to make sure the mixture doesn't boil over. Allow the mixture to cool slightly, then transfer to a blender or food processor and puree, being very careful with hot liquids in the blender, as they can overflow suddenly. Pour the mixture through a fine-mesh strainer back into the saucepan. Add the remaining 8 tablespoons butter, season with salt, and cook over medium heat, stirring occasionally, until the sauce is reduced to about 2 cups. It should be fairly thin. Keep warm until ready to use.

EDDIE'S WAY: *Serve with steamed or sautéed green beans or spinach and warm tortillas.*

CHICKEN–GREEN CHILE POTPIE IN PUFFY TORTILLA SHELLS

MAKES 8 SERVINGS

1 (3-pound) chicken, cut into
    pieces
1 tablespoon plus 1 teaspoon
    salt
3 tablespoons butter
1½ cups chopped carrots
1 cup chopped onions
1 cup chopped celery
2 jalapeños, stemmed and
    minced (remove some or all
    of the seeds and membranes
    for less heat)
1 tablespoon minced fresh
    thyme leaves
¾ teaspoon minced garlic
2 cups heavy cream
1 cup sour cream
1 cup grated white American
    cheese
3 to 4 tablespoons Blond Roux
    (page 298)
2 cups frozen peas, thawed

Puffy Tortillas
Vegetable oil for frying
8 (6-inch) flour tortillas, such
    as La Banderita
½ cup chopped roasted (see
    page 12) fresh green chiles
    or canned diced roasted
    mild green chiles for garnish

Many customers have told me this is the best potpie they've ever tried. The creamy chicken and vegetable filling, punched up with sour cream, fresh thyme, and jalapeños, is hard to beat. But what really makes it memorable is the presentation. Instead of a traditional crust, I drop flour tortillas one at a time into hot oil for just a minute, long enough for them to puff up and turn golden brown. Then I carefully crack the tops open and spoon the filling in. I recommend using La Banderita tortillas, as they are a little thicker than other brands and puff up better. If you don't want to mess with the hot oil, you can substitute baked puff pastry shells or even hot biscuits for the tortillas.

Place the chicken pieces and 1 tablespoon of the salt in a large pot, cover with water, and bring to a boil. Reduce the heat to maintain a simmer and cook just until the chicken is tender, about 30 minutes. Remove the chicken from the pot and cool slightly. Reserve 2 cups of the stock for the gravy. Remove and discard the skin and bones. Shred the meat and set aside.

Melt the butter in the pot over medium heat. Add the carrots, onions, celery, jalapeños, and remaining 1 teaspoon salt and cook, stirring frequently, for 5 to 7 minutes, until the onion is translucent. Add the thyme and garlic and cook for 1 minute. Add the reserved stock, cream, and sour cream. Bring to a boil and cook for 2 minutes. Stir in the cheese and cook until melted. Reduce the heat to medium. Stir in 3 tablespoons of the roux and simmer, stirring frequently, for 3 minutes. Stir in a little more roux if needed until the mixture reaches the desired thickness. Add the shredded chicken and the peas, reduce the heat, and simmer for 3 minutes. Taste and adjust the seasonings as desired. Keep warm.

Recipe continued

To make the puffy tortillas: Line a platter with paper towels. Heat 1½ inches of oil in a Dutch oven or large, heavy pot over high heat to 400 degrees. Add the tortillas, one at a time. Let each cook for about a minute, until puffed up and lightly browned, spooning oil over the top as they cook (do not flip).

Remove to the paper towel–lined platter to drain. Allow the oil to return to 400 degrees between each tortilla.

To serve, poke a hole in the top of each tortilla, ladle 1 to 1½ cups of the chicken mixture into the hole, and garnish with the roasted chiles.

REMOULADE-TOPPED FISH FILLETS OVER MEXICAN MAQUE CHOUX

MAKES 6 SERVINGS

Maque Choux

3 tablespoons Butter Blend
    (page 299) or equal parts
    butter and vegetable oil
½ cup finely diced red onion
1 cup finely diced poblano
    peppers
¼ cup finely diced jalapeños
    (remove some or all of the
    seeds and membranes for
    less heat)
4 cups fresh corn kernels
Salt

Fish

1 cup all-purpose flour
2 tablespoons Cajun Spice Mix
    (page 291)
¼ to ½ cup Butter Blend (page
    299) or equal parts butter
    and vegetable oil
6 (4- to 6-ounce) tilapia,
    redfish, or catfish fillets

1 recipe Creole Remoulade
    Sauce (page 212)
Chopped fresh parsley for
    garnish

On the streets of Mexico, vendors sell corn on the cob roasted on a stick and slathered with mayonnaise. I got to thinking about how maque choux—a sauté of corn and peppers popular in Louisiana—might taste with a New Orleans–style remoulade sauce. My version of maque choux substitutes Mexican peppers for the traditional bell peppers, and I use it as a base for pan-fried tilapia "bronzed" with Cajun seasonings.

———

Heat the oven to 200 degrees. Line a plate with paper towels.

To make the maque choux: Heat the butter (or butter and oil) over medium heat until the butter is melted and the foam subsides. Add the onion, poblanos, and jalapeños and cook, stirring, until soft, 5 to 7 minutes. Add the corn and cook for 5 minutes, stirring often. Season to taste with salt. Keep warm until ready to serve.

Meanwhile, make the fish: Combine the flour and seasoning in a shallow dish. Melt ¼ cup of the Butter Blend (or butter and oil) in a large nonstick skillet set over medium-high heat. Roll each fish fillet in the seasoned flour to coat on both sides, and shake off the excess.

Add enough fillets to fill the skillet without crowding.

Cook until golden brown on both sides and opaque in the center, 3 to 4 minutes per side. Transfer the fillets to the paper towel–lined plate and keep warm in the oven while you cook the rest.

Repeat with the remaining fillets, adding more Butter Blend as needed.

To serve, place ¾ cup of the maque choux in the center of each plate and top with a fish fillet. Spoon about 3 tablespoons of the sauce around the mixture. Garnish with parsley.

BLACK PEPPER–CRUSTED TILAPIA WITH ARTICHOKE AND JALAPEÑO RELISH

MAKES 8 SERVINGS

Artichoke and Jalapeño Relish

1 cup white vinegar

¼ cup olive oil

1 bay leaf

1 garlic clove, crushed

1½ teaspoons dried oregano

1 (14-ounce) can artichoke
   hearts, drained and cut into
   quarters

¼ cup capers

1 large jalapeño, quartered
   lengthwise, stemmed, seeded,
   and thinly sliced

Fish

¼ cup cracked black
   peppercorns (coarsely
   cracked in a peppermill
   or by pounding with a mallet
   between sheets of wax paper)

½ teaspoon salt

8 (4-ounce) tilapia fillets
   or other flaky white fish

¼ to ½ cup Butter Blend
   (page 299) or equal parts
   butter and vegetable oil

Mac and Cheese with Feta and
   Jalapeño (optional; page 164)

6 sprigs fresh cilantro for
   garnish (optional)

At Taqueria del Sol, we use tilapia sourced from environmentally approved regions for most of our fish dishes. It's mild, economical, and easy to work with. A while back I wanted to mimic the scales of more expensive (and endangered) Chilean sea bass, so I rolled the tilapia fillets in cracked black pepper. I really liked the spice and crunch it added, and it got me to thinking about Greek flavors. For a garnish, I made a tangy artichoke-heart relish that I spiked with some chiles, and served the fish on a bed of creamy macaroni and cheese flavored with feta to temper the tartness and spice. I love the way these contrasting flavors and textures play off one another.

The mac and cheese is really key to this dish's success.

———————

To make the relish: Place the vinegar in a bowl. While slowly pouring in a steady stream, whisk the olive oil into the vinegar. Stir in the bay leaf, garlic, and oregano. Add the artichoke hearts, capers, and jalapeño. Set aside and marinate for at least 20 minutes. The relish will keep, covered and refrigerated, for 2 weeks.

To make the fish: Combine the pepper and salt in a shallow dish. Pat the fish dry with paper towels. Press just one side of the fillets into the pepper mixture, transfer to a plate, and chill until you're ready to serve.

Heat ¼ cup of the Butter Blend (or butter and oil) in a skillet over medium-high heat until it shimmers. Add the fish in batches, pepper side down, and cook for 2 minutes. Turn the fish and cook for 2 more minutes, or until it flakes with a fork. Repeat with the remaining fillets, adding more Butter Blend as needed.

To serve, place a serving of the feta mac and cheese, if using, in the center of each plate and top with a fillet. Surround each fillet with 4 artichoke pieces and a little of the marinade. Garnish with a sprig of cilantro, if desired.

MAC AND CHEESE WITH FETA AND JALAPEÑO

MAKES 8 SERVINGS

In cafeteria lines in the South, macaroni and cheese is treated like a vegetable. Though I created this creamy, spicy dish with a subtle feta tang to go with tilapia, it's good with just about anything.

8 ounces dried macaroni

1 tablespoon butter

¼ cup finely chopped onion

2 tablespoons stemmed, chopped jalapeño (remove some or all of the seeds and membranes for less heat)

¼ cup dry white wine

2 cups heavy cream

2 tablespoons Blond Roux (page 298), at room temperature

½ cup crumbled feta cheese

½ cup grated white American cheese

Cook the macaroni according to the package directions. Drain and return to the pot.

Melt the butter in a medium saucepan over medium heat. Add the onion and jalapeño and cook until the onion is soft and translucent, 2 to 3 minutes. Increase the heat to medium-high and add the wine. Cook, stirring well, for 1 minute. Add the cream and bring to a boil. Stir in the roux and cook until the sauce is thickened, about 1 minute. Add the feta and cook, stirring, for 1 minute to melt. Remove from the heat and stir in the American cheese until melted and the sauce is smooth. Stir into the macaroni and serve warm.

SAUTÉED SNAPPER WITH CILANTRO–ROASTED PECAN PESTO

MAKES 6 SERVINGS

These snapper (or other mild fish) fillets are first marinated in a puree of celery and onion, but this step can be eliminated if you are short on time. For the pesto, I use a combination of basil and cilantro, and to round out the flavor, I add roasted jalapeño and a little sugar. Pecans give the sauce my Georgia five cents.

Serve with Yellow Rice (page 192).

───────────

Quick Lemon-Habanero Drizzle
½ cup vegetable oil
¼ cup lemon juice
2 tablespoons green habanero
   sauce, such as El Yucateco

Fish
½ cup chopped celery
2 tablespoons chopped onion
½ cup vegetable oil
Pinch of salt
6 (4-ounce) snapper fillets or
   other mild-flavored fish

9 tablespoons Cilantro–
   Roasted Pecan Pesto
   (page 167)

To make the drizzle: Mix the oil, lemon juice, and habanero sauce in a small bowl. Set aside.

To make the marinade: Place the celery, onion, oil, and salt in a blender and puree.
   Put the fish in a baking dish, add the marinade, cover, and refrigerate for 1 hour.

To finish the fish: Place a large nonstick skillet over medium-high heat and add 3 fish fillets (do not crowd). Cook for about 3 minutes per side, until cooked through. Repeat with the remaining fillets.

To serve, set each fillet on a plate and top with 1½ tablespoons pesto. Spoon some of the drizzle around each fillet.

CILANTRO—ROASTED PECAN PESTO

MAKES 2½ CUPS

1 cup pecan halves

1½ cups fresh cilantro

1½ cups fresh basil

1 jalapeño, roasted (see page 12),
   stemmed (remove some or all of the
   seeds and membranes for less heat)

1 garlic clove, peeled

1 tablespoon sugar

1½ cups vegetable oil

Salt

This pesto is good tossed in rice, pasta, and vegetables, as well as a topping for a piece of meat, fish, or chicken.

————————

Toast the pecans in a 350-degree oven for 5 to 10 minutes, stirring occasionally.

Pulse the pecans, cilantro, basil, jalapeño, garlic, and sugar several times in a food processor to finely chop. With the motor running, slowly add the oil and blend until smooth. Taste and add salt as desired. Cover and chill until ready to use. The pesto will keep, covered and refrigerated, for up to 2 weeks or frozen for several months.

MEXICAN-STYLE BARBECUED SHRIMP

MAKES 4 TO 6 SERVINGS

I don't know why Louisianans call their famous shrimp "barbecued," because the shrimp are actually cooked in a heavy skillet with loads of butter and spices. The rich, briny juices from the heads infuse the butter as it melts, creating a hot dipping sauce for crusty bread that is as tasty and hard to stop eating as the shrimp. If you can't get head-on shrimp, you can make this dish with regular shrimp, though it won't be as rich and good. Cover your table with newspapers, set the whole pan in the center, and let everyone dig in. Don't forget to have plenty of napkins, cold beer, and extra lemons and limes on hand.

---

2 pounds head-on 16/20 shrimp, unpeeled (see headnote)

1 cup vegetable oil

2 tablespoons chopped garlic

16 tablespoons (2 sticks) plus 2 tablespoons unsalted butter, at room temperature

1 serrano chile, stemmed and coarsely chopped (remove some or all of the seeds and membranes for less heat)

¼ cup chopped fresh cilantro

Juice of 1 lime

1½ teaspoons salt

½ cup diced onion

1 cup diced tomatoes

Ciabatta bread for dipping

Extra lemon and lime wedges

Fresh cilantro leaves (optional)

Place the shrimp, oil, and garlic in a large bowl, cover, and refrigerate for 1 hour.

Process 2 sticks of the butter, the serrano chile, chopped cilantro, lime juice, and salt in a food processor.

Melt the remaining 2 tablespoons butter in a large, heavy skillet set over medium heat. With a slotted spoon, remove the shrimp from the marinade, draining off the oil, and add to the pan. Increase the heat to high and cook for 2 minutes, flip the shrimp, and add the onion. Cook for 1 minute, then add the tomatoes and continue to cook for 3 minutes, stirring occasionally.

Add the herbed butter and stir until melted.

Serve with bread for dipping and lemon and lime wedges and allow everyone to peel their own shrimp at the table.

To serve individually, put a few slices of ciabatta bread on a plate, top with some of the shrimp and butter sauce, and garnish with cilantro leaves.

SHRIMP FRIED RICE TOPPED WITH BRONZED SCALLOPS AND TABASCO OIL

MAKES 6 TO 8 SERVINGS

¼ cup plus 1 tablespoon
toasted sesame oil

⅓ pound chopped raw peeled
and deveined shrimp

¼ cup chopped celery

¼ cup chopped onion

¼ cup chopped green bell
pepper

1 tablespoon Cajun Spice Mix
(page 291)

1 garlic clove, minced

2 tablespoons chopped fresh
parsley, plus more for
garnish

2 large eggs, lightly beaten

1 recipe Fluffy White Rice
(page 192), cold

Scallops

12 to 16 medium to large
scallops, adductor muscle
removed, and rinsed

1 tablespoon Cajun Spice Mix
(page 291)

2 tablespoons Butter Blend
(page 299); or equal parts
butter and vegetable oil,
plus more if needed

¼ cup vegetable oil

2 tablespoons Tabasco sauce

The first time I ever heard the word "jambalaya" was when the band I used to play with in Texas did a cover of Hank Williams's hit song by that name. That was the only word of the song we knew. None of us spoke English then, and we just made up the rest of the lyrics for it in Spanish. But I had no idea what jambalaya was until around 1990, when Steve Murrell, the best Cajun chef I know, made it for the menu at the Sundown Café. Working by his side for several years, I also learned how to make the gumbos and the étouffées and just about every other famous dish to come out of New Orleans. They were very different from anything I ever ate in Mexico, but I could identify with the spicy flavors and I loved them. Once I mastered each dish, Steve would say to me, "OK, Eddie, now destroy it!" And then I would come up with my way of making it. Sometimes I would create something completely different, like the way I make fried rice. The technique is basically Chinese, as is the sesame oil I use for sautéing. But there are also flavors straight out of bayou country, with enough chile heat to make this Mexican happy.

To quickly turn this dish into a special-occasion treat, I top it with scallops. Because the rice is so substantial, two scallops per serving are plenty. But I like this rice so much that I often eat it as a main dish without the scallops.

Heat a large skillet over medium-high heat. Add 1 tablespoon of the sesame oil and when it shimmers, add the shrimp. Cook, stirring, until pink and opaque, about 1 minute. Remove the shrimp to a plate and set aside.

Recipe continued

Add the remaining ¼ cup sesame oil to the skillet. Add the celery, onion, bell pepper, and Cajun Spice Mix and cook, stirring, for 2 minutes, or until the vegetables are soft. Add the garlic and parsley and cook for 1 minute longer. Add the beaten eggs and scramble just until they begin to set, about 30 seconds. Stir in the cooked shrimp and rice and cook until heated through. Remove from the heat and keep warm.

To make the scallops: Toss the scallops in the Cajun Spice Mix. Place the Butter Blend (or butter and oil) in a large cast-iron skillet over medium-high heat. When it shimmers, add the scallops in a single layer (cook in batches if necessary) and cook, turning once, until caramelized on each side, about 2 minutes per side.

Remove from the heat and keep warm.

Place some of the fried rice in the center of each plate. Top with 2 or 3 scallops. Mix together the oil and Tabasco and drizzle some of the Tabasco oil over the rice and scallops. Garnish with chopped parsley. Serve hot.

SHRIMP AND GRITS, MY WAY

MAKES 4 SERVINGS

One of our most popular lunch and dinner specials, shrimp and grits originated long ago in the Low Country, where it is commonly served for breakfast or brunch. Now cooks all over the South make it for any meal, and everyone does it a little differently. Some add cheese to their grits, while others sauté the shrimp with bacon, tomatoes, mushrooms, and every spice in their pantry. I prefer to keep mine simple so the fresh shrimp flavor shines through. The cream and sugar in my Creamy Grits temper the heat of the jalapeños and provide a rich, smooth contrast to the quick tomato-based sauce. The photo is on page 174.

---

2 tablespoons butter

4 large tomatoes, chopped

2 jalapeños, stemmed and minced (remove some or all of the seeds and membranes for less heat)

½ teaspoon salt

1¼ pounds raw shrimp, peeled and deveined

1 recipe Creamy Grits (page 175)

2 tablespoons chopped fresh parsley for garnish (optional)

Melt 1 tablespoon of the butter in a large skillet over medium heat. Add the tomatoes and jalapeños and cook until soft, about 5 minutes. Transfer the mixture to a food processor and puree with the salt until smooth.

Melt the remaining 1 tablespoon butter. Add the shrimp and cook until just pink, about 3 minutes. Add the tomato mixture and cook for another minute or two. Taste and adjust the seasonings as desired.

To serve, divide the grits among four plates or large bowls. Top with the shrimp and sauce. Garnish with the parsley.

CREAMY GRITS

A lot of serious food people swear by the coarse, less processed stone-ground grits, but for most dishes, I prefer the smoother texture of the quick-cooking kind. To make them even creamier, I cook them in heavy cream instead of water, and add a few tablespoons of sugar to help balance the richness. You don't have to add butter to these grits! They are really, really good this way—especially with a spicy topping for contrast, as in Shrimp and Grits, My Way (page 173). But that lighter variation, which isn't quite so rich or sweet, doesn't stray too far from the original.

---

1 quart heavy cream

1 cup quick grits (not instant)

¼ cup sugar

1½ teaspoons salt, plus
    additional as desired

Bring the cream to a boil in a large saucepan over medium-high heat. Watch carefully so it doesn't boil over. While continually whisking, add the grits and cook, whisking, for 5 minutes. Add the sugar and salt and cook, whisking frequently, for an additional 5 to 10 minutes, until the grits are tender. Serve hot.

VARIATIONS

LIGHTER CREAMY GRITS

Substitute 3 cups half-and-half for 3 cups of the cream and add 1 tablespoon of butter. Reduce the amount of sugar to 2 tablespoons, or to taste. Cook as directed above.

CREAMY BLUE CHEESE GRITS

Increase the grits to 1¼ cups and reduce the sugar to 2 tablespoons. Cook as directed above. At the end of cooking, stir in ½ to 1 cup of crumbled blue cheese (depending on how strong the cheese is). This is excellent with fried chicken.

BREADS, BEANS, RICE, AND CORN

Chapter Seven

CORN TORTILLAS *180*

—RED AND YELLOW TORTILLAS *182*

—GORDITAS *182*

BOLILLOS *185*

—YEASTY FLOUR TORTILLAS *186*

VEGGIE REFRIED BEANS *187*

CHARROS BEANS *188*

REFRIED BLACK-EYED PEAS WITH CHORIZO *190*

HOPPIN' JUAN *191*

FLUFFY WHITE RICE *192*

—YELLOW RICE *192*

—GREEN RICE *192*

HERBAL RICE *193*

MEXICAN RICE *194*

HOLY TRINITY RICE AND SAUSAGE *195*

STONE-GROUND GRITS WITH CHILES *196*

MEXICAN SPAGHETTI (SOPA DE FIDEO) *197*

Think of our breads, our grains, and our legumes as blank pages on which we can tell our own stories.

———

Mexicans and Southerners love their starch. Starches are cheap, they require no refrigeration, and they fill you up. Dried corn, beans, and rice have been the basis for both Mexican and Southern cuisines for centuries. I ate as much French bread and pasta back home in Mexico as I do in Atlanta.

Because these foods have so little flavor on their own, they give the cook tremendous freedom to make them distinctive—either with seasonings or what they're paired with on the plate. Think of our breads, our grains, and our legumes as blank pages on which we can tell our own stories. In this chapter I will show you how to make beans the way my mother did every day for our family, as well as rice cooked Mexican style and Cajun style, as I learned it from watching my Louisiana chef friend. I won't tell you how to make corn bread or biscuits—I'll leave those recipes to the Southern food experts—but I will show you how I cook grits the way I like them, which is different from how anyone else will tell you.

Once you understand my methods, you can take whatever creative liberties you like.

CORN TORTILLAS

MAKES 16 (5½-INCH) TORTILLAS

There is no gluten in corn tortillas, so you cannot overwork the dough! They are not time-consuming to make—the only equipment you'll need is a bowl, a wooden spoon, and a tortilla press (see page 9), or they can be pressed with the bottom of a heavy skillet if you have to.

---

2 cups Maseca masa harina

1 tablespoon vegetable oil

½ teaspoon salt

1½ cups warm water, plus more as needed

Line a plate with paper towels.

Combine the masa harina, oil, salt, and water in a large bowl. Stir with a wooden spoon until a ball is formed, adding more warm water as needed. (It should be the consistency of Play-Doh.) Knead the dough several times in the bowl, until it is smooth and becomes a ball that cleans the sides of the bowl as you move it around. Wet your hands if they become sticky as you are kneading. Divide into 16 (1¾-ounce) pieces. Roll each piece into a ball. Place the balls on a baking sheet, cover with a damp cloth, and set aside.

Heat an electric griddle to 350 degrees or a large, heavy skillet over medium heat.

To shape the tortillas, cut a 1-quart plastic bag into 2 pieces. Set one piece of the plastic on the bottom of the tortilla press. Place one dough ball on the plastic, top with the second piece of plastic, and press down the lid to make a 5½-inch round tortilla. Or place the dough ball between the two pieces of plastic, set a heavy skillet on top, and press down firmly to flatten. Peel off the top piece of plastic, place the tortilla in your hand, and peel off the other piece of plastic.

Add the tortilla to the griddle as soon as it is shaped and the griddle is hot. Cook on one side until the tortilla begins to bubble up and brown, 2 to 3 minutes. Flip and continue to cook for another 1 to 2 minutes, until the other side begins to brown and bubble up. Transfer to the paper towel–lined plate and cover to keep warm. Continue until all the tortillas are cooked.

VARIATIONS

RED AND YELLOW TORTILLAS

Some cooks tint the dough red by kneading a little red chile puree into it. The puree gives it extra flavor, too. You can also use paprika for this. For yellow tortillas, knead in a little Cuban Bijol Coloring and Seasoning Condiment (see page 192).

GORDITAS

These crispy little corn cakes are thicker than tortillas and made with your hands without a press. They are typically split and filled as you would a taco or a sandwich, but I often serve them plain to go with a meal, like a biscuit. They are not much different from what Southerners called hoe cakes—coarse cornmeal cakes that used to be baked in a fire on top of a hoe—in the old days. Often I knead Chicharrones (page 299) into the dough, just as Southerners stir those fried pork bits into corn bread batter for crackling bread.

To make gorditas, follow the recipe for Corn Tortillas, adding 1 teaspoon of baking powder to the dough ingredients. Mix the dough and roll into balls as directed. Flatten each ball with your hands (use plastic wrap to prevent sticking) to about $\frac{1}{3}$- to $\frac{1}{2}$-inch thickness. Then cook on a hot griddle for about 2 minutes per side as you would a tortilla. Meanwhile, heat about $\frac{1}{4}$ inch of vegetable oil in a large, heavy skillet over medium heat until it shimmers. Add the lightly cooked masa rounds a few at a time, and fry on both sides until crispy, about 1 minute. Drain on paper towels and fill as desired.

FAST, FRESH TORTILLAS AND MEXICAN ROLLS

You can make a good taco with a store-bought tortilla—
preferably one without artificial preservatives or gums. Your
best bets are usually found in the refrigerator or freezer case.
I get my tortillas made to our specifications from an excellent
factory here in Atlanta. Nowadays most cities—even smaller
ones—have their own factories, and these local products are
worth seeking out.

Still, there is nothing quite like the toasty aroma and earthy
taste of a tortilla that you have mixed and made yourself, hot
off the griddle. One bite takes me right back to the kitchens
of my mother, my grandmother, and my aunt, where I learned
to make them myself by watching. Now I sometimes make
them just for me and for the guys in the kitchen on a Saturday
morning before the lunch crowd comes.

Even though Mexicans eat tortillas made of corn or flour daily,
we are big bread eaters, too. At Latin markets and bakeries,
you will find French bread, sliced bread, and a variety of
homemade wheat rolls in many different shapes and sizes. I
don't have the patience for baking my own, except for bolillos,
the light, crispy rolls we typically use in Mexico for the sturdy
sandwiches we call tortas. I can get them in Mexican markets
here in Atlanta, but I have developed a quick, easy recipe for
making them fresh that is so much better than anything you'll
buy. I use this same dough for many things—from flour tortillas
to sopapillas—as you will see elsewhere in this book.

BOLILLOS

MAKES 18 TO 20 (2-OUNCE) ROLLS

Bolillos (buh-*lee*-os), yeast rolls that are crispy on the outside and soft and light in the middle, are made throughout Mexico and are not unlike a large Southern dinner roll. But they are used mostly for the sandwiches called tortas. Although bolillos are traditionally shaped into ovals and slashed down the middle before baking, I prefer to roll them into rounds because this shape holds fillings better. You can also roll them into smaller appetizer sizes.

I also use this recipe to make flour tortillas. Traditional flour tortillas are made with baking powder and lard, but I like the yeasty, bready flavor of these even better than the ones I used to make with my mom. These tortillas are versatile and may be fried until crispy as a base for pizza toppings, or folded over a sweet or savory filling for a deep-fried turnover.

Dough

2 tablespoons vegetable oil, plus more for greasing the pans

5 cups all-purpose flour, plus more as needed

2 tablespoons instant yeast

2 tablespoons sugar

1 tablespoon salt

2 cups very warm (120 degrees) water

4 tablespoons (½ stick) butter, melted

Coarse sea salt

Brush two large heavy-duty baking sheets, preferably nonstick, with vegetable oil. Set aside.

To make the dough: In the bowl of a stand mixer fitted with the dough hook, combine 5 cups of the flour, the yeast, sugar, salt, and the 2 tablespoons oil. Set the mixer on low speed and slowly add

the warm water. Mix until thoroughly incorporated and the dough becomes elastic, about 5 minutes. If it's too sticky, add a little more flour. Continue mixing until the dough no longer sticks to the sides of the bowl, about 10 minutes.

Remove the dough from the bowl and set on a clean surface. Knead a few times to form a smooth ball. With a sharp knife, cut the dough into 18 to 20 pieces, about 2 ounces each.

Set a piece of dough on another clean surface. With the palm of your hand, roll it vigorously into a smooth ball. Set on one of the greased baking sheets. Repeat with the remaining pieces of dough. Leave 2 to 3 inches of space between each ball, then set in a warm place, uncovered, and let rise until doubled, about 30 minutes.

Heat the oven to 400 degrees.

Brush the rolls with the butter and sprinkle with a little sea salt.

Bake 20 minutes, or until golden brown.

Remove with a spatula to a cooling rack and cool completely.

The rolls will keep for 2 to 3 days in an airtight container or frozen, wrapped airtight, for up to 2 months.

VARIATION

YEASTY FLOUR TORTILLAS

Cut 1 recipe bolillo dough into 24 (about 1¾-ounce) pieces. Roll into balls and place on a floured surface. With a rolling pin (use a small one designed for rolling tortillas if you have one; see page 9), roll back and forth over the ball of dough, rotating an inch or two between the rolls, until you have a 6-inch disk. Cook on the griddle as for Corn Tortillas (page 180), pressing with a solid spatula to flatten (they will be thicker than regular tortillas). Makes 24 tortillas.

VEGGIE REFRIED BEANS

MAKES 8 CUPS

In many Mexican homes, refried beans are made with vegetable oil because it is cheaper than the more traditional lard. I boost the beans' flavor by sautéing onion, garlic, and pickled jalapeños before adding the beans. Though pintos are most commonly used, black beans also work well. Serve them as a dip for chips, as a side dish, or in a taco (see page 77).

¼ cup olive oil

¼ cup vegetable oil

½ cup chopped onion

1 tablespoon minced garlic

1 tablespoon chopped pickled jalapeños

1½ teaspoons salt

8 cups cooked or canned pinto beans, drained

1 tablespoon ground cumin

Heat the oils in a large saucepan over medium heat until they shimmer. Add the onion, garlic, jalapeños, and salt and cook until the onion is translucent and softened, 5 to 7 minutes. Add the beans and stir together. Continue to cook for 3 more minutes, then add the cumin. Stir to combine.

Using a fork, potato masher, or other tool, mash the beans until you reach the consistency you prefer. Add a little water if it seems dry. Taste and adjust the seasonings as desired and serve hot. The refried beans can be refrigerated for up to 1 week. They can also be frozen in freezer bags or freezer-safe containers, allowing about ½ inch of head space, for 6 months or longer.

CHARROS BEANS

MAKES 8 SERVINGS

Frijoles charros—"cowboy beans"—are eaten every day in Mexico, and everybody thinks their mama makes the best. Unlike refried beans, these stewed pinto beans are whole instead of mashed. They are served in soup bowls, with a thick, rich broth that has almost a creamy texture owing to the pork fat the beans are cooked in. This dish is a lot like the soup beans and corn bread that are part of the regular diet in mountain regions of the South, only spicier. I render the fat to make lard, which I use to sauté some onion. Then I add the cooked pintos along with chopped fresh tomatoes and cilantro. To make this a main dish, serve it over rice.

---

1 pound dried pinto beans

1 teaspoon salt

4 ounces pork fat, diced

½ cup finely chopped onion

3 medium tomatoes, chopped

½ cup finely chopped fresh
   cilantro

Sort through the beans to remove any debris. Place in a colander and rinse thoroughly with cold water, then transfer to a large bowl. Add enough cold water to cover by at least 2 inches. Soak overnight, until they've doubled in size.

Drain, rinse again, place in a large pot, and cover with fresh water by at least 2 inches. Set over high heat and bring to a boil. Reduce the heat to maintain a simmer, and cook until the beans are softened but still firm, about 1 hour. Add the salt and cook for 20 to 30 minutes longer, or until completely soft.

Drain and transfer to a covered container until ready to use.

Place the pork fat in a large, heavy pot over medium heat and cook until it is rendered. Add the onion and cook in the fat until soft, 3 to 5 minutes. Add the beans, tomatoes, and cilantro. Add enough water to cover by about an inch, and simmer slowly until the water reduces and thickens, about 1 hour, adding more water if necessary. The beans should be quite soupy. Taste and adjust the seasonings as desired. Serve.

REFRIED BLACK-EYED PEAS WITH CHORIZO

MAKES 8 SERVINGS

Dried black-eyed peas are small and white with a black eye in the center, and they have a lighter flavor and texture than larger legumes. They cook much faster, too. They take well to the heavy spices of cured Spanish chorizo, and for more complexity, I add onion and garlic, along with a puree of roasted tomato and jalapeño. Like other refried beans, these can be served as a dip, a side dish, or a taco filling.

1 pound dried black-eyed peas

1 tablespoon salt

1 large tomato

1 jalapeño

½ cup plus 2 teaspoons vegetable oil

½ cup finely chopped onion

2 garlic cloves, finely chopped

8 ounces finely diced Spanish chorizo

Place the peas in a large bowl, cover by at least 2 inches of water, and soak overnight. Drain, rinse, and place in a large pot. Add the salt and enough water to cover by 2 inches. Bring to a boil over high heat, reduce the heat to medium-low, and simmer, stirring occasionally, until the peas are tender, about 45 minutes. Drain and set aside.

Heat the broiler to high.

Brush the tomato and jalapeño with 2 teaspoons of the oil and set on a baking sheet. Broil, turning several times with tongs, until they are lightly charred on all sides, about 5 minutes. Remove the stem from the jalapeño; split and remove some or all of the seeds to reduce the heat, if desired. Quarter the tomato and place in a blender with the jalapeño. Puree until smooth and set aside.

Place the remaining ½ cup oil in a large pot over medium heat. As soon as the oil shimmers, add the onion and garlic and cook until the onion is translucent and soft, 5 to 7 minutes. Add the chorizo and cook until it renders its fat, about 5 minutes more.

Add the cooked peas and tomato-jalapeño puree and cook until the peas start to break down, about 20 minutes. Mash some or all of the peas with a potato masher or fork to get the desired consistency. Taste and adjust the seasonings as desired. Serve.

HOPPIN' JUAN

MAKES 6 SERVINGS

Southerners eat hoppin' John, black-eyed peas mixed with rice, with greens on New Year's Day to bring good luck. The greens symbolize dollar bills, and the black-eyed peas represent pennies. I took that idea and came up with a chilled version, by combining our Mex-American Black-Eyed Pea Salad with leftover cooked rice. It makes a healthy, hearty side salad for just about any meat, or a vegetarian main dish.

1½ cups Mex-American Black-Eyed Pea Salad (page 230)
½ recipe Fluffy White Rice (page 192), cold or warm
1 tablespoon red wine vinegar
2 tablespoons vegetable oil
½ teaspoon salt

Combine the black-eyed pea salad, rice, vinegar, oil, and salt in a large bowl. Taste and adjust the seasonings as desired. Add more vinegar and oil if the rice seems too dry or could use a little extra tang. Serve cold or at room temperature.

FLUFFY WHITE RICE

MAKES 8 TO 10 SERVINGS

I mostly use broken rice, kernels that are broken in the milling process and sold inexpensively. I love its fluffy texture. It's available online, including on Amazon, and in Asian markets. Other white rices will also produce good results. Jasmine rice, for example, has a floral aroma that I like. I first rinse the kernels in water to wash out some of the starch so it is less sticky. The main thing to pay attention to, though, is the ratio of liquid to rice: Broken rice uses less water than long-grain.

---

2 cups broken (see headnote)
   or long-grain white rice
3 cups water for broken rice;
   4 cups for long-grain
1 tablespoon vegetable oil
½ teaspoon salt, plus
   additional as desired

Place the rice in a colander. Set in the sink and rinse until the water begins to turn clear.

Place the water, oil, and salt in a large saucepan over high heat and bring to a boil. Add the rice and cook, stirring, for 3 minutes.

Reduce the heat to medium and simmer without stirring until there is just a thin film of water on the top, 5 minutes. Cover, reduce the heat to the lowest setting, and cook for 25 minutes more, or until the rice is tender. Serve warm.

VARIATIONS

YELLOW RICE

Cuban Bijol Coloring and Seasoning Condiment (available online, in Latin markets, and in many supermarkets) is a spice blend from Cuba that contains ground cumin, annatto, corn flour, and coloring and lends a golden color and delicate flavor to many dishes, especially rice.

Follow the basic recipe, adding 1½ teaspoons Bijol seasoning and 3 bay leaves to the water before adding the rice. Remove the bay leaves before serving.

GREEN RICE

Follow the basic recipe, folding ½ to 1 cup of Poblano-Cilantro Sauce (page 207) into the warm rice.

HERBAL RICE

MAKES 8 TO 10 SERVINGS

Here is a light, healthy way to dress up plain white rice.

———————

2 tablespoons butter

1 cup chopped onions

1 jalapeño, stemmed and
   minced (remove some or all
   of the seeds and membranes
   for less heat)

1 garlic clove, minced

1 cup chopped fresh cilantro

1 recipe Fluffy White Rice
   (opposite)

Salt to taste

Melt the butter in a medium skillet over medium heat. Add the onions, jalapeño, and garlic and cook until the onions are soft and translucent, 5 to 7 minutes.

Remove from the heat and add the cilantro. Fold the mixture into the rice, season with salt, and serve.

MEXICAN RICE

MAKES 8 TO 10 SERVINGS

The Low Country of Georgia and South Carolina has its red rice. Mexico has its own versions of this dish, too. In chain restaurants, Mexican rice is often made from prefabricated mixes and is pretty bad. But I make it with fresh ingredients, and it's very similar to what you'll find all over Mexico. The trick is to first sauté the rice kernels to give them a nice nutty smell. Then add some onion and other aromatics and cook everything in a broth that's enhanced with pureed tomato, which gives the whole dish a light red tint. It's seasoned with garlic and cumin but no chiles, since it is usually served with spicy dishes. I like to make a big batch so I can add a scoop of the leftovers to chicken soup.

1 medium tomato, plus 1 cup finely chopped tomatoes

3 cups chicken stock, preferably homemade (page 99), or water

1 chicken bouillon cube if using stock, or 4 bouillon cubes if using water

1 teaspoon salt

¾ teaspoon ground white pepper

¾ teaspoon ground cumin

3 tablespoons vegetable oil

2 cups long-grain or broken white rice (see page 17)

½ cup finely chopped white onion

½ cup finely chopped green bell pepper

½ cup finely chopped carrots

1½ teaspoons minced garlic

Quarter the whole tomato and place it in a blender. Add ½ cup of the stock, the bouillon cube, salt, white pepper, and cumin. Puree until smooth. Transfer the mixture to a small saucepan and set over low heat.

Heat the oil in a medium saucepan over medium heat until it shimmers. Add the rice and stir to coat. Cook, stirring frequently, until most of the rice has turned opaque, 3 to 4 minutes. Add the onion, bell pepper, carrots, garlic, and chopped tomatoes and stir to combine. Add the puree and enough chicken stock or water to equal 3 cups total if using broken rice, or 4 cups if using long-grain rice. Bring to a boil, stirring occasionally. Reduce the heat to medium-low and cook just until there is a thin film of liquid on top, 7 to 10 minutes.

Reduce the heat to the very lowest setting. Taste and adjust the seasonings as desired. Cover tightly and cook for an additional 25 minutes without stirring, or until the rice is tender. Serve.

HOLY TRINITY RICE AND SAUSAGE

MAKES 8 SERVINGS

The trio of aromatics that people from Louisiana call the holy trinity—bell peppers, celery, and onions—is the foundation of much of Cajun cooking. I use it in this adaptation of dirty rice, along with my own sausage blend and Cuban Bijol seasoning (see page 192). True dirty rice has chopped giblets and gizzards, which I love, so if you happen to have some, chop them up and throw them in with the vegetables.

---

2 tablespoons butter

1½ cups Eddie's Breakfast
   Sausage (page 33),
   uncooked

1 cup finely chopped bell
   peppers

1 cup finely chopped celery

1 cup finely chopped onions

1½ recipes (6 cups cooked)
   Yellow Rice (page 192), hot

Salt

Melt the butter in a large skillet over medium-high heat. Add the sausage and cook, stirring, until cooked through, about 5 minutes. Add the bell peppers, celery, and onions and cook, stirring, until the vegetables are tender, 5 to 7 minutes. Transfer to a large bowl, add the rice, and stir to combine. Season to taste with salt. Serve hot.

STONE-GROUND GRITS WITH CHILES

MAKES 6 TO 8 SERVINGS

To enhance the natural corn flavor of stone-ground grits, I add the butter at the beginning of the cooking as part of the cooking liquid, along with both fresh and roasted chiles (canned is fine). These are great with eggs, or as part of a dinner plate with fried chicken or pork chops, in place of mashed potatoes or rice.

3 cups water, or more as
    needed

8 tablespoons (1 stick) butter

1½ teaspoons salt

1 cup stone-ground grits

1 cup diced roasted (see
    page 12) mild fresh green
    chiles, or canned diced
    roasted mild green chiles

½ fresh jalapeño, stemmed and
    minced (remove some or all
    of the seeds and membranes
    for less heat)

Place 3 cups of water, the butter, and salt in a large saucepan over high heat and bring to a boil. Add the grits and peppers while continually whisking. Reduce the heat to medium-low. Cook, whisking often, for about 35 minutes, or until the grits are fluffy. Add a little more water if they become too thick. Taste and adjust the seasonings as desired. Serve hot.

MEXICAN SPAGHETTI (SOPA DE FIDEO)

MAKES 4 TO 6 SIDE SERVINGS

Mexicans eat a lot of pasta. Very thin pasta or small pasta, such as alphabets, is first sautéed in oil, as for Mexican or Spanish rice. Then tomato sauce or broth is added so that the noodles absorb that liquid instead of plain water. To make it even more delicious, I add garlic and vegetables as well. If you let it stand for about 5 minutes before serving, the noodles will swell with those savory juices even more, and the consistency thickens and becomes less soupy, like spaghetti. I love to serve this in the same bowl as Real Mexican Chili con Carne (page 130). The photo is on page 131.

———————

¼ cup vegetable oil

1 tablespoon chopped garlic

8 ounces vermicelli pasta, broken in half, or alphabet pasta

1 cup finely chopped yellow onions

1 large tomato, chopped

1 bell pepper, cored, seeded, and chopped

2 cups (from 2 recipes) Salsa Frita (page 204)

4 cups chicken stock, preferably homemade (page 99)

½ teaspoon salt, plus additional as desired

Pinch of ground cumin

Heat the oil in a large stockpot over medium heat. Add the garlic and pasta and cook for 1 minute, just to coat. Add the onions, tomato, and bell pepper, stir to combine, and cook for 1 minute. Add the Salsa Frita, stock, salt, and cumin. Increase the heat to high, bring to a boil, and cook for 5 minutes. Reduce the heat to medium-low and simmer for 5 more minutes.

For a soupier pasta, remove from the heat and serve immediately.

For a spaghetti-style pasta, let the pasta sit for another 5 minutes to absorb the liquid.

SALSAS, SAUCES, RELISHES, AND CONDIMENTS

Chapter Eight

PICO DE GALLO *202*

SALSA FRESCA *202*

SALSA FRITA *204*

SALSA ASADA *204*

SALSA VERDE *205*

ROASTED TOMATILLO SAUCE *205*

TOMATO-HABANERO SAUCE *206*

  —TOMATO-HABANERO GRAVY *206*

POBLANO-CILANTRO SAUCE *207*

TAQUERIA VINAIGRETTE *207*

SPICY THOUSAND ISLAND SAUCE/DRESSING *209*

JALAPEÑO-LIME MAYONNAISE *211*

  —PICKLED JALAPEÑO MAYONNAISE *211*

  —BASIL-JALAPEÑO MAYONNAISE *211*

CREOLE REMOULADE SAUCE *212*

CREAMY LEMON—BLACK PEPPER DRESSING *212*

WATERMELON-JICAMA RELISH *213*

AROMATIC PICKLED JALAPEÑOS WITH CARROTS
  AND ONIONS *214*

SPICY BREAD AND BUTTER PICKLES *217*

Our favorite condiments have some shared history.

Mexicans are good in the kitchen because we know how to dress up pretty much anything edible, no matter how flavorless or tough, and make it exciting. Southerners have this skill as well. Our favorite condiments have some shared history.

Aztecs had been blending tomatoes and tomatillos with chiles for hundreds of years before the Spanish conquistadors discovered this combination in the 1500s and started calling it *salsa*, meaning "sauce." Salsa is what brings our dishes to life and allows us to go in a million different directions with our cooking. And salsa has outsold ketchup in the U.S. for more than twenty years. But no Mexican I know touches bottled salsa—especially since it is so easy to make and the fresh taste can't be beat.

It's simple and fun to make my own hot sauces and flavored oils, especially since I've started growing different kinds of chiles myself. But I always keep bottles of Tabasco (originally bottled by Edmund McIlhenny, a New Orleans banker, after the Civil War) in my kitchen, and usually at least a half-dozen other pepper sauces, including El Yucateco Chile Habanero sauce and Sriracha, the tangy-sweet, garlicky hot sauce that originated in Thailand.

In the pages that follow, I will share with you some of the most versatile of these condiments and other accessories that will guarantee you will never have to settle for bland.

PICO DE GALLO

MAKES 2¼ CUPS

2 cups ½-inch-dice tomatoes
   (2 large)
½ cup finely diced white onion
⅓ cup finely diced jalapeños
   (remove some or all of the
   seeds and membranes for
   less heat)
¼ cup lemon juice, or more
   as needed
¼ teaspoon salt

The vegetables in this multipurpose relish are cut by hand, so it is chunkier—better for garnishing a taco or a piece of fish than dipping a chip into.

———————

Combine the tomatoes, onion, jalapeños, lemon juice, and salt in a medium bowl. Taste and adjust the seasonings as desired. The sauce keeps for up to 2 days, covered and refrigerated.

SALSA FRESCA

MAKES 2 CUPS

The terms *salsa fresca* ("fresh sauce") and *pico de gallo* ("rooster's beak"; above) are often considered one and the same, but they have different tastes and purposes. I chop the ingredients for pico de gallo by hand, but I pulse the salsa fresca ingredients in the food processor so that it has a smoother texture that's better for dipping chips into.

———————

2 jalapeños, stemmed (remove
   some or all of the seeds and
   membranes for less heat)
¼ cup chopped fresh cilantro
2 tablespoons chopped white
   onion
4 large tomatoes, quartered
1 teaspoon white vinegar
½ teaspoon salt

Process the jalapeños, cilantro, and onion in a food processor until finely chopped. Add the quartered tomatoes and process until the mixture is fairly smooth but still has some texture. Do not overprocess. Transfer to a small bowl, add the vinegar and salt, and stir to combine. Taste and adjust the seasonings as desired. The salsa is best served within a few hours of making it, but it will keep in the refrigerator, covered, for 3 days.

Clockwise from left:
Salsa Asada (page 204),
Salsa Fresca (opposite),
and Salsa Verde
(page 205)

SALSA FRITA

MAKES ABOUT 3½ CUPS

¼ cup vegetable oil

6 large tomatoes, diced

4 or 5 jalapeños, stemmed, cut lengthwise, and thinly sliced (remove some or all of the seeds and membranes for less heat)

Salt

Frita means "fried," and salsa frita is what you get when you cook the basic salsa ingredients in sizzling oil and allow their flavors to concentrate. You can make it as chunky or smooth as you like.

———————

Heat the oil in a medium saucepan over medium-high heat until it shimmers. Add the tomatoes and jalapeños, standing back to avoid splatters. Cook, stirring frequently, until the tomatoes are very soft, 5 to 10 minutes. Taste and season with salt as desired. For a smoother salsa, puree in a food processor or blender. The salsa keeps for up to 1 week, covered and refrigerated.

SALSA ASADA

MAKES 1½ CUPS

Asada means "roasted" in Spanish. In this salsa, the flavor of the tomatoes concentrates and caramelizes, while the chile mellows. I like to include the bits of charred skin for a rustic character. The photo is on page 203.

———————

4 medium tomatoes

1 jalapeño

¼ cup chopped white onion

¼ cup chopped fresh cilantro

½ teaspoon salt

Heat the broiler to high.

Place the tomatoes and jalapeño in a shallow baking pan and broil until the skins are very dark on all sides, turning occasionally. Set aside. Quarter the tomatoes and stem the jalapeño. If desired, remove some or all of the seeds and membranes for less heat.

Place the tomatoes, jalapeño, onion, cilantro, and salt in a food processor and puree until they reach the desired consistency. Taste and adjust the seasonings as desired. The salsa will keep for up to 3 days, covered and refrigerated.

SALSA VERDE

MAKES ABOUT 1¾ CUPS

2 cups canned tomatillos, drained,
   or 1 pound fresh tomatillos, husked
   and boiled for about 5 minutes
   until soft
1 or 2 medium serrano chiles, stemmed
   (remove some or all of the seeds
   and membranes for less heat)
¼ cup chopped white onion
¼ cup chopped fresh cilantro,
   or more to taste
1 small garlic clove, peeled
½ teaspoon salt

Once fresh tomatillos are boiled, they lose their vibrant color and look and taste pretty much like canned, so I'm not ashamed to take a shortcut for this recipe. The more cilantro you add, the greener and fresher tasting this salsa will be. It's good as both a cold dip or a warm sauce for enchiladas and many other things. The photo is on page 203.

Place the tomatillos, chiles(s), onion, cilantro, garlic, and salt in a blender and puree until quite smooth. (If using fresh tomatillos, you may need to add a tablespoon or so of water to thin the salsa.) Taste and adjust the seasonings as desired. The salsa keeps for up to 3 days, covered and refrigerated.

ROASTED TOMATILLO SAUCE

MAKES 1¾ CUPS

1 pound tomatillos, husks
   removed, rinsed, and
   patted dry
1 tablespoon vegetable oil
10 dried chiles de árbol,
   stemmed (remove some
   or all of the seeds for less
   heat)
1 garlic clove, peeled
Salt

Roasting the tomatillos and toasting the dried chiles adds complexity to this simple, tangy hot sauce that can wake up a bland bowl of refried beans in an instant.

Heat the oven to 375 degrees.

Brush the tomatillos with the oil and roast for 10 minutes, or until softened. Toast the chiles de árbol in a dry skillet over medium-high heat for a few minutes on each side until slightly darkened.

Place the tomatillos, chiles de árbol, and garlic in a blender. Puree until smooth and transfer to a bowl or container. Season to taste with salt. Set aside at room temperature, or cover and refrigerate and bring back to room temperature before using. The sauce keeps for up to 3 days, covered and refrigerated.

TOMATO-HABANERO SAUCE

MAKES ABOUT 4 CUPS

I keep a container of this basic Mexican-style fresh tomato sauce on hand to heat and serve with eggs, to mix with sausage for a sauce to go over pasta or rice, or as a base for a stew or soup that might be thickened with a roux. This sauce is supposed to be thin. If it seems too watery, boil it down until it is the consistency you want. A fresh stemmed jalapeño or other chile can be used in place of the habanero.

---

5 to 6 medium tomatoes
(about 1½ pounds)

1 habanero (see headnote)

2 tablespoons vegetable oil

¼ cup finely diced onion

1 garlic clove, crushed

1 teaspoon salt

1 cup chicken stock,
preferably homemade
(page 99)

Place the tomatoes and habanero in a large saucepan, cover with water, and bring to a boil over high heat. Boil just until the tomato skins start to crack. Drain in a colander. Remove the stem from the habanero.

Transfer the tomatoes and habanero to a blender and puree until smooth.

Heat the oil in a medium saucepan over medium heat until it shimmers. Add the onion, garlic, and salt and cook until the onion is translucent and soft, 3 to 5 minutes. Add the tomato puree and the stock, increase the heat to high, and boil for 3 minutes more. Taste and adjust the seasonings as desired. The sauce keeps for up to 3 days, covered and refrigerated.

VARIATION

TOMATO-HABANERO GRAVY

Substitute 1 tablespoon butter for the oil, melt, add the tomato puree with all the ingredients except the stock, and cook for 3 minutes, or until slightly thickened. Taste and adjust the seasonings as desired. The sauce keeps for up to 5 days, covered and refrigerated.

POBLANO-CILANTRO SAUCE

MAKES 2 CUPS

1 jalapeño, stemmed (remove
    some or all of the seeds and
    membranes for less heat)
1 poblano pepper, cored,
    stemmed, and seeded
1 cup chopped fresh cilantro
1 garlic clove, peeled
1½ cups vegetable oil
Pinch of salt

This smooth, emerald-green sauce is almost like a Mexican pesto, pungent with herbs and a mild chile zing. It is versatile and especially good for dressing up plain white rice, pasta, a fish fillet, a grilled chicken breast, or a steak.

————————

Puree the jalapeño, poblano, cilantro, and garlic in a blender. With the machine running, slowly add the oil. Season with the salt. The sauce keeps for up to 1 week, covered and refrigerated.

TAQUERIA VINAIGRETTE

MAKES 2¼ CUPS

Fresh jalapeños and lots of black pepper add extra bite to our house vinaigrette, which I use for our green salads and a host of other things. It's also a good marinade for chicken or fish. It lasts for months in the refrigerator, so I recommend making a big batch.

————————

¾ cup red wine vinegar
1 jalapeño, stemmed
1 teaspoon salt
1½ teaspoons ground black
    pepper
1½ cups vegetable oil

Put the vinegar, jalapeño, and salt in a blender and puree. Strain through a fine-mesh strainer into a medium bowl. Whisk in the black pepper, then slowly add the oil, whisking until emulsified. Taste and adjust the seasonings as desired.

Transfer to a jar. The dressing will keep, covered and refrigerated, for at least a month.

MAYONNAISE-BASED SAUCES AND DRESSINGS

I put mayonnaise on sandwiches in Mexico, but the idea of using it as a salad dressing or anything else never occurred to me until I went to work for a Tex-Mex chain in Texas. There I got my first taste of Thousand Island dressing. It was a revelation. I memorized how the cooks did it so I could make it for myself, and it is one of my favorite condiments to this day. Since moving to Georgia, I have learned just how versatile this condiment can be. Southerners are insane for mayonnaise. They mix it in their pimento cheese and their fillings for deviled eggs. They make tartar sauce and a Louisiana-style remoulade to go with fried fish. I now make my own versions of all of these, using mayo as the base.

People get into arguments about which mayonnaise brand is the best. Many swear by Duke's, a South Carolina product that's been around for 100 years. I am not so particular, as long as it is full-bodied without added chemicals—not that light stuff! I always have several flavored mayonnaises on hand to give my food a different twist. Here are some of the ones I use most frequently—to dress a wedge of iceberg lettuce, garnish a taco, or use as dip for raw vegetables.

SPICY THOUSAND ISLAND SAUCE/ DRESSING

MAKES ABOUT 2½ CUPS

Besides hard-boiled eggs, onion, celery, and pickle relish, this classic gets a few shots of habanero hot sauce as well. It's especially good on a Potato-Crusted Chicken Taco (page 80) with lettuce and tomato. The photo is on page 210.

———————

2 large eggs

2 large stalks celery, chopped into a few pieces

¼ cup chopped onion

1 cup mayonnaise

½ cup ketchup

½ cup sweet pickle relish

½ teaspoon ground black pepper

¼ teaspoon granulated garlic (or garlic powder, not garlic salt)

½ to 1½ teaspoons red habanero sauce, such as El Yucateco, or other hot sauce

Pinch of salt

Place the eggs in a small saucepan and cover with cold water. Bring to a rolling boil and cook for 1 minute. Turn off the heat and let the eggs rest in the water until you can immerse your hand in it, about 20 minutes. Pour off the water and cover the eggs in cold water. Set aside for 5 minutes. Peel the eggs. Grate them with a box grater (or chop them).

Meanwhile, puree the celery and onion in a food processor. Transfer to a bowl. Add the mayonnaise, ketchup, pickle relish, pepper, garlic, and habanero sauce (start with the smaller amount). Stir in the grated hard-boiled eggs. Add the salt and taste and adjust the seasonings as desired. The sauce keeps, covered and refrigerated, for up to 3 days.

Top to bottom: Basil-Jalapeño Mayonnaise (opposite), Creole Remoulade Sauce (page 212), Pickled Jalapeño Mayonnaise (opposite), Spicy Thousand Island Sauce/Dressing (page 209), Base for Creamy Lemon–Black Pepper Dressing (page 212)

JALAPEÑO-LIME MAYONNAISE

MAKES 2¼ CUPS

Blending mayonnaise with hot chiles is a great way to soften the chiles' flavor. Here are three variations on this pairing with distinctive results. I specify a blender for one and a food processor for the others, depending on how much texture I want. If I am going to squeeze the mayo through a bottle, then I want it as smooth as possible, but if I am going to spread it or spoon it on, I might want some little pieces. This is up to you.

This versatile mayonnaise is great in Fried Chicken Tacos (page 78) and Cheeseburger Tacos (page 75).

———————

2 cups mayonnaise

¼ cup lime juice

1 jalapeño, roasted on a skillet without oil (see page 13) and stemmed (remove some or all of the seeds and membranes for less heat)

Pinch of salt

Place the mayonnaise, lime juice, jalapeño, and salt in a blender and puree. Taste and adjust the seasonings as desired. Refrigerate in an airtight container for up to 1 week.

VARIATIONS

PICKLED JALAPEÑO MAYONNAISE

Puree 2 cups mayonnaise, ½ cup drained pickled sliced jalapeños, and 1 tablespoon brine from the jalapeños in a food processor until blended.

Taste and adjust the seasonings as desired. Use in Nashville Hot Chicken Tacos (page 82). Makes 2¼ cups.

———————

BASIL-JALAPEÑO MAYONNAISE

Puree 2 cups mayonnaise; 1 roasted jalapeño (see page 12), stemmed (remove some or all of the seeds and membranes for less heat); ½ cup chopped fresh basil; and the juice of 1 lemon in a food processor. Season to taste with salt. Use this on a chicken or turkey sandwich. Makes 2¼ cups.

CREOLE REMOULADE SAUCE

MAKES ABOUT 1½ CUPS

¾ cup mayonnaise

6 tablespoons Creole mustard

2 tablespoons dry white wine

2 tablespoons finely chopped onion

2 tablespoons finely chopped celery

1 tablespoon stemmed and finely chopped jalapeño (remove some or all of the seeds and membranes for less heat)

1½ teaspoons Worcestershire sauce

A traditional Louisiana-style remoulade is based on the classic French sauce but usually has Creole mustard, a grainy mustard produced in Louisiana and widely sold throughout the Southeast. If you can't find it, Dijon or any good stone-ground mustard is fine. I give my remoulade extra kick with fresh jalapeño.

————————

Combine all the ingredients in a small bowl. The remoulade keeps for up to 1 week, covered and refrigerated.

CREAMY LEMON–BLACK PEPPER DRESSING

MAKES 1½ CUPS

1 cup mayonnaise

Flavor Base

¼ cup lemon juice

1 tablespoon finely chopped pickled jalapeños (optional)

½ cup sugar

1½ teaspoons ground black pepper

Pinch of salt

This sweet-and-sour sauce with a peppery bite takes less than five minutes to make and is terrific over hot and cold vegetables (see Melted Cabbage with Carrots, page 243) or drizzled on a Guacamole Mini Taco (page 49). I also use this formula to dress Jalapeño Coleslaw (page 223).

————————

Place the mayonnaise a small bowl. Whisk in the flavor base ingredients. Taste and adjust the seasonings as desired. The dressing keeps, covered and refrigerated, for up to 1 week.

WATERMELON-JICAMA RELISH

MAKES 3 CUPS

2 cups diced watermelon,
    seeds removed

1 cup peeled and diced jicama

¼ cup finely chopped fresh
    cilantro

¼ cup stemmed and finely
    diced jalapeños (remove
    some or all of the seeds and
    membranes for less heat)

Juice of 1 lime

½ teaspoon salt

A little sweet and a little hot, this crunchy and refreshing mixture can serve as a garnish for grilled fish or chicken if diced small, or a relish or side salad if cut into a larger dice.

―――――――――

Combine the watermelon, jicama, cilantro, jalapeños, lime juice, and salt in a medium bowl. Taste and adjust the seasonings as desired. Cover and refrigerate until ready to serve. The relish keeps for up to 2 days, covered and refrigerated.

AROMATIC PICKLED JALAPEÑOS WITH CARROTS AND ONIONS

MAKES 11 CUPS (2¾ QUARTS)

I keep pickled jalapeños on hand at all times to add as a quick garnish. Here I use sugar and oil to mellow and soften the bite, so the jalapeños can be served like a vegetable on their own.

4 cups white vinegar

2 cups water

2 cups sugar

1½ tablespoons salt

4 cinnamon sticks

10 garlic cloves, peeled

6 bay leaves

10 jalapeños, stemmed and split or sliced into ¼-inch-thick rounds

2 large onions, peeled and cut into eighths

1 pound carrots, peeled and cut into ½-inch-thick rounds

1 cup vegetable oil

Combine the vinegar, water, sugar, salt, cinnamon sticks, garlic, and bay leaves in a large saucepan. Bring to a boil over high heat. Reduce the heat to a simmer and cook, stirring occasionally, for about 10 minutes, until syrupy. Add the jalapeños, onions, and carrots and bring back to a boil. Boil for 8 minutes, or until the vegetables are tender-crisp.

Turn off the heat and cool to room temperature. Transfer to a large glass or other nonreactive container, stir in the oil, and refrigerate for 24 hours before serving or for up to 1 month, covered and refrigerated.

SPICY BREAD AND BUTTER PICKLES

MAKES 2 TO 3 QUARTS

David Waller, one of our longtime chefs from North Carolina who is in charge of our catering operation, makes these pickles from an old family recipe to go with a variety of dishes he serves at parties, like pimento cheese–stuffed eggs (page 46). And they also sometimes show up in a taco filled with barbecue. When making these myself, I add jalapeños and onion for extra spice, or toss in whole chiles de árbol just for color.

———————

3 pounds pickling cucumbers

2 teaspoons salt

4 cups white vinegar

2½ cups sugar

3 jalapeños, stemmed and
   sliced into ¼-inch-thick
   rounds, or 3 whole dried
   chiles de árbol

1 small white onion, thinly
   sliced (optional)

1 garlic clove, crushed

1 teaspoon ground turmeric

1 teaspoon black peppercorns

1 teaspoon mustard seeds

Partially peel the cucumbers, cutting away thin lengthwise strips of skin. Thinly slice them crosswise. Place in a large bowl and toss with the salt. Cover with ice and refrigerate for 1 hour. Drain but do not rinse.

In a large saucepan, combine the vinegar, sugar, chiles, if using, onion, if using, garlic, turmeric, peppercorns, and mustard seeds. Bring to a boil over high heat. Add the cucumbers, return to a boil, and cook for 1 minute. Remove from the heat. Taste and adjust the seasonings as desired.

Cool to room temperature, transfer to glass quart jars, and refrigerate. The pickles keep for up to 1 month, covered and refrigerated.

SALADS, SLAWS, AND HOT VEGETABLE SIDES

Chapter Nine

LEMON-GARLIC DELTA SALAD *222*

JALAPEÑO COLESLAW *223*

GREEN PEA SALAD WITH ROASTED CHILES
    AND RED ONION *225*

ORANGE-ALMOND SALAD WITH SWEET
    SERRANO-LIME DRESSING *226*

GREEN PEACH SALAD WITH SIMPLE LIME
    DRESSING *229*

MEX-AMERICAN BLACK-EYED PEA SALAD *230*

BLACK BEAN AND CORN SALAD WITH
    CILANTRO-MINT DRESSING *232*

ROASTED POTATO SALAD WITH MUSTARD-ORANGE
    DRESSING *233*

"THE GEORGE" *234*

EDDIE'S TURNIP GREENS *236*

COLLARDS WITH ANDOUILLE *237*

COLLARDS AND BLACK-EYED PEAS WITH
    LEMON-HABANERO DRESSING *238*

OKRA AND HAM, RANCHERO STYLE *240*

KITCHEN-SINK SUCCOTASH *241*

MELTED CABBAGE WITH CARROTS *243*

FOIL-ROASTED BEETS AND VIDALIA ONIONS
    WITH BUTTER, LIME, AND SEA SALT *244*

ROASTED CAULIFLOWER WITH JALAPEÑOS
    AND BLUE CHEESE *246*

ANCHO MASHED POTATOES *247*

If we're making a meal just for ourselves, Mike and I will often skip the meat.

A few years ago, I started a little garden because I wanted to grow different kinds of chiles—the really hot kinds that are hard to find—to make pepper sauce. One of our managers and a dishwasher from rural Mexico know a lot more about this gardening stuff than I do, and they pitched in to help. They keep the plants watered and weeded when I can't get to them. Besides chiles, we have harvested tomatoes, beans, and tomatillos. No telling what we will have growing by next year. It's something we all enjoy and take pride in.

My business partner, Mike Klank, is a sucker for fresh produce, just like I am. I think it is one of the reasons we hit it off when I first started working for him three decades ago. He's like a lot of the Southern friends I have now who have great memories of big Sunday suppers with a dozen different fresh vegetables on the table, many fresh from the backyard or the neighborhood produce truck.

If we're making a meal just for ourselves, Mike and I will often skip the meat and make a Southern-style vegetable plate with a helping of rice or beans, some tortillas or corn bread, and maybe—if we get lucky—some fresh sliced tomatoes from our own little garden. I may bring out a bottle of Tabasco for extra seasoning like they do all over the South or—better yet—some of my own pepper vinegar made with chiles that are too hot even for me to eat straight off the vine.

LEMON-GARLIC DELTA SALAD

MAKES 4 SERVINGS

On my first trip to Greenville, Mississippi, to participate in the annual Delta Hot Tamale Festival, I went to dinner one night with a group of people at Doe's Eat Place, a restaurant in an old grocery store that is famous for its steaks and Mississippi-style hot tamales. But what I remember most about that meal was the salad. It was very simple—just chopped lettuce, tomato, and onion drenched in a tart and refreshing dressing with a heavy garlic flavor. The secret, the regular customers told me, was the very well–seasoned wooden salad bowl that the chefs had been using to toss it in for about fifty years. This salad tasted exactly like one that is served all over the west coast of Mexico. I suspect that the Mexican migrant workers who came to Mississippi a long time ago to work the cotton fields—the same ones who, by legend, introduced tamales to the Delta—made this salad. Some people use limes but I prefer the milder flavor of lemons, like they use at Doe's.

The texture of the salad changes after you toss it. It immediately wilts, and that is the idea. I restore some of the texture with the crunch of fresh red onions. I like to use a wooden bowl for this, but any bowl will work.

---

2 garlic cloves

1 tablespoon salt

¼ cup lemon juice

½ cup vegetable oil

1 head iceberg lettuce, cored, washed, dried, and chopped

1 cup thinly sliced red onions

½ cup finely diced tomato

On a cutting board, smash the garlic with the flat side of a knife blade and peel away the skins. Mince the garlic, gather it into a pile, then dump the salt on top. Using the side of the knife, scrape the mixture against the board until it forms a paste.

Place the garlic pulp in a large bowl, then add the lemon juice. Slowly add the oil in a steady stream, whisking until emulsified. Add the lettuce, onions, and tomato. Toss and let sit for 5 to 10 minutes, allowing the lettuce to wilt—but not too much.

EDDIE'S WAY: *Toss in 1 sliced fresh jalapeño, which is true to the Mexican way. Sliced avocado or cooked shrimp or both are also delicious with this combination.*

JALAPEÑO COLESLAW

MAKES 8 TO 10 SERVINGS

This slaw is just the right balance of sweet and heat to go with just about everything. It's a key ingredient in our Memphis taco, and a side dish on many of our plates. If you need to bring a side dish to a potluck cookout but don't want to turn on the stove, look no further than this recipe!

9 cups thinly sliced green cabbage, about ½ head (or a 16-ounce bag grated)

¾ cup grated carrots (about 2 medium)

1 tablespoon finely chopped pickled jalapeño

1 cup mayonnaise

½ cup sugar

¼ cup lemon juice

1½ teaspoons ground black pepper

Salt

Combine the cabbage, carrots, and pickled jalapeño in a large bowl. Add the mayonnaise, sugar, lemon juice, and pepper and toss to combine. Season to taste with salt. Refrigerate for 30 minutes before serving, or overnight. The coleslaw will lose its crispness the longer it sits in the refrigerator, but it will keep, covered and refrigerated, for several days after you make it.

GREEN PEA SALAD WITH ROASTED CHILES AND RED ONION

MAKES 8 SERVINGS

You see variations on this pea salad at many old Southern buffet lines and church socials, but I learned to make this in South America. It gets its kick from roasted chiles and red onion and it tastes great with Steak Churrasco with Chimichurri Sauce (page 148). You can serve it immediately, but it's better if it's been chilled for an hour or two to allow the flavors to blend.

---

2 large eggs

¼ cup roasted (see page 12), skinned, cored, seeded, and chopped poblano pepper

2 tablespoons roasted (see page 12), skinned, stemmed, and chopped jalapeño (remove some or all of the seeds and membranes for less heat)

4 cups frozen green peas, thawed

3 tablespoons diced red onion

⅔ cup mayonnaise

¼ teaspoon salt

Place the eggs in a small saucepan and cover with cold water. Bring to a rolling boil and cook for 1 minute. Turn off the heat and let the eggs rest in the water until you can immerse your hand in it, about 20 minutes. Pour off the water and cover the eggs in cold water. Set aside for 5 minutes. Peel the eggs.

Chop the eggs and transfer to a large bowl. Add the chopped peppers, peas, onion, mayonnaise, and salt. Stir to combine. Taste and adjust the seasonings as desired. Cover and refrigerate for 1 to 2 hours to blend the flavors.

ORANGE-ALMOND SALAD WITH SWEET SERRANO-LIME DRESSING

MAKES 8 SERVINGS

My love, Orfa, lives in Colombia, South America, and I travel there to visit her every few months. She is the pickiest woman on the planet. On one visit, I made this cool little salad, and she loved it so much, she asked me to make her a gallon of the dressing to tide her over till the next time I came to see her. You don't need to have a chef's skills to make it. Just throw everything in a blender and that is it! It's sweet and sour and a little spicy, and goes really well with salads that have some fruit, like this one.

4 seedless oranges

1 head romaine lettuce, washed, dried, and torn into bite-size pieces, and refrigerated until ready to use

Sweet Serrano-Lime Dressing (opposite)

½ cup toasted, sliced almonds

Cut off the tops and bottoms of the oranges. Cut off the white pith with a sharp knife. Cut the segments free from the membranes.

Divide the chilled lettuce among eight serving plates. Arrange the orange segments on the lettuce. Drizzle with the dressing and garnish with the toasted almonds. Serve immediately.

SWEET SERRANO-
LIME DRESSING

MAKES 2 CUPS

1 cup sugar

½ cup lime juice

¾ cup olive oil

¼ cup vegetable oil

1 or 2 serrano chiles, stemmed (remove
some or all of the seeds
and membranes for less heat)

Pinch of salt

Put all the ingredients in a blender and puree. Taste and adjust the seasonings as desired. Chill until ready to use. The dressing will keep, covered and refrigerated, for 1 week.

GREEN PEACH SALAD WITH SIMPLE LIME DRESSING

MAKES 4 SERVINGS

If all the peaches at the market are hard as rocks, you don't have to wait two days for them to ripen. Instead you can thinly slice them and toss them with a simple lime vinaigrette and salt for a refreshing salad. The peach slices are crisp and tart but loaded with flavor, and the lime and salt help to soften them. For this reason the salad will hold its texture for several days in the refrigerator. For a little heat and green color, I toss in some finely chopped serranos, although the salad is also good without them. In Mexico we do something similar with unripe mangoes and papayas, slicing them and sprinkling them with lime juice and chile salt. These are common street snacks, as are other tropical fruits treated this way.

I like to serve a scoop of cottage cheese on the side, to balance the heat of the peppers and tartness of the lime and fruit.

½ cup vegetable oil

¼ cup lime juice

½ teaspoon sea salt,
   or to taste

2 cups thinly sliced unripe
   peaches

2 to 3 finely chopped serrano
   chiles (optional)

4 cabbage leaves (optional)

Cottage cheese or other soft,
   fresh cheese (optional)

In a medium bowl, whisk the oil, lime juice, and salt until emulsified. Toss the peach slices and chiles, if using, with the dressing. Cover and chill for at least 10 minutes before serving.

Place a cabbage leaf, if using, on each of four plates and top with the peaches. Season with an extra sprinkling of sea salt, if desired. Add a scoop of cottage cheese, if desired.

MEX-AMERICAN BLACK-EYED PEA SALAD

MAKES 8 TO 10 SERVINGS

This relish is served in homes all over the South, and everywhere you go, it's a little different. I've seen it called Texas caviar, Georgia caviar, and Mississippi caviar. That goes to show how much the cooks in Texas and the South value their peas! The tangy marinade complements fried fish and pork well, and the multicolored peppers help dress up the plates. Any starchy bean or pea will absorb the vinegar-based marinade, as will corn. The dish is very adaptable to what you have on hand.

4 cups cooked or canned black-eyed peas, drained

½ cup finely diced red bell pepper

½ cup finely diced green bell pepper

½ cup finely diced red onion

1 to 2 stemmed and finely diced serrano chiles (remove some or all of the seeds and membranes for less heat)

½ cup vegetable oil

¼ cup red wine vinegar

1 tablespoon finely chopped fresh parsley

½ teaspoon salt

Combine all the ingredients in a large bowl. Cover and refrigerate for at least 1 hour before serving. Taste and adjust the seasonings as desired. Serve chilled or at room temperature.

BLACK BEAN AND CORN SALAD WITH CILANTRO-MINT DRESSING

MAKES 6 TO 8 SERVINGS

Corn and beans make a complete protein, and they taste good together, too, tossed in this fresh-tasting herbal dressing. You can use any legume in place of the black beans here. The photo is on page 220.

Cilantro-Mint Dressing

¼ cup packed fresh cilantro
    leaves
¼ cup packed fresh mint
    leaves
½ to 1 medium jalapeño,
    stemmed (remove some
    or all of the seeds and
    membranes for less heat)
¼ cup vegetable oil

Salad

1 tablespoon vegetable oil
1 serrano chile, stemmed and
    diced (remove some or all of
    the seeds and membranes
    for less heat)
¼ cup diced onion
2 cups fresh corn kernels
2 cups cooked or canned black
    beans, drained
¼ cup cider or white vinegar
½ teaspoon salt

To make the dressing: Put the cilantro, mint, jalapeño, and oil in a food processor or blender and process until smooth. Set aside or refrigerate until ready to use.

To make the salad: Heat the oil in a large skillet over medium heat. Add the serrano chile and onion and cook for 1 minute. Add the corn kernels, cook for 3 minutes more, and remove from the heat.

Place in a medium bowl to cool slightly. Add the black beans, vinegar, salt, and dressing and toss to combine. Taste and adjust the seasonings as desired.

ROASTED POTATO SALAD WITH MUSTARD-ORANGE DRESSING

MAKES 6 TO 8 SERVINGS

These roasted potatoes, which are turned into a salad that goes especially well with Oven-Baked Memphis-Style Ribs (page 145), are tossed in a dressing made of mayonnaise, orange marmalade, and a little yellow mustard. The hints of bitter citrus from the marmalade tie together the flavors of the potatoes and spicy pork.

———————

3 pounds assorted new potatoes, halved lengthwise

3 tablespoons vegetable oil

1 tablespoon ground black pepper

1½ teaspoons salt

Dressing

1 cup mayonnaise

3 tablespoons orange marmalade

1 tablespoon yellow mustard

Heat the oven to 425 degrees.

Toss the potatoes with the oil, pepper, and salt in a shallow roasting pan. Roast for 30 to 35 minutes, until tender.

To make the dressing: Whisk together the mayonnaise, orange marmalade, and mustard in a large serving bowl. Toss with the potatoes. Serve warm or at room temperature.

"THE GEORGE"

Years ago one of our longtime managers, George Trusler, used to sit at the bar after the lunch rush and get the kitchen to fix him a bowl of my Turnip Greens and mix in some of the Charros Beans (page 188) and Mexican Rice (page 194). Sometimes his friends would join him, and they would ask for the same thing. Since the dish didn't have a name, they would just ask for "The George." Other customers would ask what they were having, and the name stuck. "The George" is not on the menu, but if you order it, any of our employees will know exactly what you mean and will get it for you. In the summertime it's really good to make a vegetable plate of it, with some sliced homegrown tomatoes on the side.

EDDIE'S TURNIP GREENS

MAKES 6 SERVINGS

In Mexico we ate our share of leafy greens—mostly cooked instead of raw in salads. Spinach and chard were both popular. Lamb's quarters, amaranth leaves, squash vines, and beet greens have been important sources of nourishment in Mexico since ancient times and still are, especially among the poor. We cook the turnip greens on the Taqueria del Sol menu much the way my family used to fix lamb's quarters—we knew them as *quelites*—in chicken stock flavored with tomatoes and spices instead of in stock seasoned with ham hock. But we do serve them in bowls with the "potlikker" they are cooked in, which is also common in Southern restaurants. They are equally good with tortillas or corn bread. Never in my wildest dreams would I have imagined that this little soup I concocted nearly thirty years ago would create such a sensation, but I am very glad that it did. (See photo, page x.)

---

1 pound cleaned, stemmed, and chopped turnip greens

4 tablespoons (½ stick) butter

⅔ cup chopped onion

1 teaspoon chopped garlic

1 teaspoon ground chile de árbol or cayenne pepper, or more to taste

1¼ cups diced tomatoes

2½ cups chicken stock, preferably homemade (page 99)

Salt

Place the greens in a large pot and cover with water by 1 inch. Bring to a boil over high heat. Reduce the heat to maintain a simmer and cook until just tender, about 45 minutes. Drain well and set aside.

Wipe out the pot and melt the butter over medium heat. Add the onion, garlic, and chile de árbol and cook, stirring, until the onion is softened, 5 to 7 minutes. Add the tomatoes and cook for 5 minutes. Add the cooked greens and chicken stock, increase the heat to high, and boil for 5 minutes. Reduce the heat to medium-low and simmer for 15 minutes, or until very tender. Taste and add salt as desired. Serve in bowls with the liquid, like a soup.

COLLARDS
WITH ANDOUILLE

MAKES 6 TO 8 SERVINGS

Collard leaves are thicker and heartier than turnip greens, but the two are prepared and served in similar ways in the South. For this recipe I cook the greens twice, as for turnip greens, but I cook them for a shorter time in the beginning because I want to serve them on the plate instead of in a bowl. For the second cooking, I use less liquid and cook the greens until they're no longer soupy but still retain some good juice. The andouille really complements the meaty flavor of the collards.

12 cups chopped, cleaned
    collards (from a 1-pound
    bag or a 2-pound bunch with
    whole leaves and stems),
    thick stems removed
3 tablespoons butter
½ cup chopped white onion
1 teaspoon coarsely ground
    chile de árbol or red chile
    flakes
1 tablespoon chopped garlic
½ teaspoon salt
2 cups sliced andouille
    sausage, cut into half-moons
1½ cups diced tomatoes
2 cups chicken stock,
    preferably homemade
    (page 99)
¼ teaspoon ground cumin
⅛ teaspoon ground white
    pepper

Put the collards in a large pot, cover with water by 1 inch, and set over high heat. Bring to a boil and cook until wilted, 10 to 15 minutes. Remove, drain well, and set aside.

Wipe out the pot and melt the butter over medium heat. Add the onion, chile de árbol, garlic, and salt and cook, stirring, until the onion is translucent, 3 to 5 minutes. Add the sausage and cook for 2 minutes. Add the tomatoes and cook for 5 minutes. Add the chicken stock, cumin, and white pepper, increase the heat to high, and boil for 1 minute. Add the cooked collards, reduce the heat to low, and simmer for 10 minutes or longer, until the collards reach the desired tenderness. Taste and adjust the seasonings as desired.

COLLARDS AND BLACK-EYED PEAS WITH LEMON-HABANERO DRESSING

MAKES 6 TO 8 SERVINGS

Collards and field peas (usually black-eyed peas but also lady peas, purple hull peas, and many other Southern varieties) are commonly served together on the same plate. Here they are combined in a light, lemony dressing spiked with habanero for a great vegetarian dish.

---

12 cups chopped, cleaned
   collards (from a 1-pound
bag or a 2-pound bunch with
   whole leaves and stems),
   thick stems removed
2 tablespoons butter
½ cup thinly sliced white onion
1 cup cooked or canned black-
   eyed peas, or other field
   peas, drained
Salt
Lemon-Habanero Dressing
   (opposite)

Place the collards in a large pot and cover with water by 1 inch. Set over high heat, bring to a boil, and cook until wilted, 10 to 15 minutes. Remove, drain well, and set aside.

Wipe out the pot and melt the butter over medium heat. Add the onions and cook, stirring, until tender, 3 to 5 minutes.

Add the collards and cook, stirring, for 2 minutes. Add the black-eyed peas and cook, stirring, until warmed through, about 2 minutes more. Toss with the Lemon-Habanero Dressing to taste, adjust salt as desired, and serve.

LEMON-HABANERO DRESSING

MAKES 1½ CUPS

½ cup finely diced onion

½ to 1 habanero, stemmed and minced
   (remove some or all of the seeds and
   membranes for less heat)

¼ cup minced fresh parsley

½ cup lemon juice

½ cup vegetable oil

Pinch of salt

Combine the onion, habanero, parsley, and lemon juice in a small bowl. Whisk in the vegetable oil to blend. Add the salt. Taste and adjust the seasonings as desired.

OKRA AND HAM, RANCHERO STYLE

MAKES 6 SERVINGS

Mexicans grow a lot of okra, but we don't eat a lot of it. It is exported to the U.S., and I have learned to like it since I have lived in Georgia. The gelatinous substance in the pods helps thicken this stew, which also includes ham, tomatoes, and lots of spice. Sautéing the vegetables in lard gives this dish a country flavor. Served over rice, it tastes almost like gumbo and is a hearty side dish or even a meal in itself. I also like leftovers for breakfast, with a fried egg and Texas toast—extra thick–sliced white bread—for sopping up the savory juices.

---

3 tablespoons lard, preferably homemade (page 299)

2 pounds okra, trimmed and sliced into ½-inch-thick rounds (about 3 cups)

1 cup finely diced white onions

¼ cup finely diced serrano chiles (remove some or all of the seeds and membranes for less heat)

½ teaspoon salt

1½ cups diced smoked ham

2 cups finely diced tomatoes

1½ teaspoons ground cumin

1 teaspoon ground white pepper

½ cup water

Melt the lard over medium heat in a large skillet. Add the okra, onions, serranos, and salt and cook until the onions are soft and translucent, 5 to 7 minutes. Add the ham and cook for 1 minute. Add the tomatoes and cook for 3 minutes.

Add the cumin, white pepper, and water; bring to a boil, reduce the heat, and simmer for 2 minutes, or until the vegetables are tender. Taste and adjust the seasonings as desired. Serve hot.

KITCHEN-SINK SUCCOTASH

MAKES 6 TO 8 SERVINGS

My version of succotash uses all ingredients that are staples in my home country as well as in the South. It is very colorful, healthy, and easy to make, and it tastes like summer. Also, you can add any leftover vegetable you think might work.

---

6 tablespoons (¾ stick) butter

1 cup thinly sliced white onions

½ teaspoon salt

½ cup diced red bell pepper

½ cup diced green bell pepper

½ cup diced yellow bell pepper

2 cups diced zucchini

2 cups corn kernels

1 cup diced tomatoes

1 cup baby limas, lady peas, or other beans or peas

2 jalapeños, stemmed and minced (remove some or all of the seeds and membranes for less heat)

Melt the butter in a large skillet over medium heat. Add the onions and salt and cook until soft and translucent, 5 to 7 minutes. Add the bell peppers and cook for 2 minutes. Add the zucchini and cook for 2 minutes. Add the corn and cook for 2 minutes. Add the tomatoes, limas, and jalapeños and stir to combine. Taste and adjust the seasonings as desired. Cover and continue to cook for 3 minutes, or until the vegetables are tender. Serve hot.

MELTED CABBAGE WITH CARROTS

MAKES 6 SERVINGS

We ate a lot of cabbage in Mexico, both raw and cooked, because it was economical and also because it's so sturdy that it does not require long refrigeration. A lot of people don't like it cooked because they find it strong tasting and smelly. Here I offer a simple and delicious solution. Steam it in a pot with butter, sugar, and shredded carrot for color. When the cabbage is done, it's so tender it melts in your mouth and the leaves taste slightly sweetened. Most of the melted butter and sugar remains in the pot.

---

2 cups water

1 medium cabbage, cored and quartered

2 large carrots, sliced very thin using a mandoline or very sharp knife

½ cup sugar

1½ teaspoons salt

8 tablespoons (1 stick) unsalted butter

Creamy Lemon–Black Pepper Dressing (page 212; optional)

Mint-Jalapeño Drizzle (page 154; optional)

Put the water and cabbage in a large pot. Put the carrots on top. Add the sugar and salt on top, then the butter. Cover tightly and bring to a boil over high heat. Reduce the heat to medium and continue to cook at a brisk simmer for 15 to 20 minutes, until the cabbage is very tender. Serve warm, topped with some of the dressing if desired, and surround with some of the drizzle if desired.

EDDIE'S WAY: *Serve with Blue Cornmeal–Crusted Chicken with Mint-Jalapeño Drizzle (page 154).*

While the cabbage cooks, quick-fry the boneless chicken breasts in the cornmeal coating. Set a chicken breast on top of a mound of the cabbage, top it with some of the creamy dressing, and spoon the mint drizzle around the edge. The entire dish, including both sauces, can be made in less than an hour.

FOIL-ROASTED BEETS AND VIDALIA ONIONS WITH BUTTER, LIME, AND SEA SALT

MAKES 4 TO 8 SERVINGS

I like to roast beets at the same time as onions and serve them together so that their sweetness complements each other. Georgia's naturally sweet Vidalias don't need much sugar—but a little helps with the caramelization. If I'm using a different yellow onion, I add another teaspoon or so of sugar to each packet.

---

1 tablespoon sea salt

½ cup sugar

4 large beets, stemmed and trimmed

4 Vidalia onions or other sweet onions (see headnote), peeled

8 tablespoons (1 stick) butter

¼ cup chopped fresh mint leaves (optional)

Lime wedges for garnish

Sea salt for garnish

Heat the oven to 425 degrees.

Mix the salt and sugar together in a small bowl.

Cut sixteen 8-inch-square pieces of aluminum foil and place two together so you have eight double-thicknesses of foil. Set the beets and onions on the squares of foil, one per square. Top each with 1 tablespoon butter and 1 tablespoon of the sugar/salt mixture. Sprinkle with mint leaves if desired.

Wrap each tightly and set on a baking sheet. Bake until tender, 45 to 60 minutes. Remove from the oven. Peel off the foil. Cut the beets into halves or quarters and the onions into bite-size pieces. Serve the beets with a mound of onions on the side. Squeeze with lime juice and sprinkle with coarse sea salt.

Note: The foil-wrapped beets and onions can also be roasted directly in the coals while you are grilling. This can take up to 1½ hours, depending on how hot your fire is.

ROASTED CAULIFLOWER WITH JALAPEÑOS AND BLUE CHEESE

MAKES 4 TO 6 SERVINGS

Roasting brings out cauliflower's sweet, nutty flavor and creamy texture. After tossing the florets in a little oil with chiles and onions, I spread them in a roasting pan and cover it with foil for the first half of the roasting time to keep the cauliflower from burning or drying out. Then I uncover the pan and allow the cauliflower to caramelize slightly. It's good served plain, but stirring in some butter and blue cheese really takes it over the top.

---

1 medium head cauliflower, broken into florets (about 6 cups)

½ cup chopped white onion

¼ cup stemmed and minced jalapeños (remove some or all of the seeds and membranes for less heat)

2 tablespoons vegetable oil

½ teaspoon salt

⅓ cup crumbled blue cheese

2 tablespoons butter

Heat the oven to 425 degrees.

Toss the cauliflower, onion, jalapeños, oil, and salt in a large bowl. Spread the vegetables in a roasting pan, cover with foil, and cook for 15 minutes. Remove the foil and cook for 20 to 25 minutes longer, until the florets are soft and begin to turn golden.

Transfer the vegetables to a serving bowl, add the cheese and butter, and stir to combine. If desired, smash gently. Serve hot.

ANCHO MASHED POTATOES

MAKES 8 SERVINGS

Ancho puree gives a smoky, subtle heat and a nice salmon-colored tint to these creamy potatoes. Make sure the puree is ready to go before the potatoes are cooked. It is my favorite side dish to serve with Eddie's Pork with Roasted Jalapeño Gravy (page 142). Always mash hot potatoes with warm or room-temperature ingredients to prevent the potatoes from turning gummy.

---

3 pounds russet potatoes, peeled and cut into 1-inch pieces (about 8 cups)

1 tablespoon salt

3 ounces cream cheese, at room temperature

2 ounces white American cheese or Monterey Jack, grated, at room temperature

4 tablespoons (½ stick) butter, at room temperature

1 tablespoon Ancho Chile Puree (page 292)

1 cup whole milk, hot, plus more if needed

Bring a large pot of water to a boil over medium-high heat. Add the potatoes and salt and cook until the potatoes are easily pierced with a fork, 15 to 20 minutes. Drain. Place in a large bowl or baking pan and, using a potato masher, mash with the cream cheese, American cheese, butter, and chile puree until smooth. Stir in the hot milk, a little at a time, until you reach the preferred consistency. Taste and adjust the seasonings as desired.

DRINKS TO COOL YOU DOWN AND WARM YOU UP

Chapter Ten

WESTSIDE RITA *252*
SKINNY RITA *253*
FRESH SWEET-AND-SOUR MIX *253*
FROZEN LIMEADE MARGARITA *254*
—CHILE SEA SALT *254*
MEXICAN MINT JULEP *255*
EDDIE PALMER *257*
TEQUILA-MANGO SMOOTHIE *258*
—LEMON SYRUP *258*
MICHELADAS *260*
—RED MICHELADA MIX *261*
—GREEN MICHELADA MIX *262*
—YELLOW MICHELADA MIX *262*
BASIL LIMONADA *263*
AGUAS FRESCAS (MEXICAN FRUIT COOLERS) *264*
MEXICAN CINNAMON TEA *267*
MEXICAN COFFEE *269*

Margaritas are an American creation.

In the region of Mexico where my family and I lived—the northeast part of the country—temperatures hovered around the 90s and 100s for months at a time, and few people in my neighborhood had air-conditioning. I saw snow only once. When my little brother looked out the window, he thought someone had dumped sugar all over our patio!

My mother, like most mothers in the neighborhood, kept a clay pitcher filled with water on the windowsill. The water stayed cold all the time. I loved the taste—it was like drinking out of a creek. On the streets there were many more options. We enjoyed fresh fruit drinks called *aguas frescas*, meaning "fresh waters."

In high school my buddies and I mixed Squirt, a grapefruit-flavored soft drink, with a cheap tequila for a quick buzz. This was the closest thing to a margarita I had before I crossed the border into the U.S., where I discovered that margaritas, like most other versions of Mexican food you find here, are an American creation.

We have our own ways of mixing our margaritas at the restaurant, and in this chapter I tell you how we do it. I also include a selection of other drinks that I think go best with my style of cooking and eating—cold and hot, with and without alcohol, some steeped in tradition and others straight out of my head.

WESTSIDE RITA

MAKES 1 DRINK

Kosher salt

2 fresh lime wedges or slices

2 ounces Herradura Reposado
tequila

1 ounce Patrón
Citrónge Orange Liqueur

3 ounces Fresh Sweet-and-
Sour Mix (opposite)

Ice

My business partner, Mike Klank, designed this potent citrusy
drink, named for Taqueria del Sol's first location on Atlanta's
Westside, using one of the most reliable tequilas for margarita
making, along with an orange liqueur that is basically a triple sec
made in Mexico.

Reposado (meaning "rested" in Spanish) tequilas are aged slowly
in oak barrels, which gives the liquor its golden color. Herradura
Reposado is our brand of choice for classic margaritas and is
good with most citrus-based cocktails.

_____

Pour some kosher salt onto a small saucer. Wet the rim of a
12-ounce old-fashioned glass with one of the lime wedges and dip
the rim in the salt. Pour the tequila, liqueur, and sweet-and-sour
mix into a shaker with ice. Shake vigorously and pour into the glass.
Garnish with the other lime wedge.

SKINNY RITA

MAKES 1 DRINK

2 ounces Herradura Silver
    tequila
1 ounce Cointreau liqueur
1 ounce Fresh Sweet-and-Sour
    Mix (below)
2 ounces lime juice
Ice
Fresh lime slice or wedge for
    garnish

Light-tasting silver, or *blanco*, tequila is the base of this variation for people who prefer their margaritas less sweet.

———————

Pour the tequila, liqueur, sweet-and-sour mix, and lime juice into a shaker with ice. Shake vigorously and pour into a margarita glass. Garnish with the lime.

FRESH SWEET-AND-SOUR MIX

MAKES 2 CUPS

Here is a small-batch version of the sweet-and-sour mix we use for our margaritas at Taqueria del Sol.

———————

¾ cup water
¾ cup sugar
½ cup lemon juice
½ cup lime juice

Combine the water and sugar in a medium saucepan over high heat. Bring to a boil, stirring until the sugar dissolves.

Remove from the heat and cool to room temperature. Add the lemon and lime juices and stir to combine. Refrigerate in an airtight container for up to 1 week.

FROZEN LIMEADE MARGARITA

MAKES 6 TO 8 DRINKS

Kosher salt or Chile Sea Salt
(below)
Lime wedge for rubbing the
rims
6 cups crushed ice
1 (12-ounce) can frozen
limeade
½ to ¾ cup gold or silver
tequila
¼ cup triple sec or other
orange liqueur
Lime wedges or slices for
garnish (optional)

In 1971 the Dallas restaurateur Mariano Martinez
revolutionized the cocktail industry when he invented the
world's first frozen margarita machine. The Smithsonian's
National Museum of American History considers this so
important that they now have that original machine on display.
We churn out tons of frozen margaritas from our own machines.
But you can make a very good one in your home blender using
frozen limeade. It's actually better to use the concentrate than
fresh-squeezed lime juice in this case because the extra ice
dilutes it so much you can hardly taste it.

—————

Pour some salt onto a small saucer. Wet the rims of six to eight
margarita glasses with the lime wedge and dip the rims in the salt.

Fill a blender with ice. Add the limeade, tequila, and triple sec and
blend. Pour into glasses and garnish with lime wedges, if desired.

CHILE SEA SALT

MAKES ⅓ CUP

¼ cup sea salt
2 tablespoons ground chile de árbol
or cayenne pepper

—————

Mix together the salt and chile de árbol. Store at room temperature
in a covered container for up to 3 months.

MEXICAN MINT JULEP

MAKES 1 DRINK

Jose Cuervo Reserva de la Familia (or other añejo tequila) is oak cured and has a slight bourbon taste. So why not use it to make a mint julep with a Mexican twist?

_____

6 fresh mint leaves

1 teaspoon confectioners'
   sugar

2 teaspoons water

Cracked ice

2½ ounces Jose Cuervo
   Reserva de la Familia
   or other añejo tequila

Muddle 4 of the mint leaves, the sugar, and water in a chilled 10- to 12-ounce Tom Collins or beer glass. Fill the glass with ice. Pour in the tequila. Stir until the glass mists. Garnish with the remaining mint leaves and serve.

EDDIE PALMER

MAKES 8 TO 10 DRINKS

At Taqueria del Sol, we take pride in serving fresh-made tea. Years ago I came across an Arnold Palmer, which is half tea and half lemonade. The famous golfer used to order it at country club bars and that's how it got its name. I like mine with tequila and lime juice.

---

2 quarts fresh-brewed hot
   black tea
1 cup sugar, plus additional
   as desired
½ cup lime juice
1 cup Hornitos Reposado
   tequila
Ice cubes
Lime wedges

Combine the tea and sugar in a large pitcher and stir until the sugar is dissolved. Taste and add more sugar if you like your tea sweeter. Cool to room temperature. Stir in the lime juice and tequila.

Serve in tumblers over ice, with lime wedges for garnish.

TEQUILA-MANGO SMOOTHIE

MAKES 1 DRINK

This is similar to a frozen margarita, with a tropical twist. I like to dip the rim in a mixture of salt and chile de árbol first so the salt and the spiciness contrast with the fruit.

½ lemon or lime wedge

Chile Sea Salt (page 254)

1 cup diced mango

1½ ounces gold tequila

1½ ounces Lemon Syrup
   (below)

6 ounces ice cubes

Rub the rim of a margarita glass with the lemon wedge. Pour the chile salt onto a small plate and dip the rim into the salt.

Puree the mango, tequila, lemon syrup, and ice cubes in a blender until smooth. Pour into the glass and serve.

LEMON SYRUP

MAKES 1½ CUPS

1 cup sugar

¾ cup water

½ cup lemon juice

Combine all the ingredients in a small container and stir until the sugar dissolves. Cover and store in the refrigerator up to 1 week.

RED, GREEN, AND YELLOW MICHELADAS

Micheladas—beer mixed with a spicy, refreshing blend of peppers and usually tomatoes—are made for Sunday mornings after a night of partying. Instead of a Bloody Mary, this is what we Mexicans drink. When you have a hangover, the best thing you can do is drink another beer. At least that's what works for me! It levels the sugar and takes the dizziness away. There's lots of vitamin C in the peppers and the citrus, so it rehydrates you very fast. If you're having a party, make all three of these micheladas and let guests choose. Even if you didn't have any alcohol the night before, this is a great drink.

MICHELADA

MAKES 1 DRINK

2 lime wedges

Coarse salt (optional)

Ice

1 to 2 tablespoons lime juice

4 ounces Red, Green, or Yellow Michelada
   Mix (recipes follow)

6 ounces Corona or other pale lager
   (I like Corona Light)

Rub the rim of a 16-ounce beer glass with 1 lime wedge and dip the rim into a saucer of coarse salt, if desired. Fill the glass with ice. Add the remaining ingredients and stir. Garnish with the remaining lime wedge.

RED MICHELADA MIX

MAKES 6 DRINKS

1 (6-ounce) can tomato paste

1 red jalapeño, stemmed and cut in half
(remove some or all of the seeds and
membranes for less heat)

½ cup chopped red bell pepper

½ cup chopped celery

¾ teaspoon granulated onion

¾ teaspoon ground white pepper

¼ teaspoon granulated garlic

½ cup lemon juice

2 cups water

Puree all the ingredients in a blender until smooth. Pour through a fine-mesh strainer into a container and refrigerate for up to 3 days, until ready to use.

GREEN MICHELADA MIX

MAKES 6 DRINKS

¾ cup diced green bell pepper

¼ cup chopped celery

1 tablespoon green habanero sauce,
   such as El Yucateco

¾ teaspoon ground white pepper

¾ teaspoon granulated onion

¼ teaspoon granulated garlic

½ cup lemon juice

2 cups water

Proceed as directed for Red Michelada Mix.

YELLOW MICHELADA MIX

MAKES 6 DRINKS

¾ cup chopped yellow bell pepper

¼ cup chopped celery

1 habanero, stemmed and cut in half
   (remove some or all of the seeds and
   membranes for less heat)

1 small yellow tomato, chopped (about
   ½ cup)

¾ teaspoon granulated onion

¾ teaspoon ground white pepper

¼ teaspoon granulated garlic

½ cup lemon juice

2 cups water

Proceed as directed for Red Michelada Mix.

BASIL LIMONADA

MAKES 4 DRINKS

Because limes are mostly seedless, you can just quarter them and puree them, peel and all. The peels give the drink a fresh, slightly bitter taste. This also makes a good base for a cocktail— just add a splash of tequila, vodka, or gin. Or if you like bubbles, use sparkling water instead of plain water.

———————

½ cup sugar

4 cups water

1 tablespoon chopped fresh basil

2 to 3 limes, quartered

Ice

Place the sugar and water in a large pitcher and stir until the sugar dissolves. Measure out 1 cup.

Place the basil and limes in a blender with the 1 cup sugar water and puree. Pour the mixture through a fine-mesh strainer back into the pitcher with the sugar water, mashing with a whisk or wooden spoon to eliminate any pulp.

Taste and add more sugar, if desired. Serve over ice.

AGUAS FRESCAS (MEXICAN FRUIT COOLERS)

MAKES 8 DRINKS

Aguas frescas, water-based fruit drinks, are a cool way to make your fresh fruit go further—especially in the summertime when you might have a larger watermelon than you know what to do with, or peaches that are starting to shrivel. These Mexican street drinks are traditionally very sweet and thin, but you can easily adjust the water and sugar to your taste and the sweetness of your fruit. Watermelon is the classic and is hard to beat. But I also like the tropical flavors of mangoes and peaches together. We always have fresh oranges at the restaurant—which are free for the taking in big wooden bowls—and I sometimes peel and chop the extras to blend into a cold drink as a healthier alternative to a soda. You can get creative by adding a handful of mint or other herb, or fresh ginger. Substitute sparkling water for plain if you prefer bubbles. Serve these aguas frescas with a lemon or lime wedge if you like more acidity.

½ cup sugar

4 cups water

4 cups chopped fruit
  (watermelon, cantaloupe,
  pineapple, papaya,
  strawberries, oranges,
  peaches, mangoes, or any
  combination)

Ice cubes

Lemon or lime wedges
  (optional)

Stir the sugar and water together in a large pitcher until the sugar dissolves. Measure out 1 cup. Puree the fruit and the 1 cup sugar water in a blender. Pour the mixture through a fine-mesh strainer back into the pitcher with the sugar water, mashing with a whisk or wooden spoon to eliminate any pulp.

Taste and add more sugar, if desired. Serve over ice, with a lemon or lime wedge, if desired.

*Watermelon and Orange
Aguas Frescas and Basil
Limonada (page 263)*

MEXICAN CINNAMON TEA

MAKES 5 CUPS

Mexican cinnamon sticks (*canela*) are softer, lighter in color, and easier to grind than the cinnamon sticks sold in the U.S. Besides using canela for cooking, we often boil it for tea. We drink it in the morning, after a heavy meal, or anytime, as you would hot tea. Cinnamon is rich in nutrients, and this tea is also used for medicinal purposes. Because it is naturally sweet, not everyone adds sugar, but I like to put a few spoonfuls in mine. You can boil this and keep it in the refrigerator and reheat whenever you like. Canela can be found in any Latin market or online. This tea is also good with regular cinnamon sticks.

———————

6 cups water
1½ ounces canela (Mexican cinnamon sticks)
Sugar
Milk or cream (optional)

Fill a medium saucepan with 5 cups of the water. Add the cinnamon sticks and boil over high heat for 8 minutes. Add the remaining 1 cup of water, reduce the heat to medium-low, and simmer for 2 minutes. Add sugar to taste and a splash of milk or cream if you like. Serve hot. The tea can be covered and refrigerated for up to 1 week and reheated.

MEXICAN COFFEE

MAKES 1 DRINK

This after-dinner cocktail can easily double as dessert. In Mexico, this is often served at funerals. With everything else in this drink, don't waste the good tequila on it—any cheap brand will do.

———————

½ cup hot coffee

2 tablespoons sweetened condensed milk

1 ounce gold or other inexpensive tequila

Whipped cream for topping

Ground cinnamon for sprinkling

Stir together the coffee, condensed milk, and tequila. Top with as much or as little whipped cream as you like and sprinkle with ground cinnamon.

SWEET TREATS FOR MY SOUTHERN FRIENDS

Chapter Eleven

NATILLA *274*

TROPICAL FLAN WITH RUM CARAMEL *276*

CHOCOLATE CHIMICHANGAS
  WITH TEQUILA CREAM SAUCE *278*
    —WHITE CHOCOLATE CHIMICHANGAS
    WITH RASPBERRY SAUCE *280*

SWEET POTATO CHEESECAKE *281*

MEXICAN BREAD PUDDING (CAPIROTADA) *282*

ANCHO CHILE PRALINES *285*

GREEN CHILE–APPLE-PINEAPPLE TURNOVERS
  WITH LIME ZEST GLAZE *286*
    —BUTTERY PASTRY DOUGH *287*

Some of these desserts are more Southern than Mexican, and some are more Mexican than Southern.

I've never been big on dessert. When I want something sweet, I'm more likely to make myself something simple, like Green Peach Salad with Simple Lime Dressing and a scoop of cottage cheese (page 229).

Southerners have a big sweet tooth, though, and over the years, I have challenged myself to develop desserts that satisfy their cravings, but with a Mexican twist. Like most Mexican families, we didn't have an oven, just a gas stovetop, so things like cakes and flans were something you had to order in restaurants, which we never went to. A piece of chocolate, a candied sweet potato, or a simple stirred custard was about as sophisticated a dessert as we'd ever get, unless it was a holiday, a birthday, or a funeral. On those occasions we would have sweet tamales filled with fruits and nuts and topped with sprinkles. For Lent we had *capirotada*, our traditional bread pudding.

Rather than attempt to reproduce those dishes, I turn to them to help inspire me to create something new, with tastes a Southerner will love. And people go crazy for them no matter where they are from. Some of these desserts are more Southern than Mexican, and some are more Mexican than Southern. They are ways for me to show hospitality Eddie style.

NATILLA

MAKES 6 TO 8 SERVINGS

Other than the oranges offered from big wooden bowls on the table, Taqueria del Sol has one dessert, which you will not see on the menu: natilla. It's a creamy, refreshing vanilla pudding infused with cinnamon, which is popular throughout Mexico. I like to eat it warm, straight out of the pan, on a cold day. But most people like it chilled, and that is how we serve it. Traditionally it's thickened with egg yolks, but years ago I wanted to create a lighter version and switched to cornstarch. It was very popular at our previous restaurant, Sundown Café. I started making pans of it at Taqueria del Sol for customers who remembered it from our earlier restaurant and begged us to put it on the menu. Now it's available every day—but you have to know to ask for it.

½ cup cold whole milk

½ cup cornstarch

4 cups half-and-half

1 cup sugar

1½ teaspoons vanilla

1 cinnamon stick

Chocolate syrup for drizzling

Ground cinnamon for sprinkling

Combine the milk and cornstarch in a small bowl and whisk until smooth. Set aside.

Stir the half-and-half, sugar, vanilla, and cinnamon stick together in a medium saucepan over medium heat. When the mixture begins to bubble, about 5 minutes, gradually add the cornstarch mixture in a steady stream, stirring constantly with a wooden spoon until it begins to form thick ribbons.

Remove from the heat. Discard the cinnamon stick.

Pour the mixture into a medium serving dish or into 6 to 8 small individual bowls. Cover with plastic wrap and refrigerate until cold.

To serve, drizzle with chocolate syrup and sprinkle with cinnamon.

TROPICAL FLAN WITH RUM CARAMEL

MAKES 8 TO 12 SERVINGS

Flan is so often associated with Mexican cooking that I initially resisted making it myself. How could I possibly improve it? Then I had the idea to infuse the creamy custard with passion fruit puree, which Latin markets sell in the frozen foods section, along with mango puree. (I keep them both on hand for smoothies, marinades, and other things.) And I add a shot of rum or brandy to the caramel. I love the result, and you will, too—the tropical fruit adds an unexpected twist that is perfectly complemented by the caramel. My method is much easier than most, since you can just throw all the custard ingredients into a blender while you make the caramel (also easy, so long as you watch the pan). Any concentrated fruit puree can be used for the custard, though I don't recommend fresh fruit, as it may be too watery and the flavor won't be as intense.

———————

Heat the oven to 350 degrees, with a rack in the center.

To make the caramel: Combine the sugar, water, and rum in a large skillet. Turn the heat to medium. Without stirring, wait for the mixture to turn brown around the edges, then swirl the pan around so that it caramelizes evenly (you can stir at this point).

When it becomes a deep amber color, remove from the heat and pour into a 2-quart baking dish to evenly coat the bottom, leaving a little in the skillet if making the fruit garnish. Set the dish in a larger dish. Let cool.

To make the fruit garnish: Immediately add the fruit for the garnish to the pan with the caramel, swirling and stirring to coat. Cool, transfer to a covered container, and refrigerate.

Meanwhile, set a kettle of water on to boil.

To make the custard: Puree the eggs, condensed milk, milk, and fruit puree in a blender until smooth.

Caramel

1 cup sugar

½ cup water

2 tablespoons rum, brandy, or
   other liqueur (optional)

Fruit Garnish (optional)

1 or 2 mangoes, peaches, or
   other fruit, peeled, seeded,
   and thinly sliced

Custard

7 large eggs

1 (14-ounce) can sweetened
   condensed milk

1 cup whole milk

½ cup frozen passion fruit
   puree, thawed (or mango
   puree, or orange juice
   concentrate)

Pour the custard mixture over the caramel. Carefully pour the boiling water into the larger pan so that it reaches halfway up the sides of the baking dish.

Bake for 50 to 60 minutes, until the center is set but still slightly jiggly. Carefully remove the custard dish from the larger pan.

Cover with plastic wrap and chill for at least 4 hours. Loosen the edges of the flan and invert onto a serving platter.

If desired, arrange the fruit slices over the top when ready to serve. Cut the flan into slices and serve on plates drizzled with some of the caramel.

CHOCOLATE CHIMICHANGAS WITH TEQUILA CREAM SAUCE

MAKES 8 SERVINGS

The deep-fried burrito better known as the chimichanga has been standard on Tex-Mex and Southwest restaurant menus for decades. If you make them with chocolate, these fried pouches become a dessert that is hard to stop eating, especially if you present them the way I do, in a silky, spiked custard sauce.

––––––––––

Working with 1 tortilla at a time, wrap in a paper towel and heat in the microwave for 10 seconds, until soft. Transfer to a work area. Spread ¼ cup chocolate chips across the tortilla, leaving a 1-inch border on each side. Brush the top edge and sides of the tortilla with a little egg white. Fold in the sides of the tortilla, then fold the bottom up, over, and around the chocolate. Roll the tortilla up toward the top edge like an egg roll and press to seal. Place it seam side down on a large plate. Repeat with the remaining 7 tortillas and chocolate chips. Chill in the refrigerator, covered, for at least 20 minutes or up to 24 hours.

Line a baking sheet with paper towels and set aside. Place a cooling rack on top. Heat 1 inch of vegetable oil in a large skillet over high heat until it is 375 degrees. Add the chimichangas, seam side down, in 1 layer, working in batches. Fry until golden brown, about 3 minutes, turning once if necessary. Drain on the cooling rack. Return the oil to 375 degrees between each batch. Dust with confectioners' sugar while still warm.

To serve, spread ¼ cup cream sauce on a plate. Drizzle decoratively with 1 to 2 teaspoons chocolate syrup. Top with a warm chimichanga.

8 (6-inch) flour tortillas

2 cups miniature chocolate chips

1 egg white, beaten

Vegetable oil for frying

Confectioners' sugar for dusting

2 cups Tequila Cream Sauce (page 280), chilled

Chocolate syrup for drizzling

From top: Chocolate Chimichangas and White Chocolate Chimichangas with Raspberry Sauce (page 280)

TEQUILA CREAM SAUCE

MAKES 3 CUPS

1 large egg, plus 1 large egg yolk

2 tablespoons cornstarch

¾ cup whole milk

Pinch of salt

2 cups heavy cream

½ cup sugar

2 tablespoons gold or other inexpensive
tequila, or to taste

2 tablespoons orange liqueur, such as
triple sec, Cointreau, or Grand Marnier,
or to taste

¼ teaspoon vanilla

1 cinnamon stick

This recipe makes more sauce than you'll need for Chocolate Chimichangas. But don't worry: It won't go to waste. Drizzle the leftover sauce over angel food cake or fresh strawberries.

———————

Whisk together the egg, egg yolk, cornstarch, ½ cup of the milk, and the salt in a large bowl until smooth.

Put the cream, sugar, tequila, orange liqueur, vanilla, and cinnamon stick into a medium, heavy-bottomed saucepan over high heat. Bring to a boil. Remove from the heat.

Continually whisking the egg mixture, pour about half of the hot cream mixture in a steady stream into it. Then whisk this mixture back into the saucepan with the remaining cream mixture.

Return the saucepan to the stove over medium heat and cook, whisking constantly, until the mixture thickens and comes to a simmer, about 3 minutes. Remove from the heat. Pour through a fine-mesh strainer into a bowl, discard the cinnamon stick, and stir in the remaining ¼ cup milk. Let the sauce cool to room temperature before covering with plastic wrap and chilling for at least 1 hour before serving. The sauce will keep, covered and refrigerated, for up to 4 days.

VARIATION

WHITE CHOCOLATE CHIMICHANGAS WITH RASPBERRY SAUCE

Proceed as directed for Chocolate Chimichangas, using mini white chocolate chips instead of dark chocolate chips for the filling. To make the sauce, heat 2 cups raspberries with 1 cup sugar in a saucepan just until the sugar melts. Puree in a blender, strain out the seeds if you like, and chill it until you're ready to serve.

SWEET POTATO CHEESECAKE

MAKES ONE 10-INCH CHEESECAKE (12 TO 16 SERVINGS)

Mexicans and Southerners alike love candied sweet potatoes and cream cheese–filled pies. So I wanted to mix those ideas into one great dessert. This luxurious cheesecake is the best of both worlds and is the only dessert you'll need to serve at your next holiday dinner.

Crust

½ cup sugar

2 cups graham cracker crumbs

8 tablespoons (1 stick) unsalted butter, at room temperature

Filling

3 cups peeled, cooked, and mashed or pureed sweet potatoes (see page 140; from about 2 pounds raw), or unsweetened canned puree

24 ounces (three 8-ounce packages) cream cheese, at room temperature

¾ cup sugar

8 large eggs

½ cup heavy cream

1½ teaspoons vanilla

¼ teaspoon ground cloves

Heat the oven to 350 degrees, with a rack in the center. Wrap several layers of heavy-duty foil around the bottom of a 10-inch springform pan.

To make the crust: Place the sugar, graham crackers, and butter in a food processor and pulse to combine. Press the mixture into the pan. Bake for 10 minutes, or until lightly browned. Set aside to cool.

Increase the oven temperature to 425 degrees.

Place a roasting pan large enough to hold the springform pan in the oven. Pour in ½ inch of water.

To make the filling: Put the sweet potatoes, cream cheese, sugar, eggs, cream, vanilla, and cloves in a large bowl. With an electric mixer, beat on medium speed until well combined and smooth, stopping to scrape down the sides of the bowl once.

Pour into the baked crust. Set the cheesecake in the water bath. Loosely cover the cheesecake with foil and bake for 1 hour to 1 hour and 20 minutes, or until set.

Remove from the oven and from the water bath, and let cool. Cover and refrigerate for at least 4 hours or overnight before slicing and serving. The cheesecake can be refrigerated, covered, for up to 5 days.

MEXICAN BREAD PUDDING (CAPIROTADA)

MAKES 6 TO 8 SERVINGS

Syrup

1 pound piloncillos (see
    headnote), cane sugar,
    turbinado sugar, or brown
    sugar
3 cups water
2 cinnamon sticks, preferably
    Mexican (canela)
6 cloves

8 ounces French bread or
    4 bolillo rolls (page 185),
    cut into ¼-inch-thick pieces
4 tablespoons (½ stick) butter,
    melted
1 cup golden raisins
1 cup coarsely chopped pecans
1½ cups crushed animal
    crackers
1 cup crumbled queso fresco
    or grated Monterey Jack
    cheese
¾ cup shredded sweetened
    coconut
Ice cream (optional)
Colored sprinkles (optional)

Bread pudding is served all over the South—in the finest restaurants and in the humblest cafés. Mexicans love bread pudding, too, but for us it's a special treat we typically eat only during Lent. It is not like any bread pudding you have had in the U.S., but the flavors should taste very familiar—a little like the inside of a cinnamon roll, with the gooeyness of pecan pie. The exact ingredients vary with whatever's in the cook's kitchen cabinet that needs to be used up, but they usually include toasted and buttered bread, dried fruits, nuts, and mild cheese. My mother often added animal crackers, and I still find their crunchy texture works well in this mixture. Whereas my mother steamed her bread pudding on top of the stove, I bake mine.

Instead of being held together by an eggy custard, the pudding is drenched in a warm syrup spiced with cinnamon and cloves that is made by melting *piloncillos*—unrefined sugar molded in cones and sold in Mexican markets or online—with water. Turbinado or brown sugar works just as well. There is deep religious meaning behind the main ingredients: The bread symbolizes Christ's body, the syrup is his blood, the cinnamon and cloves are the wood and the nails of the cross, and the melted cheese signifies the holy burial shroud. As serious as its message is, the dish is very festive and often served with ice cream and colored sprinkles. This bread pudding is even good for breakfast as a coffee cake.

———————

To make the syrup: Combine the piloncillos, water, cinnamon sticks, and cloves in a medium saucepan set over medium-high heat. Bring to a boil, reduce the heat to maintain a simmer, and simmer for 5 to 10 minutes, until slightly thickened. Remove from the heat; cover and let steep while you prepare the remainder of the dish. This step can be done a day ahead.

Heat the broiler to high, with one rack set in the middle of the oven and one 4 or 5 inches from the broiler source.

Brush the bread with 2 to 3 tablespoons of the butter. Place the pieces in a single layer on a sheet pan and set under the broiler until lightly toasted, about 1 minute (watch carefully). Remove from the oven and set aside until ready to use.

Set the oven temperature to 325 degrees. Brush a deep 8-inch square pan or 2-quart casserole dish with the remaining 1 to 2 tablespoons butter.

Place one-third of the bread in a single layer in the baking dish. Top with one-third of the raisins, pecans, animal crackers, cheese, and coconut. Remove the spices from the syrup and ladle one-third of the syrup over the mixture. Let the syrup soak into the bread for about 15 minutes, then repeat the layering with the remaining ingredients two more times, finishing with the syrup. Let the syrup soak into the bread for 15 minutes.

Cover the pan tightly with foil and bake for 45 minutes, then uncover and bake for 10 minutes longer, or until the top of the pudding is golden brown. Serve warm or at room temperature, with ice cream and garnished with sprinkles, if desired. The pudding will keep for several days, tightly covered, at room temperature.

ANCHO CHILE PRALINES

MAKES 15 TO 20 PRALINES

The U.S. produces about 75 percent of the world's pecans, and Mexico comes in second. Pecans are the key ingredient in pralines, the creamy, caramel-like confections sold in candy stores and restaurants all over New Orleans and much of the rest of the South, including Texas, where I first tried them. I have added a hint of smoky, tingly heat to them with a spoonful of ground ancho chile. Even big spice companies like McCormick now sell ground ancho chile, but I prefer the flavor of freshly ground (see page 14).

---

14 ounces light brown sugar
   (about 2 cups packed)
⅔ cup evaporated milk
2 cups chopped pecan halves
2 tablespoons unsalted butter
1 tablespoon vanilla
1½ teaspoons ground ancho
   chile

Line two baking sheets with parchment paper and set aside.

Combine the brown sugar and milk in a large saucepan over medium-high heat and cook, stirring constantly, until the mixture reaches 235 to 238 degrees on a candy thermometer, about 4 minutes.

Stir in the pecans, butter, vanilla, and ground chile and continue cooking, stirring, for 1 minute. Remove from the heat and set aside for 2 minutes.

Drop heaping tablespoonfuls onto the baking sheets. Set aside until firm, 15 to 20 minutes. Store in an airtight container at room temperature for up to 1 week.

GREEN CHILE–APPLE-PINEAPPLE TURNOVERS WITH LIME ZEST GLAZE

MAKES 6 LARGE TURNOVERS

Filling

2 tablespoons butter

3 cups peeled, cored, and
finely chopped apples
(Granny Smith, Jonagold,
Winesap, or other baking
apples)

1 cup finely chopped fresh
pineapple

¼ cup finely chopped roasted
(see page 12) and peeled
New Mexico chiles, fresh
or canned (drain well)

¼ cup plus 1 tablespoon sugar

1 teaspoon ground cinnamon

Pinch of ground nutmeg

Pinch of ground cloves

Pinch of salt

Double recipe Buttery Pastry
Dough (opposite), chilled

1 egg yolk, beaten with
1 teaspoon water

All-purpose flour for sprinkling

Lime Zest Glaze

2 cups confectioners' sugar

4 teaspoons whole milk

1 teaspoon grated lime zest

These turnovers are like a cross between Southern fried pies and
Mexican empanadas, with a filling that blends local and tropical
fruit with just enough chile to add a subtle kick. Other mild to
medium-hot chiles will work when Hatch chiles aren't in season,
including the canned ones in the supermarket.

————————

To make the filling: Melt the butter in a medium saucepan over
medium heat. Add the apples, pineapple, and chiles and cook, stirring
frequently, for 3 minutes. Stir in ¼ cup of the sugar, the cinnamon,
nutmeg, cloves, and salt. Reduce the heat to low and simmer for
5 minutes, or until the apples are tender and most of the liquid is
gone. Set aside to cool. The filling will keep, covered and refrigerated,
overnight.

To make the turnovers: Heat the oven to 400 degrees, with a rack in
the center. Remove one dough ball from the refrigerator. Divide it into
three evenly sized balls. Sprinkle a work surface with flour and use a
rolling pin to roll each ball into a ⅛-inch-thick circle 7 to 8 inches in
diameter. Place a small plate or saucer over the pastry and trim the
edges with a knife to make a neater circle, if you like.

Place about 3 tablespoons of filling in the center of each circle,
leaving any liquid behind. Fold over the pastry, seal the edges, and
crimp. Brush the tops and edges with some of the beaten egg yolk
and sprinkle the turnovers with some of the remaining 1 tablespoon
sugar. Cut several air vents on top of each with a sharp knife.

Place the pastries on a baking sheet lined with parchment paper
and bake until golden, 30 to 35 minutes. Transfer to a cooling rack.
While the first batch is baking, repeat with the remaining dough ball
and filling, place on another baking sheet, and bake and cool as before.

Meanwhile, to make the glaze: Whisk all the ingredients together
in a bowl. Set aside for at least 5 minutes before drizzling over the
cooled turnovers.

BUTTERY PASTRY DOUGH

**MAKES 1 DOUBLE-CRUST PIE CRUST
OR ENOUGH FOR 6 LARGE TURNOVERS**

2 cups all-purpose flour

1 teaspoon baking powder

½ teaspoon salt

1½ sticks (6 ounces) cold unsalted butter,
   cut into small cubes

3 to 4 tablespoons ice water

Whisk the flour, baking powder, and salt together in a large bowl. Lightly work in the butter with your fingertips until coarse crumbs form, with some streaks of fat remaining.

Sprinkle the water evenly over the mixture and mix lightly with a fork until it is all absorbed and the dough just holds together. Add a little more water if needed to create a dough ball. Divide into 2 balls, wrap each ball in plastic wrap, and refrigerate for at least 1 hour. Or freeze for up to 2 months and thaw overnight in the refrigerator before using.

BASIC RECIPES

Chapter Twelve

COATING MIXES *290*
   —SEASONED FLOUR COATING *290*
   —SPICY-HOT COATING *290*
   —CRUNCHY POTATO COATING *290*
   —CRACKER COATING *290*
   —EXTRA-CRISPY COATING *290*

CAJUN SPICE MIX *291*

ANCHO (OR GUAJILLO) CHILE PUREE *292*

THREE GREAT SOUTHERN BARBECUE SAUCES
  WITH HINTS OF MEXICO *293*
   —MEMPHIS-STYLE BARBECUE SAUCE *293*
   —WACO BARBECUE SAUCE *294*
   —ATLANTA BARBECUE SAUCE *294*

HOT CHILE PEPPER VINEGAR *296*

CHILE DE ÁRBOL VINEGAR *296*

BLOND ROUX *298*

BUTTER BLEND *299*

HOMEMADE LARD AND CHICHARRONES *299*

COATING MIXES

Texture is as important as flavor in my dishes—especially when it comes to tacos. My coating mixtures can be mixed and matched with various meats and vegetables before frying or sautéing, adding both flavor and crunch. They keep for 3 months tightly covered and are great to have on hand when you are short on ideas for dinner. Use as directed in the recipes that call for them, or swap them out. Then add gravy, a ribbon of flavored mayonnaise, or a drizzle of a simple sauce, and you have created your own masterpiece!

SEASONED FLOUR COATING

In a container, combine 2 cups all-purpose flour with $4\frac{1}{2}$ teaspoons ground black pepper and $1\frac{1}{2}$ teaspoons salt. Makes 2 cups.

SPICY-HOT COATING

In a container, combine 2 cups all-purpose flour with $1\frac{1}{2}$ teaspoons ground cayenne pepper, $\frac{1}{2}$ teaspoon dried oregano, $\frac{1}{2}$ teaspoon granulated garlic, $\frac{1}{2}$ teaspoon granulated onion, $\frac{1}{2}$ teaspoon ground white pepper, and $\frac{1}{2}$ teaspoon salt. Makes 2 cups.

CRUNCHY POTATO COATING

In a container, combine $1\frac{1}{4}$ cups flaked instant mashed potatoes with $\frac{3}{4}$ cup all-purpose flour and 1 teaspoon salt. Makes 2 cups.

CRACKER COATING

In a container, combine 2 cups coarsely ground saltine crackers with 1 cup Maseca masa harina and 1 tablespoon ground black pepper. Makes 3 cups.

EXTRA-CRISPY COATING

In a food processor, pulse 1 cup panko crumbs until it reaches the consistency of coarse meal. Transfer to a container and stir in $\frac{1}{2}$ cup all-purpose flour, $\frac{1}{2}$ cup Maseca masa harina, $\frac{1}{4}$ cup cornstarch, and $1\frac{1}{2}$ teaspoons salt. Makes about 2 cups.

CAJUN SPICE MIX

MAKES ½ CUP

2 tablespoons salt

2 tablespoons dried oregano

2 tablespoons granulated onion

2 teaspoons paprika

1½ teaspoons cayenne pepper

1½ teaspoons ground white
   pepper

1½ teaspoons dried basil

1½ teaspoons granulated
   garlic

1½ teaspoons dried thyme

Mix all the ingredients well. Store tightly covered for up to 3 months.

ANCHO (OR GUAJILLO) CHILE PUREE

MAKES ABOUT 1 CUP

I keep containers of chile puree in the refrigerator to add to sauces, chilis, and mashed potatoes. I even add it to chocolate and desserts. Guajillos can be substituted for the anchos in this formula. Use this method to experiment with different combinations of your own. Don't let the peppers cook for longer than 15 minutes as they can turn bitter. Make a big batch at one time and freeze the extra in ice cube trays or small containers.

---

8 dried ancho chiles
8 dried chiles de árbol

Combine the chiles in a medium saucepan and cover with 4 cups water. Bring to a boil over high heat and cook until the chiles are soft, about 15 minutes. Remove the stems from the peppers and transfer the peppers with about ½ cup of the cooking liquid to a blender and puree. Add more of the cooking liquid if necessary to create a smooth puree. Press through a fine-mesh strainer and discard the solids. Store the puree in a tightly covered jar in the refrigerator for up to 2 weeks or in the freezer for up to 2 months.

THREE GREAT SOUTHERN BARBECUE SAUCES WITH HINTS OF MEXICO

Barbecue sauce in the South is a lot like salsa in Mexico—every region has its own, and every recipe will vary from one cook to the next. I enjoy playing with different sauce combinations just as I do with salsas. Many pit masters keep their recipes top secret, but I don't mind telling you how I make mine. These three sauces go well with all kinds of smoked and grilled meats but have the different flavors I associate with the three cities that have most shaped my thinking on Southern barbecue.

MEMPHIS-STYLE BARBECUE SAUCE

MAKES 4 CUPS

1 tablespoon vegetable oil

½ cup chopped onion

1½ teaspoons chopped garlic

1½ teaspoons ground chile de árbol or cayenne pepper or red pepper flakes

1 lemon

4 cups ketchup

¼ cup Worcestershire sauce

2 teaspoons chopped pickled jalapeños

1½ teaspoons ground black pepper

8 tablespoons (1 stick) butter

1 teaspoon salt

1½ ounces tequila (optional)

This thick red sauce simmered with Worcestershire, onion, and strong spices stands up well to a rack of ribs or a platter of pulled pork. The juice and squeezed rind of a whole lemon give it a zesty undertone. A splash of tequila adds another layer.

I use this spicy tomato-based sauce for Memphis Tacos (page 67).

———

Heat the oil in a medium saucepan over medium heat until it shimmers. Add the onion, garlic, and chile de árbol and sauté for 3 to 5 minutes, until the onion is translucent. Reduce the heat to low. Cut the lemon in half and discard the seeds. Add the juice of the lemon and the lemon halves to the pan. Add the ketchup, Worcestershire sauce, jalapeños, and black pepper and cook for 5 minutes, stirring occasionally. Stir in the butter and salt and continue to cook, stirring occasionally, until the butter is melted and incorporated into the sauce. Stir in the tequila, if using. Remove and discard the lemon halves and simmer for 5 more minutes. Taste and adjust the seasonings as desired. The sauce keeps for 2 weeks or longer, covered and refrigerated.

WACO BARBECUE SAUCE

MAKES ABOUT 5 CUPS

4 cups ketchup

1 tablespoon lemon juice

1 tablespoon white vinegar

1 tablespoon Worcestershire sauce

1 tablespoon green habanero sauce,
   such as El Yucateco

4 tablespoons (½ stick) butter

1 tablespoon ground black pepper

1 tablespoon granulated onion

1½ teaspoons granulated garlic

1 cup water

This smooth, peppery sauce, with splashes of acid and the spices used for brisket rub, is especially good with barbecued brisket (page 65).

———————

Combine all the ingredients in a medium saucepan. Cook over low heat, stirring frequently, for 5 to 10 minutes, until the butter is melted. Keep warm until ready to serve. The sauce keeps for 2 weeks or longer, covered and refrigerated.

ATLANTA BARBECUE SAUCE

MAKES ABOUT 6½ CUPS

36 ounces Coca-Cola

1 cup light or dark brown sugar

8 tablespoons (1 stick) butter

½ cup apple cider vinegar

¼ cup Worcestershire sauce

1 tablespoon ground chile de árbol
   or cayenne pepper

1 tablespoon granulated onion

1½ teaspoons granulated garlic

3 cups ketchup

Salt

When boiled, the cola reduces to a rich syrup that adds a complex component to the tomato base. This sauce goes well with beef, pork, or chicken.

———————

Pour the cola into a medium saucepan and bring to a boil over high heat. Boil until reduced to 1 cup, about 45 minutes.

Reduce the heat to medium. Add the sugar and butter and continue to cook, stirring occasionally, until the butter and sugar are melted and the mixture is syrupy, 3 to 4 minutes. Add the apple cider vinegar, Worcestershire sauce, chile de árbol, granulated onion, and granulated garlic and whisk to combine.

Remove from the heat, stir in the ketchup, and set aside for 5 minutes, or until ready to use. Season to taste with salt. The sauce keeps for 2 weeks or longer, covered and refrigerated.

HOT CHILE PEPPER VINEGAR

MAKES 1½ CUPS

At any Southern meat and three–type restaurant, you will see bottles of vinegar filled with chile peppers on the table, usually beside the Tabasco, for customers to season their turnip greens and other vegetables. This is a great way to use whatever hot peppers you have growing. The hotter the better.

————————

6 ounces fresh small hot
   chiles, any kind
1½ cups white vinegar
¼ teaspoon salt

Wash the chiles thoroughly and pat dry. Prick with a fork. Place them into a sterilized 1-pint jar. In a bowl, combine the vinegar and salt and stir until the salt has dissolved. Pour over the peppers and seal with a lid. Store the vinegar at room temperature for at least 24 hours before using. The vinegar can be stored in the refrigerator for up to 6 months.

CHILE DE ÁRBOL VINEGAR

MAKES 1¼ CUPS

The seasoned rice vinegar lends a subtle sweetness to this spicy vinegar.

————————

3 dried chiles de árbol,
   stemmed
1¼ cups seasoned rice vinegar

Place the peppers in a small saucepan and cover with water. Bring to a boil and cook for 10 to 15 minutes, until softened. Drain. Place the peppers and vinegar in a blender and puree. Pour through a fine-mesh strainer. Refrigerate in an airtight container for up to 6 months.

BLOND ROUX

MAKES ABOUT ⅓ CUP OR ENOUGH TO THICKEN 1 QUART LIQUID

I like sauce and gravy—and lots of it. You can thicken sauces and gravies with a paste of flour (or cornstarch) and cold water, or make a *beurre manié* the way the French do, by blending softened butter and flour with your fingers or a spoon, and stirring in bits at the end of the cooking. You have to be very careful with these methods, though, because if you don't cook the sauce long enough, it will have a raw flour taste. But you will never have this problem if you make a blond, or white, roux, as cooks do in Louisiana. In a blond roux, the butter and flour mixture is cooked, and it thickens without imparting much flavor and with little risk of lumps forming. Unlike the more time-consuming dark roux used for gumbo, this cream-colored roux is hard to mess up and takes only a few minutes to make.

---

4 tablespoons (½ stick)
  unsalted butter
6 tablespoons all-purpose flour

Melt the butter in a small saucepan set over medium heat. Add the flour all at once and whisk vigorously until smooth. When the mixture thins and starts to bubble, reduce the heat to low. Cook for 1 to 2 minutes, whisking slowly, until the mixture smells nutty and toasty and is still lightly colored. Cook for 2 more minutes, stirring occasionally. Cool at least to room temperature before adding to hot liquids.

The roux stores well, tightly covered, in the refrigerator for up to 1 month.

For 1 cup roux: 12 tablespoons butter and 1 cup plus 2 tablespoons all-purpose flour. (Thickens 3 quarts liquid.)

For ¼ cup roux: 3 tablespoons butter and 4 tablespoons plus 2 teaspoons all-purpose flour. (Thickens 3 cups liquid.)

BUTTER BLEND

MAKES 2 CUPS

16 tablespoons (2 sticks)
   unsalted butter, melted
1½ teaspoons salt
1 cup vegetable oil

Combine the butter and salt in a blender. With the machine running, slowly add the oil until combined. Transfer to a container. The butter blend will keep, covered and refrigerated, for up to 2 weeks.

HOMEMADE LARD AND CHICHARRONES

MAKES ABOUT 2 CUPS LARD AND 3 CUPS CHICHARRONES

When you make lard yourself, you know it's the cleanest and healthiest cooking oil you can get because there are no chemicals. You can make lard with any kind of pork fat. Leaf lard, which is the fat around the kidneys, is considered the best but it is hard to find.

This lard is great for making refried beans or biscuits, or for cooking meats or eggs. The chicharrones can be cooked with some green salsa and served with fresh Corn Tortillas (page 180).

———————

2 pounds pork fat or fatback
   from a Boston butt (pork
   shoulder; see headnote),
   with some meat on it, cut
   into 1-inch pieces
1½ cups water
1½ tablespoons salt

Bring the fat, water, and salt to a boil in a medium pot over medium-high heat. Cook until all the water has evaporated, 15 to 20 minutes. Reduce the heat to medium and continue cooking until some of the lard renders, about 30 minutes. Reduce the heat to medium-low and continue to cook, stirring occasionally, for another 15 minutes, or until the meat is crispy but not browned. Remove the meat and crispy bits with a slotted spoon, and refrigerate in an airtight container until ready to use. The chicharrones will keep, covered and refrigerated, for up to 1 week. Place the lard in a separate container and refrigerate until ready to use. The lard will keep, refrigerated, for up to 3 months, or frozen for up to 1 year.

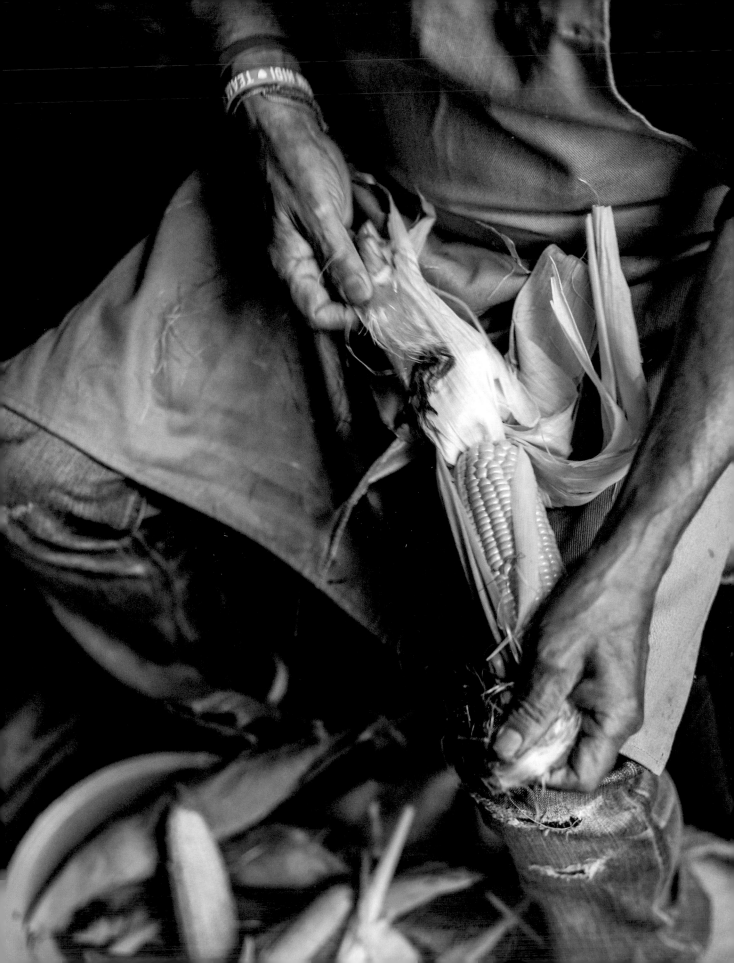

INDEX

Note: Page references in *italics* indicate photographs.

A

aguas frescas (Mexican fruit coolers), 264, *265*

almond-orange salad with sweet serrano-lime dressing, 226, *227*

ancho (chile)
about, 13
chicken tacos with red onion and jalapeño escabeche, 84
mashed potatoes, *152*, 247
pralines, *284*, 285
puree, 292
three-chile homemade chorizo, 31

appetizers
Cajun boiled peanuts, *40*, 41
chunky Mexican-style guacamole, *44*, 45
deviled eggs with Mexican flavors, *47*, 48
deviled eggs with pimento cheese and spicy bread and butter pickles, 46
fried green tomatillos with peach-habanero sauce, 54
guacamole mini tacos, 49, *49*
homemade tostadas and chips, 53
Mexican "sushi" roll-ups, 56, *57*
smoked salmon–chipotle pizza on fry bread, 58, *59*
sweet and tangy ceviche tostadas, *49*, 51
Taqueria del Sol jalapeño-cheese dip, 42, *43*
tomato and pickled pork skin tostadas, *49*, 52

apple-pineapple–green chile turnovers with lime zest glaze, 286, *287*

artichoke and jalapeño relish, *162*, 163

Atlanta barbecue sauce, 294

avocado(s)
about, 10
chunky Mexican-style guacamole, *44*, 45
-cilantro drizzle, 101
the dishwasher's soup (Mexican-cocktail seafood soup), 132–33, *133*
ham and egg torta, 34, *35*
Mexican "sushi" roll-ups, 56, *57*

B

basil
cilantro–roasted pecan pesto, *166*, 167
-jalapeño mayonnaise, *210*, 211
limonada, 263, *265*

bean(s)
black, and corn salad with cilantro-mint dressing, *220*, 232
black, enchiladas with cilantro-avocado drizzle, 100
black, pork, and peanut butter chili, 128
canned, cooking with, 16
charros, 188, *189*
collards and black-eyed peas with lemon-habanero dressing, 238, *239*
dried, soaking, 16
hoppin' Juan, 191
kitchen-sink succotash, 241
Mex-American black-eyed pea salad, 230, *231*
for recipes, 16
red, and rice, Creole, burritos, 107–8
refried black-eyed peas with chorizo, 190
veggie refried, 187
veggie tacos, 77

beef
brisket tacos, 74
cheeseburger tacos, 75
Cubano tacos, 70, *71*
meatloaf with tomato-habanero gravy, 146, *147*
real Mexican chili con carne, 130, *131*
sloppy José tacos, 72, *73*
slow-cooker barbacoa tacos party platter, 68, *69*
steak churrasco with chimichurri sauce, 148, *149*
tacos, crispy, 74
Texas chicken-fried steak with Tabasco cream gravy, 151–53, *152*
Waco chili, 127
Waco tacos, 65

beer, in red, green, and yellow micheladas, 260, *261*

beets and Vidalia onions, foil-roasted, with butter, lime, and sea salt, 244, *245*

black-eyed pea(s)
and collards with lemon-habanero dressing, 238, *239*
hoppin' Juan, 191
refried, with chorizo, 190
salad, Mex-American, 230, *231*

black pepper
–crusted tilapia with artichoke and jalapeño relish, *162*, 163
–lemon dressing, creamy, *210*, 212

blender, 8

blond roux, 298

blue cornmeal–crusted chicken with mint-jalapeño drizzle, 154, *155*

bolillos, *184*, 185–86

bread(s)
bolillos, *184*, 185–86
fry, smoked salmon–chipotle pizza on, 58, *59*
for Mexican dishes, 183
pudding, Mexican (capirotada), 282–83
see also tortilla(s)

burritos, Creole red beans and rice, 107–8

butter, substitutes for, 19

butter blend, 299

buttermilk fried chicken with green chile–horseradish sauce, 156

buttery pastry dough, 287

C

cabbage
jalapeño coleslaw, 223
melted, with carrots, *242*, 243

Cajun boiled peanuts, *40*, 41

Cajun hash, 28, *29*

Cajun spice mix, 291

caldo de pollo (chicken soup), 116, *117*

capirotada (Mexican bread pudding), 282–83

caramel, rum, tropical flan with, 276–77, *277*

carrots
Cajun hash, 28, *29*
chicken–green chile potpie in puffy
tortilla shells, *158*, 159–60
jalapeño coleslaw, 223
melted cabbage with, *242*, 243
and onions, aromatic pickled jalapeños
with, 214, *215*
cast-iron skillet, 8–9
cauliflower, roasted, with jalapeños and blue
cheese, 246
cayenne pepper
Cajun spice mix, 291
spicy-hot coating, 290
ceviche tostadas, sweet and tangy, *49*, 51
charros beans, 188, *189*
cheese
American, for dips and sauces, 18
ancho mashed potatoes, *152*, 247
black bean enchiladas with cilantro-
avocado drizzle, 100
blue, and jalapeños, roasted cauliflower
with, 246
blue, grits, creamy, 175
cheeseburger tacos, 75
chicken enchilada casserole with lemon-
cream sauce, 98–99
corn, and poblano tamales, 102–3, *103*
Cubano tacos, 70, *71*
enchiladas Mexicanas, 94–95, *97*
enchiladas with morita pepper sauce, 96
Fritos chilaquiles, 27
-jalapeño dip, Taqueria del Sol, 42, *43*
mac and, with feta and jalapeño, *162*,
164
Mexican, types of, 17–18
Mexican bread pudding (capirotada),
282–83
my breakfast muffins, 24, *25*
New Mexican chiles rellenos, 109–10,
111
pimento, 48
pimento, and spicy bread and butter
pickles, deviled eggs with, 46
sloppy José tacos, 72, *73*
smoked Gouda, and Vidalia onions, pork
broth with, 126

sweet potato cheesecake, 281
Tex-Mex-style enchiladas, 95
veggie tacos, 77
zucchini and corn soup with Brie, 118
cheesecake, sweet potato, 281
chicharrones
about, 19
homemade, 299
pork hot tamales, *103*, 104–6
chicken
ancho, tacos with red onion and jalapeño
escabeche, 84
blue cornmeal–crusted, with mint-
jalapeño drizzle, 154, *155*
buttermilk fried, with green chile–
horseradish sauce, 156
cracker, tacos with Tabasco-honey
drizzle, 80
enchilada casserole with lemon-cream
sauce, 98–99
filling, basic, 99
fried, tacos, 78
–green chile potpie in puffy tortilla
shells, *158*, 159–60
Nashville hot, tacos, 82
potato-crusted, tacos with spicy
Thousand Island dressing, *79*, 80
soup (caldo de pollo), 116, *117*
stock, basic, 99
tenders, for tacos, 80
verde tacos, 81
chilaquiles, Fritos, 27
chile(s)
about, 10
ancho chicken tacos with red onion and
jalapeño escabeche, 84
ancho mashed potatoes, *152*, 247
ancho (or guajillo) puree, 292
buying and storing, 11
canned and bottled, about, 14
dried, toasting and grinding, 14
dried, types of, 13–14
fresh, roasting, 12–13
fresh, types of, 11–12
green, –apple-pineapple turnovers with
lime zest glaze, 286, *287*
green, –horseradish sauce, 157

green, stew, 129
growing at home, 14
heat levels, 10–11
hottest varieties of, 14
morita pepper sauce, 96, *97*
New Mexican, rellenos, 109–10, *111*
pepper, hot, vinegar, 296, *297*
pork hot tamales, *103*, 104–6
red (or green) posole, 124–25, *125*
roasted tomatillo sauce, 205
sea salt, 254
sloppy José tacos, 72, *73*
stone-ground grits with, 196
sweet serrano-lime dressing, 227
three-, homemade chorizo, 31
see also chipotle(s); habanero(s);
jalapeño(s); poblano(s)
chile(s) de árbol
about, 13
ancho (or guajillo) puree, 292
chile sea salt, 254
red (or green) posole, 124–25, *125*
roasted tomatillo sauce, 205
sauce, 83
spicy bread and butter pickles, *216*, 217
vinegar, 296, *297*
chili
con carne, real Mexican, 130, *131*
pork, peanut butter, and black bean, 128
Waco, 127
chili powders, note about, 19
chimichangas
chocolate, with tequila cream sauce,
278, *279*
white chocolate, with raspberry sauce,
279, 280
chimichurri sauce, *149*, 150
chipotle(s)
about, 13
in adobo, about, 14
mayonnaise, 59, *59*
–smoked salmon pizza on fry bread,
58, *59*
three-chile homemade chorizo, 31
chocolate
chimichangas with tequila cream sauce,
278, *279*

chocolate (*continued*)
  white, chimichangas with raspberry
    sauce, *279*, 280
cilantro
  about, 15
  -avocado drizzle, 101
  chicken verde tacos, 81
  chimichurri sauce, *149*, 150
  green rice, 192
  herbal rice, 193
  -mint dressing, 232
  -poblano sauce, 207
  –roasted pecan pesto, *166*, 167
cinnamon
  Mexican, tea, *266*, 267
  Mexican bread pudding (capirotada),
    282–83
  sopapillas, 26
coating mixes
  cracker, 290
  crunchy potato, 290
  extra-crispy, 290
  seasoned flour, 290
  spicy-hot, 290
coffee, Mexican, *268*, 269
cola, in Atlanta barbecue sauce, 294
coleslaw, jalapeño, 223
collards
  with andouille, 237
  and black-eyed peas with lemon-
    habanero dressing, 238, *239*
cooking oils, 19
corn
  and black bean salad with cilantro-mint
    dressing, *220*, 232
  chowder, poblano, with shrimp, *120*,
    121
  kitchen-sink succotash, 241
  poblano, and cheese tamales, 102–3,
    103
  remoulade-topped fish fillets over
    Mexican maque choux, 161
  and zucchini soup with Brie, 118
cornmeal
  about, 16
  blue, –crusted chicken with mint-
    jalapeño drizzle, 154, *155*

fried green tomatillos with peach-
  habanero sauce, 54
mix, self-rising, about, 17
New Orleans fried oyster tacos, 88
precooked, about, 17
waffles, 30, *32*
corn products, types of, 16–17
see also specific types
crab, in Mexican "sushi" roll-ups, 56, *57*
cracker chicken tacos with Tabasco-honey
  drizzle, 80
cracker coating, 290
Creole red beans and rice burritos, 107–8
Creole remoulade sauce, *210*, 212
crispy carnitas, 76
crispy mini taco shells, 50
croutons, tortilla, 119, *119*
crunchy potato coating, 290
Cubano tacos, 70, *71*
cucumbers, in spicy bread and butter
  pickles, *216*, 217

D

dairy, 17–18
see also cheese; sour cream
desserts
  ancho chile pralines, *284*, 285
  chocolate chimichangas with tequila
    cream sauce, 278, *279*
  green chile–apple-pineapple turnovers
    with lime zest glaze, 286, *287*
  Mexican bread pudding (capirotada),
    282–83
  natilla, 274, *275*
  sweet potato cheesecake, 281
  tropical flan with rum caramel, 276–77,
    277
  white chocolate chimichangas with
    raspberry sauce, *279*, 280
deviled eggs
  with Mexican flavors, *47*, 48
  with pimento cheese and spicy bread
    and butter pickles, 46
dips and spreads
  chunky Mexican-style guacamole, *44*, 45
  pimento cheese, 48

Taqueria del Sol jalapeño-cheese dip,
  42, *43*
see also mayonnaise-based dips, sauces
  and dressings
the dishwasher's soup (Mexican-cocktail
  seafood soup), 132–33, *133*
dressings
  cilantro-mint, 232
  lemon–black pepper, creamy, *210*, 212
  lemon-habanero, 239
  mayonnaise-based, about, 208
  mustard-orange, 233
  spicy Thousand Island, 209, *210*
  sweet serrano-lime, 227
drinks
  aguas frescas (Mexican fruit coolers),
    264, *265*
  basil limonada, 263, *265*
  Eddie Palmer, *256*, 257
  fresh sweet-and-sour mix, 253
  frozen limeade margarita, 254
  Mexican cinnamon tea, *266*, 267
  Mexican coffee, *268*, 269
  Mexican mint julep, 255
  red, green, and yellow micheladas, 260,
    261
  skinny rita, 253
  tequila-mango smoothie, 258, *259*
  Westside rita, 252, *252*
drizzles
  cilantro-avocado, 101
  mint-jalapeño, 154, *155*
  quick lemon-habanero, 165

E

Eddie Palmer, *256*, 257
Eddie's breakfast sausage, *32*, 33
Eddie's pork with roasted jalapeño gravy,
  142
Eddie's turnip greens, *79*, 236
egg(s)
  chorizo with, 31
  deviled, with Mexican flavors, *47*, 48
  deviled, with pimento cheese and spicy
    bread and butter pickles, 46
  Fritos chilaquiles, 27

green pea salad with roasted chiles and red onion, *224*, 225

and ham torta, 34, *35*

my breakfast muffins, 24, *25*

spicy Thousand Island sauce/dressing, 209, *210*

electric griddle, 9

electric spice or coffee grinder, 9

enchilada(s)

    black bean, with cilantro-avocado drizzle, 100

    casserole, chicken, with lemon-cream sauce, 98–99

    cheese, with morita pepper sauce, 96

    Mexicanas, 94–95, *97*

    Tex-Mex-style, 95

    variation ideas, 95

equipment, 8–9

escabèche, red onion and jalapeño, 85

extra-crispy coating, 290

F

famous fish tacos, 86

fish

    black pepper–crusted tilapia with artichoke and jalapeño relish, *162*, 163

    the dishwasher's soup (Mexican-cocktail seafood soup), 132–33, *133*

    fillets, remoulade-topped, over Mexican maque choux, 161

    sautéed snapper with cilantro–roasted pecan pesto, 165, *166*

    smoked salmon–chipotle pizza on fry bread, 58, *59*

    sweet and tangy ceviche tostadas, *49*, 51

    tacos, famous, 86

flan, tropical, with rum caramel, 276–77, *277*

flour coating, seasoned, 290

flour tortillas, yeasty, 186

fluffy sweet potatoes, 140, *141*

fluffy white rice, 192

foil-roasted beets and Vidalia onions with butter, lime, and sea salt, 244, *245*

food processor, 8

fried chicken tacos, 78

fried green tomatillos with peach-habanero sauce, 54

Fritos

    chilaquiles, 27

    sloppy José tacos, 72, *73*

frozen limeade margarita, 254

fruit

    coolers, Mexican (aguas frescas), 264, *265*

    tropical flan with rum caramel, 276–77, *277*

    see also specific fruits

G

garlic

    -habanero mayonnaise, 52

    -lemon Delta salad, 222

ginger-tamarind sauce, 57, *57*

gorditas, 182

gravy

    ranchero brown, 143

    roasted jalapeño, 142

    Tabasco cream, *152*, 153

    tomato-habanero, *147*, 206

green michelada mix, 262

green peach salad with simple lime dressing, *228*, 229

green pea salad with roasted chiles and red onion, *224*, 225

green posole, 125, *125*

green rice, 192

greens

    collards and black-eyed peas with lemon-habanero dressing, 238, *239*

    collards with andouille, 237

    turnip, Eddie's, *79*, 236

    see also lettuce

griddle, electric, 9

grits

    about, 17

    creamy, 175

    creamy, lighter, 175

    creamy blue cheese, 175

    shrimp and, my way, 173, *174*

    stone-ground, with chiles, 196

guacamole, chunky Mexican-style, *44*, 45

guacamole mini tacos, 49, *49*

guajillo(s)

    about, 13

    pork hot tamales, *103*, 104–6

    puree, 292

    red (or green) posole, 124–25, *125*

    three-chile homemade chorizo, 31

H

habanero(s)

    about, 11

    -garlic mayonnaise, 52

    -lemon dressing, 239

    -peach sauce, 55

    -tomato gravy, *147*, 206

    -tomato sauce, 206

ham

    and egg torta, 34, *35*

    and okra, ranchero style, 240

hash, Cajun, 28, *29*

Hatch chiles. *See* New Mexico chile(s)

herbs

    chimichurri sauce, *149*, 150

    herbal rice, 193

    in Mexican dishes, 15

    storing, 15

    see also cilantro; mint

holy trinity rice and sausage, 195

hominy

    about, 16

    red (or green) posole, 124–25, *125*

hoppin' Juan, 191

horseradish–green chile sauce, 157

I

indoor smoker and wood chips, 9, 64

J

jalapeño(s)

    about, 11–12

    aromatic pickled, with carrots and onions, 214, *215*

    and artichoke relish, *162*, 163

    -basil mayonnaise, *210*, 211

jalapeño(s) (*continued*)
and blue cheese, roasted cauliflower
with, 246
-cheese dip, Taqueria del Sol, 42, *43*
chimichurri sauce, *149*, 150
cilantro-mint dressing, 232
coleslaw, 223
and feta, mac and cheese with, *162*, 164
Fritos chilaquiles, 27
green chile–chicken potpie in puffy
tortilla shells, *158*, 159–60
green chile–horseradish sauce, 157
green chile stew, 129
jarred pickled, about, 14
-lime mayonnaise, 211
-mint drizzle, 154, *155*
pickled, mayonnaise, *210*, 211
ranchero brown gravy, 143
and red onion escabeche, 85
and red onion escabeche, ancho chicken
tacos, 84
remoulade-topped fish fillets over
Mexican maque choux, 161
roasted, gravy, 142
salsa asada, *203*, 204
salsa fresca, 202, *203*
salsa frita, 204
shrimp and grits, my way, 173, *174*
spicy bread and butter pickles, *216*, 217
spicy tomato soup, 122, *123*
Taqueria vinaigrette, 207
jicama-watermelon relish, 213, *213*

K

ketchup-based sauces
Atlanta barbecue sauce, 294
Memphis-style barbecue sauce, *144*, 293
spicy Thousand Island sauce/dressing,
209, *210*
Waco barbecue sauce, 294
kitchen-sink succotash, 241

L

lard
cooking with, 18–19

homemade, 299
lemon(s)
–black pepper dressing, creamy, *210*, 212
-cream sauce, 98
fresh sweet-and-sour mix, 253
-garlic Delta salad, 222
-habanero dressing, 239
-habanero drizzle, quick, 165
in Mexican dishes, 15
syrup, 258
lettuce
fried chicken tacos, 78
guacamole mini tacos, 49, *49*
lemon-garlic Delta salad, 222
Nashville hot chicken tacos, 82
New Orleans fried oyster tacos, 88
orange-almond salad with sweet
serrano-lime dressing, 226, *227*
for recipes, 15
lime(s)
basil limonada, 263, *265*
dressing, simple, green peach salad
with, *228*, 229
Eddie Palmer, *256*, 257
fresh sweet-and-sour mix, 253
frozen limeade margarita, 254
-jalapeño mayonnaise, 211
Key, about, 15
Persian, about, 15
-serrano dressing, sweet, 227
skinny rita, 253
Westside rita, 252, *252*
zest glaze, green chile–apple-pineapple
turnovers with, 286, *287*

M

mac and cheese with feta and jalapeño, *162*,
164
mango
-tequila smoothie, 258, *259*
tropical flan with rum caramel, 276–77,
277
margarine, cooking with, 19
margaritas
frozen limeade, 254
skinny rita, 253

Westside rita, 252, *252*
masa and masa harina
about, 16
corn, poblano, and cheese tamales, 102–3,
103
corn tortillas, 180, *182*
cracker coating, 290
extra-crispy coating, 290
gorditas, 182
pork hot tamales, *103*, 104–6
red and yellow tortillas, 182, *182*
mayonnaise-based dips, sauces, and dressings
basil-jalapeño mayonnaise, *210*, 211
buying mayonnaise for, 208
chipotle mayonnaise, 59, *59*
creamy lemon–black pepper dressing,
210, 212
Creole remoulade sauce, *210*, 212
garlic-habanero mayonnaise, 52
jalapeño-lime mayonnaise, 211
mustard-orange dressing, 233
peach-habanero sauce, 55
pickled jalapeño mayonnaise, *210*, 211
poblano tartar sauce, 87
spicy Thousand Island dressing, 209, *210*
sweet pickle remoulade, 89
tamarind-ginger sauce, 57, *57*
meat. *See* beef; pork
meatloaf with tomato-habanero gravy, 146, *147*
Memphis spice rub, 145
Memphis-style barbecue sauce, *144*, 293
Memphis-style ribs, oven-baked, *144*, 145
Memphis tacos, *66*, 67
Mex-American black-eyed pea salad, 230, *231*
Mexican bread pudding (capirotada), 282–83
Mexican chili con carne, real, 130, *131*
Mexican cinnamon tea, *266*, 267
Mexican-cocktail seafood soup (the
dishwasher's soup), 132–33, *133*
Mexican coffee, *268*, 269
Mexican fruit coolers (aguas frescas), 264,
265
Mexican mint julep, 255
Mexican rice, 194
Mexican spaghetti (sopa de fideo), *131*, 197
Mexican-style barbecued shrimp, 168, *169*
Mexican "sushi" roll-ups, 56, *57*

michelada mix
    green, 262
    red, 261
    yellow, 262
micheladas, red, green, and yellow, 260, *261*
mint
    -cilantro dressing, 232
    -jalapeño drizzle, 154, *155*
    julep, Mexican, 255
molcajete/tejolete, 9
morita pepper(s)
    about, 14
    sauce, 96, *97*
muffins, my breakfast, 24, *25*
mulato chiles, about, 14
mushrooms. *See* shiitakes
mustard
    Creole remoulade sauce, *210*, 212
    -orange dressing, 233

N

Nashville hot chicken tacos, 82
natilla, 274, *275*
New Mexico chile(s)
    about, 12
    green chile–apple-pineapple turnovers
        with lime zest glaze, 286, *287*
    rellenos, 109–10, *111*
    sloppy José tacos, 72, *73*
New Orleans fried oyster tacos, 88
nuts
    ancho chile pralines, *204*, 285
    Cajun boiled peanuts, *40*, 41
    cilantro–roasted pecan pesto, *166*, 167
    Mexican bread pudding (capirotada),
        282–83
    orange-almond salad with sweet
        serrano-lime dressing, 226, *227*

O

oils, for cooking, 19
okra and ham, ranchero style, 240
onion(s)
    and carrots, aromatic pickled jalapeños
        with, 214, *215*

holy trinity rice and sausage, 195
lemon-garlic Delta salad, 222
red, and jalapeño escabeche, 85
types of, 15
Vidalia, and beets, foil-roasted, with
    butter, lime, and sea salt, 244, *245*
Vidalia, and smoked Gouda cheese, pork
    broth with, 126
orange liqueur
    frozen limeade margarita, 254
    skinny rita, 253
    Westside rita, 252, *252*
orange(s)
    aguas frescas (Mexican fruit coolers),
        264, *265*
    -almond salad with sweet serrano-lime
        dressing, 226, *227*
    -mustard dressing, 233

P

paprika
    Cajun spice mix, 291
    enchiladas Mexicanas, 94–95, *97*
parsley, in chimichurri sauce, *149*, 150
pasta
    mac and cheese with feta and jalapeño,
        162, 164
    Mexican spaghetti (sopa de fideo), *131*,
        197
pastry dough, buttery, 287
peach(es)
    green, salad with simple lime dressing,
        228, 229
    -habanero sauce, 55
    tropical flan with rum caramel, 276–77,
        277
peanut butter, pork, and black bean chili,
    128
peanuts, Cajun boiled, *40*, 41
pea(s)
    chicken–green chile potpie in puffy
        tortilla shells, *158*, 159–60
    green, salad with roasted chiles and red
        onion, *224*, 225
    kitchen-sink succotash, 241
    see also black-eyed pea(s)

pecan(s)
    ancho chile pralines, *284*, 285
    Mexican bread pudding (capirotada),
        282–83
    roasted, –cilantro pesto, *166*, 167
peppers
    green michelada mix, 262
    holy trinity rice and sausage, 195
    kitchen-sink succotash, 241
    Mex-American black-eyed pea salad,
        230, *231*
    Mexican "sushi" roll-ups, 56, *57*
    pimento cheese, 48
    red michelada mix, 261
    tomato and pickled pork skin tostadas,
        49, 52
    yellow michelada mix, 262
    see also chile(s)
pesto, cilantro–roasted pecan, *166*, 167
pickled jalapeño mayonnaise, *210*, 211
pickled jalapeños with carrots and onions,
    aromatic, 214, *215*
pickles
    spicy bread and butter, *216*, 217
    spicy bread and butter, and pimento
        cheese, deviled eggs with, 46
pico de gallo, 202
pimento cheese, 48
pineapple-apple–green chile turnovers with
    lime zest glaze, 286, *287*
pizza, smoked salmon–chipotle, on fry
    bread, 58, *59*
poblano(s)
    about, 12
    -cilantro sauce, 207
    corn, and cheese tamales, 102–3, *103*
    corn chowder with shrimp, *120*, 121
    green pea salad with roasted chiles and
        red onion, *224*, 225
    green rice, 192
    ranchero brown gravy, 143
    tartar sauce, 87
pork
    broth with Vidalia onions and smoked
        Gouda cheese, 126
    butt, about, 18
    carnitas tacos, 76

pork (*continued*)

  chicharrones, about, 19

  chops, pan-fried, with ranchero brown gravy, 143

  crispy carnitas, 76

  Eddie's, with roasted jalapeño gravy, 142

  green chile stew, 129

  homemade lard and chicharrones, 299

  hot tamales, *103*, 104–6

  lard, cooking with, 18–19

  meatloaf with tomato-habanero gravy, 146, *147*

  Memphis tacos, *66*, 67

  oven-baked Memphis-style ribs, *144*, 145

  peanut butter, and black bean chili, 128

  red (or green) posole, 124–25, *125*

  skin, pickled, and tomato tostadas, *49*, 52

  tenderloin, spiced, with sweet potatoes, chile glaze, and shiitakes, 138–40, *141*

  Waco chili, 127

  see also ham; sausage(s)

posole, red (or green), 124–25, *125*

potato(es)

  ancho mashed, *152*, 247

  Cajun hash, 28, *29*

  chorizo with, 31

  coating, crunchy, 290

  -crusted chicken tacos with spicy Thousand Island dressing, *79*, 80

  Cubano tacos, 70, *71*

  roasted, salad with mustard-orange dressing, *144*, 233

  sweet, cheesecake, 281

  sweet, fluffy, 140, *141*

potato masher, 9

potpie, chicken–green chile, in puffy tortilla shells, *158*, 159–60

pralines, ancho chile, *284*, 285

puddings

  Mexican bread (capirotada), 282–83

  natilla, 274, *275*

Q

queso Cotija, about, 17

queso fresco, about, 17

queso quesadilla, about, 17

R

raspberry sauce, white chocolate chimichangas with, *279*, 280

red and yellow tortillas, 182, *182*

red michelada mix, 261

red (or green) posole, 124–25, *125*

refried black-eyed peas with chorizo, 190

relish

  artichoke and jalapeño, *162*, 163

  Mex-American black-eyed pea salad, 230, *231*

  pico de gallo, 202

  watermelon-jicama, 213, *213*

remoulade

  sauce, Creole, *210*, 212

  sweet pickle, 89

  -topped fish fillets over Mexican maque choux, 161

rice

  green, 192

  herbal, 193

  hoppin' Juan, 191

  Mexican, 194

  in Mexican dishes, 17

  Mexican "sushi" roll-ups, 56, *57*

  and red beans, Creole, burritos, 107–8

  and sausage, holy trinity, 195

  shrimp fried, topped with bronzed scallops and Tabasco oil, 171–72

  white, fluffy, 192

  yellow, 192

roux, blond, 298

rum caramel, tropical flan with, 276–77, *277*

S

salads

  black bean and corn, with cilantro-mint dressing, *220*, 232

  black-eyed pea, Mex-American, 230, *231*

  green pea, with roasted chiles and red onion, *224*, 225

  green peach, with simple lime dressing, *228*, 229

  hoppin' Juan, 191

  lemon-garlic Delta, 222

  orange-almond, with sweet serrano-lime dressing, 226, *227*

  roasted potato, with mustard-orange dressing, *144*, 233

  see also coleslaw

salmon, smoked, –chipotle pizza on fry bread, 58, *59*

salsas

  asada, *203*, 204

  fresca, 202, *203*

  frita, 204

  verde, *203*, 205

salt, 19

salt, chile sea, 254

sandwiches. *See* torta

sauces

  Atlanta barbecue, 294

  chile de árbol, 83

  chimichurri, *149*, 150

  cilantro–roasted pecan pesto, *166*, 167

  Creole remoulade, *210*, 212

  green chile–horseradish, 157

  lemon-cream, 98

  Memphis-style barbecue, *144*, 293

  morita pepper, 96, *97*

  peach-habanero, 55

  poblano-cilantro, 207

  poblano tartar, 87

  roasted tomatillo, 205

  spicy Thousand Island, 209, *210*

  sweet pickle remoulade, 89

  Tabasco cream gravy, *152*, 153

  tamarind-ginger, 57, *57*

  tequila cream, *279*, 280

  tomato-habanero, 206

  Waco barbecue, 294

  see also drizzles; gravy; salsas

sausage(s)

  Cajun hash, 28, *29*

  chorizo with eggs, 31

  chorizo with potatoes, 31

collards with andouille, 237

Eddie's breakfast, *32*, 33

my breakfast muffins, 24, *25*

refried black-eyed peas with chorizo,
190

and rice, holy trinity, 195

three-chile homemade chorizo, 31

scallops, bronzed, and Tabasco oil, shrimp
fried rice with, *170*, 171–72

seafood

soup, Mexican-cocktail (the
dishwasher's soup), 132–33, *133*

see also fish; shellfish

sea salt, chile, 254

seasoned coating mixes. *See* coating mixes

seasoning blends

Cajun spice mix, 291

making your own, 19

Memphis spice rub, 145

serrano(s)

about, 12

-lime dressing, sweet, 227

salsa verde, *203*, 205

shellfish

the dishwasher's soup (Mexican-cocktail
seafood soup), 132–33, *133*

hot shrimp tacos, 83

Mexican-style barbecued shrimp, 168,
169

Mexican "sushi" roll-ups, 56, *57*

New Orleans fried oyster tacos, 88

poblano corn chowder with shrimp, *120*,
121

shrimp and grits, my way, 173, *174*

shrimp fried rice topped with bronzed
scallops and Tabasco oil, *170*,
171–72

shiitakes, sweet potatoes, and chile glaze,
spiced pork tenderloin with, 138–40, *141*

shrimp

the dishwasher's soup (Mexican-cocktail
seafood soup), 132–33, *133*

fried rice topped with bronzed scallops
and Tabasco oil, *170*, 171–72

and grits, my way, 173, *174*

hot, tacos, 83

Mexican-style barbecued, 168, *169*

poblano corn chowder with, *120*, 121

skinny rita, 253

sloppy José tacos, 72, *73*

slow cooker, 9

slow-cooker barbacoa tacos party platter,
68, *69*

smoker, indoor, and wood chips, 9, 64

smoking foods indoors, 64

smoothie, tequila-mango, 258, *259*

snapper, sautéed, with cilantro–roasted
pecan pesto, 165, *166*

sopa de fideo (Mexican spaghetti), *131*,
197

sopapillas, 26

soups

chicken (caldo de pollo), 116, *117*

the dishwasher's (Mexican-cocktail
seafood soup), 132–33, *133*

Eddie's turnip greens, *79*, 236

poblano corn chowder with shrimp, *120*,
121

pork broth with Vidalia onions and
smoked Gouda cheese, 126

red (or green) posole, 124–25, *125*

tomato, spicy, 122, *123*

zucchini and corn, with Brie, 118

see also chili; stews

sour cream

in lemon-cream sauce, 98

Mexican (*crema*), about, 18

spice mixes

Cajun, 291

Memphis spice rub, 145

note about, 19

spice or coffee grinder, 9

squash. *See* zucchini

stand mixer, 9

steak churrasco with chimichurri sauce,
148, *149*

stews

green chile, 129

see also chili

succotash, kitchen-sink, 241

"sushi" roll-ups, Mexican, 56, *57*

sweet-and-sour mix, fresh, 253

sweet and tangy ceviche tostadas, *49*, 51

sweet pickle remoulade, 89

sweet potato(es)

cheesecake, 281

Cubano tacos, 70, *71*

fluffy, 140, *141*

syrup, lemon, 258

T

Tabasco

cream gravy, *152*, 153

-honey drizzle, cracker chicken tacos
with, 80

tacos

ancho chicken, with red onion and
jalapeño escabeche, 84

beef, crispy, 74

beef brisket, 74

cheeseburger, 75

chicken verde, 81

cracker chicken, with Tabasco-honey
drizzle, 80

Cubano, 70, *71*

fish, famous, 86

fried chicken, 78

fried oyster, New Orleans, 88

guacamole mini, 49, *49*

Memphis, 67

Nashville hot chicken, 82

pork carnitas, 76

potato-crusted chicken, with spicy
Thousand Island dressing, *79*, 80

shrimp, hot, 83

sloppy José, 72, *73*

slow-cooker barbacoa, party platter,
68, *69*

veggie, 77

Waco, 65

wrapping in foil, 64

taco shells, crispy mini, 50

tamales

corn, poblano, and cheese, 102–3, *103*

pork, hot, *103*, 104–6

tamale steamer, 9

tamarind-ginger sauce, 57, *57*

Taqueria del Sol jalapeño-cheese dip, 42, *43*

Taqueria vinaigrette, 207

tartar sauce, poblano, 87

tea
    Eddie Palmer, *256*, 257
    Mexican cinnamon, *266*, 267
tequila
    cream sauce, *279*, 280
    Eddie Palmer, *256*, 257
    frozen limeade margarita, 254
    -mango smoothie, 258, *259*
    Mexican coffee, *268*, 269
    Mexican mint julep, 255
    skinny rita, 253
    Westside rita, 252, *252*
Texas chicken-fried steak with Tabasco
    cream gravy, 151–53, *152*
Tex-Mex-style enchiladas, 95
thermometer, 9
tilapia, black pepper–crusted, with
    artichoke and jalapeño relish, *162*, 163
tomatillo(s)
    about, 15
    canned, using, 15
    fried green, with peach-habanero sauce,
        54
    roasted, sauce, 205
    salsa verde, *203*, 205
tomato(es)
    caldo de pollo (chicken soup), 116, *117*
    charros beans, 188, *189*
    chicken enchilada casserole with lemon-
        cream sauce, 98–99
    collards with andouille, 237
    Cubano tacos, 70, *71*
    deepening flavor of, 16
    the dishwasher's soup (Mexican-cocktail
        seafood soup), 132–33, *133*
    Eddie's turnip greens, *79*, 236
    fresh, for recipes, 15–16
    fried chicken tacos, 78
    guacamole mini tacos, 49, *49*
    -habanero gravy, *147*, 206
    -habanero sauce, 206
    ham and egg torta, 34, *35*
    kitchen-sink succotash, 241
    lemon-garlic Delta salad, 222

Mexican rice, 194
Mexican spaghetti (sopa de fideo), *131*,
    197
Nashville hot chicken tacos, 82
New Orleans fried oyster tacos, 88
okra and ham, ranchero style, 240
and pickled pork skin tostadas, *49*, 52
pico de gallo, 202
real Mexican chili con carne, 130, *131*
red michelada mix, 261
salsa asada, *203*, 204
salsa fresca, 202, *203*
salsa frita, 204
shrimp and grits, my way, 173, *174*
soup, spicy, 122, *123*
yellow michelada mix, 262
torta, ham and egg, 34, *35*
tortilla press and rolling pin, 9
tortilla(s)
    chicken enchilada casserole with lemon-
        cream sauce, 98–99
    chips, homemade, 53
    chocolate chimichangas with tequila
        cream sauce, 278, *279*
    corn, 180, *182*
    Creole red beans and rice burritos,
        107–8
    croutons, 119, *119*
    homemade tostadas, 53
    kneading seasoning into dough for, 95
    Mexican "sushi" roll-ups, 56, *57*
    red and yellow, 182, *182*
    shells, puffy, chicken–green chile potpie
        in, *158*, 159–60
    sweet and tangy ceviche tostadas, *49*, 51
    tomato and pickled pork skin tostadas,
        49, 52
    white chocolate chimichangas with
        raspberry sauce, *279*, 280
    yeasty flour, 186
    see also enchilada(s); tacos
tostadas
    homemade, 53
    sweet and tangy ceviche, *49*, 51

tomato and pickled pork skin, *49*, 52
tropical flan with rum caramel, 276–77, *277*
turnip greens, Eddie's, *79*, 236
turnovers, green chile–apple-pineapple,
    with lime zest glaze, 286, *287*

V

vegetables. *See specific vegetables*
veggie refried beans, 187
veggie tacos, 77
vinaigrette, Taqueria, 207
vinegar
    chile de árbol, 296, *297*
    hot chile pepper, 296, *297*

W

Waco barbecue sauce, 294
Waco chili, 127
Waco tacos, 65
waffles, cornmeal, 30, *32*
watermelon
    aguas frescas (Mexican fruit coolers),
        264, *265*
    -jicama relish, 213, *213*
Westside rita, 252, *252*
white chocolate chimichangas with
    raspberry sauce, *279*, 280

Y

yeasty flour tortillas, 186
yellow and red tortillas, 182, *182*
yellow michelada mix, 262
yellow rice, 192

Z

zucchini
    and corn soup with Brie, 118
    kitchen-sink succotash, 241

"Eddie Hernandez is a charismatic weaver of food cultures, threading together his native Mexican flavors with the strong strands of American Southern food. *Turnip Greens & Tortillas* is an ode to meals that pull at your heartstrings and take you to a place that is familiar and grounding."
— HUGH ACHESON, CHEF, AUTHOR